Shropshire Airfields

Toby Neal

LANGRISH
CAIGER
PUBLICATIONS

First published 2005 by Langrish Caiger Publications, PO Box 1916, Telford, Shropshire, TF7 5XZ. Email *langrishcaiger@aol.com*

This second edition 2008.

Cover design by Michelle Dalton.

Printed by WPG, Welshpool.

ISBN: 978-0-9548530-4-4

Main cover picture: Unidentified RAF officer with a Spitfire at RAF Atcham in 1941 (via Andre Bar). Also: Avro 504 at Shawbury aerodrome, circa 1917 (Harry C. Harvey); derelict airfield buildings at RAF Tilstock; and American pilot Warren R. Lobdell with his P47 "The Flying Ute" at Atcham in 1944.

Back cover: Gloster Gauntlet at RAF Tern Hill in 1938 (Don Tyrer); and a hangar being built at RAF Shawbury in about 1936 (Josie Morris).

Contents

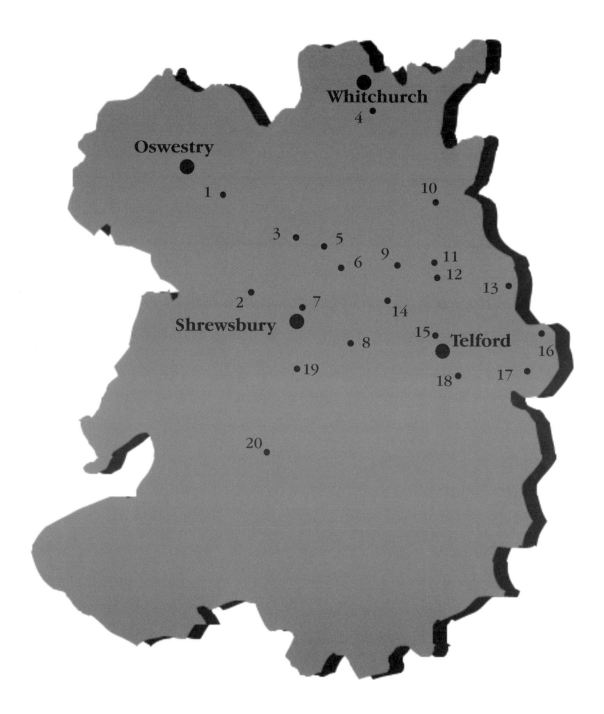

Oswestry

Whitchurch

Shrewsbury

Telford

1. Rednal.
2. Montford Bridge/Forton.
3. Sleap.
4. Tilstock/Whitchurch Heath/Prees Heath.
5. Bridleway Gate.
6. Shawbury.
7. Monkmoor.
8. Atcham.
9. Hodnet.
10. Tern Hill.
11. Hinstock/Ollerton/HMS Godwit.
12. Peplow/Childs Ercall.
13. Chetwynd.
14. High Ercall.
15. Bratton.
16. Weston Park.
17. Cosford.
18. Brockton.
19. Condover.
20. Midland Gliding Club (Long Mynd).

Foreword

Shropshire, with its ancient villages, medieval towns, castles, and countless evocative historical sites, has a wonderful heritage.

But there is an often overlooked aspect of its heritage which is within living memory. The county's countryside is dotted with airfields – places of drama and tragedy and extraordinary tales.

Most of them flourished during wartime and then faded away. They each have fascinating stories and going back to them now you stand and wonder... and imagine. I have visited them all, thanks to a 160-mile round trip on my bicycle to raise cash for the 1987 Wings Appeal.

During my RAF career, I was fortunate to fly from Shawbury and Cosford for nearly six years, and, following Air Traffic Control training at Shawbury, spent six years as Flight Commander at Tern Hill (where I had the additional responsibility for Chetwynd) controlling Shawbury's helicopters, before becoming the Senior Air Traffic Control officer at Cosford for four years.

My interest led to me researching and compiling a series of articles for RAF Shawbury's magazine about the old airfields of Shropshire and I was pleased to share what I had discovered with Toby Neal when he did his own series in the Shropshire Star in the late 1990s.

His book is, as far as I know, the first time the full story of this slice of Shropshire's history has been compiled into one book. Every page is a gripping and sometimes moving account of the endeavours of the thousands of men and women who served at these places.

By knowing the great things they did, we honour their memories.

Flt Lt Ian Pride MBE RAF (Retd.)
Lilleshall

Introduction

With every day that passes, Britain's old airfields fade away a little more, thanks to the encroachment of nature, slow decay, or the more rapid destruction brought about by new development.

Memories, too, are fading, as the generation they served is itself in its twilight. Yet the fascination about them is as strong as ever.

The first edition of *Shropshire Airfields* was well received, both by veterans and a younger generation wanting to learn more. And, as I hoped, it led to further memories, information, and rare photographs coming to light.

Time, then, for a second, revised and updated edition, including this new material. So I shall start by saying a big thank you to all the contributors who have provided much valuable and interesting information and photos.

A particular treasure trove came from Andre Bar, who kindly shared with me some extraordinary pictures from Belgian sources showing RAF Atcham in its Spitfire days.

I have also taken the opportunity to include more information from official records and, while a book such as this can never provide a complete picture – some of Shropshire's larger air bases are worthy of books in themselves – I hope to have produced a comprehensive overview.

There are two kinds of histories. One is of facts and dates. The other is of memories, anecdotes, and impressions.

Shropshire's airfields were places where thousands of men and women lived, worked, had fun, experienced danger and adventure, and in many cases lost their lives.

The skies were crowded as they had never been before, and have never been since. For a while, during the Blitz, some of the county's air bases were front line stations. A number were bombed. But they hit back as well. Nightfighters took on the bombers of the Luftwaffe as the German raiders attacked targets in the north of England, and scored a number of "kills". And bombers took off from Shropshire and headed into the dangerous territory of occupied Europe, typically to drop propaganda leaflets, in operations codenamed "nickelling".

However the main role of stations in the county was that of training. Here Spitfire pilots honed their skills before joining operational squadrons. Thunderbolts roared across the skies as American airmen prepared for combat. Rookie bomber crews were put through their paces and glider and tug combinations perfected their craft in the run-up to the major airborne assaults of 1944 and 1945. It was vital work, and it was dangerous. Dozens of young men met their deaths as their

planes plunged to earth. Bad luck, bad weather, bravado, inexperience... all claimed lives.

My father Richard Neal, who trained briefly at RNAS Hinstock in the summer of 1943, was just one of the vast number of young men and women from all over Britain and from all over the world for whom Shropshire was, for a time, their home during the war.

Today not many people, perhaps even in Hinstock itself, are aware that for a few short years there was a Royal Naval Air Station at Hinstock. Armed with good directions and after a drive of a mile or two down a country lane, there it is, unmistakably an airfield and with the magnificent three-storey control tower continuing to dominate the flying field, now sympathetically converted into a luxury home. Some hangars and airfield buildings still stand. It is a fascinating piece of local history and just one of the 19 airfields – 20 if you include the gliding club on the Long Mynd – which are dotted around the county.

They are places of extraordinary tales. Heard about the airfield which was built by circus elephants? Or the remarkable double tragedy when a bomber crashed into a control tower, and then only a few weeks later exactly the same thing happened? Or the strange case in which an RAF man stole an aircraft and then sent it into a death dive into his billet?

Much has been swept away over the decades. Yet, with only the exception of Monkmoor, on the edge of urban Shrewsbury, the county's air bases have escaped the fate of many old airfields across the nation which have been comprehensively built on for housing and industry.

For what is often perceived as a rather "out of the way" county, Shropshire has a rich aviation heritage with a number of aviation pioneers to be proud of. Indeed, according to aviation historian and author Mike Grant, Shropshire can boast the first British national to fly.

Ernie Maund with his aircraft at Craven Arms. This picture from his great - grandson Gay Baldwin has the date 1907 written on the back.

History has, says Mike, overlooked the achievements of one Ernest Maund, who assembled a monoplane in his garage and cycle shop in Craven Arms and took it to a large field at nearby Stokesay where he made a successful take-off and landed safely after a short flight.

It is claimed that the date of this feat was July 14, 1904 – more than four years before the flight by Samuel F. Cody (on October 16, 1908) which has gone into all the history books. Unfortunately, beyond handed-down anecdote, and assertion, there is an absence of evidence, and my own feeling is that the 1904 date, only a few months after the Wright brothers' feat, is too early to be credible.

There is, however, some tantalising evidence pointing to Maund having flown before 1908.

Separately, his granddaughter Vikki Wilding and great-grandson Gay Baldwin have shown me different photos of Maund and his machine, both of which bear the date 1907 on the back, as well as a ticket for a flight at "Craven Arms Aero Club", again bearing a 1907 date on the reverse. If this date is correct and if the aircraft did fly successfully – it is said that it made a flight of treetop height – then it would secure Maund's place in British history.

Yet on the other hand, since the first edition of this book Graham Neale has pointed out to me a picture in *"The Racing Campbells"* which shows Malcolm Campbell standing by an aircraft identical to that by which Maund posed. The book says Campbell built it in 1910.

Does this disprove the claims for Maund? Not necessarily. It is another of those jigsaw pieces of history which can't easily be made to fit. What we do know is that Maund advertised himself as "Britain's No. 1" aviator and that there exists a bill, obviously from the family business, dated December 31, 1910, from "A. Maund and Co., agents for all the Best Makes of Cars, Motor Cycles and Cycles. Aeroplanes Supplied and Repaired."

Other Shropshire pioneers of flight include Arthur Phillips of Market Drayton, who patented a vertical take-off aircraft in December 1908. His unmanned machine did fly. In 1910 a Santos-Dumont type monoplane was built by 17-year-old Willy Groves at Crown Works, Shrewsbury. He told his daughter in later years that the aircraft did fly successfully.

But the first aircraft flight in Shropshire which is truly well documented, through photos, postcards, and newspaper accounts, was on July 31, 1911, when an aircraft taking part in an air race, piloted by one James Valentine, caused a sensation when it landed at Brockton, near Madeley, on its journey from Manchester to Bristol. A crowd estimated at 8,000 flocked to the scene and saw the plane before it resumed its journey the same evening.

This book is based on a series of features about Shropshire airfields which I wrote for the *Shropshire Star* between 1998 and 2003, and includes material which could not be fitted in then, and which has come in since.

In many ways, this series was just in time. Almost all those I interviewed who gave me their first hand accounts have since died, my own father among them. The series also turned up a number of extremely rare pictures which might otherwise not have come to light, which in more

Picture: Ray Farlow

This fuzzy picture of James Valentine taking off on July 31, 1911, is the first known photo of an aircraft in flight in Shropshire. *(Thomas Griffiths collection)*

me to use airfield maps he prepared and various pictures.

Others have also been generous in helping with pictures. Apart from the individuals, whom I credit by name in the captions or in the text, aviation historians like Phil Ede, Michael Davies, and Alec Brew (who has written his own book on Shropshire airfields) have all given me a willing hand.

That's the thing about Shropshire's old airfields – those who know about them want others to know about them, and aviation historians like these have uncovered much rare material.

There remain some gaps. During wartime, photography at military bases was not encouraged and film was difficult to get anyway. Photos taken of the smaller airfields are like gold dust. Maybe there are some still out there, but as the wartime generation fades away, the danger is their children and grandchildren will not appreciate the rarity value of the photos they leave behind.

The airfields themselves are in danger too. While it would obviously be silly to expect all the surviving airfield buildings, which are now mostly derelict shells, to be kept, it would be a shame if they were needlessly swept away.

Shropshire Airfields is not a blow-by-blow, unit-by-unit account. Rather, it aims to give an overall picture which will fire the imaginations of the casually curious and whet the appetites of military historians and researchers.

I hope this book promotes and encourages interest in the disappeared airfields of Shropshire and, by so doing, helps create an environment in which memorabilia about them is treasured and retained and, where practical, evocative buildings like the surviving old control towers are preserved – both as structures of architectural and historical interest, and also as a tribute to the men and women who served at Shropshire's airfields during those dark days years ago.

than one case are the only known pictures of particular airfields. In *Shropshire Airfields* I have largely used the material as it was used in those features. In other words, some of the memories and anecdotes quoted in these pages are from the lips of folk who have now passed on, and some of the "modern" photos of the airfield sites date from the late 1990s and first three years of the new millennium. If things have changed since and I know about those changes, I've mentioned that.

The written material in this book has come from various sources – things people have told me in interview and letters, additional research by myself at the National Archives, and my underlying "guiding light" in the form of a series of articles written a few years ago by Flight Lieutenant Ian Pride, an RAF officer who did much research into the county's airfields, which has been invaluable. Ian, who is now retired, also allowed

Toby Neal

September 2008

Atcham

Atcham airfield was Shropshire's wartime "Little America." For three years it was home to thousands of young Americans who impressed, in various ways, all Salopians who came into contact with them. Huge Thunderbolt fighters roared over the countryside as the American pilots trained for combat in Europe. A number of them went on to become aces.

Their intensive programme at Atcham included all phases of combat, with simulated dogfights, and dive bombing and ground attacks using ranges at Llanbedr, Wales. The 48 Thunderbolts (although at one time there were up to 150 there) amassed a huge number of flying hours – 9,208 in June 1944 for example – and there were many fatal accidents.

For pilots whose initial training was in the clear skies of the American Midwest, English weather was a shock. But the local landmark, the Wrekin, was put to use. If the base commander could see the hill, then it was a flying day.

As with most wartime airfields, the accommodation for around 1,600 service personnel was dispersed around the surrounding countryside and also in Atcham's case at the neighbouring stately home, Attingham Hall, the seat of Lord Berwick, where some found themselves put up in the stables.

The sick quarters were alongside the A5 (now the B5061), virtually opposite the mouth of the Ironbridge road junction, and the operations block was in a copse just off the Ironbridge road. There was an emergency operations block between Norton and Wroxeter, and an officers mess, dining room, fuel compound and various other buildings south of the Horseshoe Inn at Uckington.

Today Atcham industrial estate occupies the site which was at the hub of the airfield. All the old buildings in this part of the air base have been demolished as a result of the redevelopment of the estate, although a few of the dispersed buildings survive here and there. The control tower was

Open air maintenance of Thunderbolts during the winter of 1943/44 or 1944/45. *(Ervin Miller)*

demolished many years ago. Although the three runways have been dug up, the B4394 road is built on the line of the old main runway for about a third of the runway's original length.

Chiefly remembered as an American airfield, Atcham in fact opened as an RAF Spitfire base on August 20, 1941. It was handed over to the Americans on June 15, 1942. At this time American pilots were flying Spitfires and the first Eighth Air Force casualty in Europe came at Atcham when a Spitfire crashed on final approach.

Towards the end of 1942 Atcham began the training role which was to last almost to war's end. The principal unit was the 495th Fighter Training Group, formed in December 1943 with two squadrons of P47s. Atcham was returned to the RAF in March 1945 and closed the following year. Many of the huts and buildings were converted into homes as a temporary measure to ease the post-war housing crisis. Each

ward of the sick quarters, for instance, made about three homes, and the mortuary was turned into a bungalow.

Of all Shropshire's wartime airfields, Atcham is by far the best recorded photographically. No doubt this was thanks to the relaxed attitude the Americans had to such matters in comparison to the RAF.

Down the decades American veterans have made the occasional visit to the site, and have had mixed reactions on their arrival.

Among the last was Harry A. Marlow, who was at Atcham in 1942 and made his one and only return there in October 2001. There was little that remained familiar and when he went to see the old station headquarters building it was a pile of rubble, having been demolished just weeks, or maybe even days, beforehand.

Like the veterans themselves, Shropshire's airfields are fading away.

War diary

1941

August 15: The Equipment Officer, P/O Hollingsworth, arrived at Atcham with half a dozen equipment assistants and began collecting stores from all over the county, borrowing transport where possible.

The station is by no means complete. There is no mains water, no electricity, the messes are not ready, and the stores are only 50 per cent complete, about half of the barrack blocks can be occupied.

The aerodrome itself is further advanced and, apart from a final top dressing of rubber chippings, the runways are ready and the perimeter track is finished.

August 20: Station officially opened.

August 27: Tonight the first bus service from Norton crossroads to Shrewsbury put on by Midland Red started. "This service should be well patronised by airmen and enable them to get in and out of Shrewsbury without hitchhiking."

August 30: "The C/O flew over in his Tiger Moth from Ternhill and brought the new senior sector controller with him – S/L Spencer, who went round the station and seemed depressed. He will like it better when he is actually installed."

September 9: The sector operations room at Tern Hill closed this morning and operational control of the Atcham sector was transferred to the E.O.R. at Atcham. The E.O.R. is in a field a mile from the aerodrome, near Wroxeter, the ancient Roman city of Uriconium. The main operations room is still under construction.

September 27: At the 0815 hours working party the C/O spoke and instructed all ranks not in possession of a weapon to improvise a bludgeon within 48 hours. 131 Squadron arrived by air from Tern Hill.

September 28: There was an unfortunate accident this afternoon when a Spitfire of 131 Squadron taking off apparently failed to see a Miles Magister on the runway, collided with it when just airborne and killed the two occupants of the Magister, P/O Chubb and Sgt Lee.

October 9: The camp is again a sea of mud due to the fact of heavy rain on unmade roads.

October 20: Flt/Lt Gonay force landed on Prestatyn Golf Course due to lack of fuel. "Some members regard this as very bad form. Others think it rather improves the short 14th."

October 28: A Beaufighter on a delivery flight piloted by an American ATA pilot crashed half a mile south of the aerodrome – presumably intending to land, stalled, and dived in. Pilot killed.

November 28: Italian prisoners of war noticed in fields near the aerodrome, gathering root crops. Complaint was made to the authorities on security grounds.

December 5: No 131 Sqn was rearming with Spitfire Vbs.

December 7: Sgt Metcalfe of 131 Sqn returning from local formation flying became separated from his formation in a sudden and violent snow storm, collided with the base of the Wrekin and was killed.

December 18: During a large scale operation by Bomber and Fighter Commands against the port of Brest, 131 Squadron aircraft provided cover for the Colerne sector.

December 31: Station strength 87 WOs and SNCOs, 1,155 airmen and 89 officers.

(The "war diaries" in this book are merely excerpts and highlights from official records to give a flavour of wartime station life. They are not meant to be complete operational diaries)

Spitfire of 131 Squadron. The squadron code was NX

Henri Picard is thought to have been the Spitfire pilot involved in a tragic accident at Atcham on September 28, 1941. Picard was executed in 1944 after taking part in The Great Escape.

Jean Ester

Atcham was a desolate and rather muddy place in the early days. With the south Shropshire hills forming the backdrop, a stationwagon is in position.

All the photographs of Atcham's "Spitfire days" in this book are courtesy of Andre Bar, of Sprimont, Belgium, and are from the collection of "Belgians in the RAF and SAAF 1940-45 Association" of which Andre is founder (website address www.bamfbamrs.be/RAF/index.htm). Most of them record the Belgian flight of 131 Squadron, and are important in Belgian wartime history as these pilots became the core of the all-Belgian 350 Squadron later. All the photos were taken during 131 Squadron's stay at Atcham

Spitfire being prepared for take-off

"Smets, de Puysseler" (presumabl
this original caption refers to the p
standing)

Flight commander Henri Gonay, who made an unscheduled landing on Prestatyn golf course. He was shot down by flak and killed in 1944 while leading an attack by Typhoons on shipping off Jersey

This little Austin must have been acquired locally – UX is a Shropshire plate prefix

Note the parachute on the wing

War diary

1942

January 1: The New Year Honours list contained the name of the station commander, who was made OBE (not named, but possibly J. Heber-Percy).

January 11: Station cinema opened.

February 8: 131 Sqn air part of 18 Spitfire Vbs flew to Llanbedr, their new station.

February 17: Air part of 350 Belgian Squadron 12 Spitfires flew from Valley to Atcham on posting here. One pilot overran after landing with considerable damage to the first aircraft.

February 19: The remainder of the air party of No 350 (Belgian) Squadron arrived this afternoon and assumed normal day state. "The Officers' Mess resembles a cafe in Brussels."

March 1: "Wrekin" exercises, i.e. airfield defence exercises, continued. "A feature of the defence was the siting of Spitfire Vb aircraft with their tails on trestles and their guns trained on possible zones of enemy attack."

April 15: 350 (B) Squadron left for Debden.

April 18: No 232 Sqn officially forming at Atcham.

May 16: 232 Sqn left Atcham for Llanbedr. After lunch 131 Sqn left for Tangmere.

May 25: Some officers went rook shooting in the rain and got a bag of about 150. Much jollification afterwards.

June 4: Group Captain Garrity, W/C Smith and Colonel Miller and Major Castle (USASC) arrived to discuss handing over this station to No 31 Pursuit Group US Army Air Corps.

June 5: "Instructions received from 9 Group that RAF personnel must be cut to 200. All sections sweat and produce cogent reasons why they cannot possibly be deprived of a single man."

June 10: We are notified that trains will arrive with first contingent of US at 1910 and 2130 hours. Buses borrowed from Shawbury and High Ercall. One way traffic roads are mapped out through drome and communal sites. Convoy arrived on station and was met at watchtower by C/O and reception committee. After kit dumped at alloted billets men had a meal and retired, all pretty well worn. Crossing made in Queen Eliz in five days.

June 13: Americans (most of whom are from Georgia, Louisiana and points south) complain of the cold in our flaming June. Fires are requested and as a result fires were relighted.

June 15: Atcham officially handed over to USAAC, the American pilots flying Spitfire 1s.

June 17: "Changeover to American conditions continues. RAF no longer know Spitfires as Spitfires or 'Spits', they have become 'pursuit ships'. Similarly, the Intelligence Officer has become 'Information' and the Sqn Ldr Admin. answers to 'Executive Major'. Telephone conversations between RAF personnel are terminated 'You're welcome' or 'You bet' and fried toast is served with maple syrup."

War diary

1942

June 20: "We are notified that a number of Spitfire Vbs will be arriving this day from the US. In no time 35 arrive and are landed bloodlessly. The whole of the field is packed with Spitfires, Masters, Ansons, Fairchilds and Dominies – during which time a Wellington elects to do circuits and bumps. The Duty Pilot ages visibly."

June 27: Visit from the US Ambassador Mr J.G. Winant accompanied by General Eaker and General Spaatz.

June 28: The 308th cracked up four planes today, one turning completely over in a wheat field, but nobody was injured.

June 29: Lieut. Giacomini of 308th killed in a crash when his Spitfire Vb span in on approach (one account said the crash was apparently due to mechanical failure). He died on way to hospital.

July 10: Two Spitfires F/O Gray and 1st Lt Hill USA came in simultaneously and despite shrill cries from the watch tower and many red lights persisted in completing a composite mayo landing. Two Spitfires written off but both pilots comparatively unscathed.

July 14: Officers meeting in the morning. In the past 16 days, 21 planes have been destroyed or badly damaged, most of them by 308 Squadron. That's too many, and due to carelessness, says Col. Hawkins.

July 15: Eight aircraft of 308 Sqn USAAF left Atcham for Tangmere.

July 17: Lieut. Kerr of 309th killed during an oxygen hop. It appeared that something went wrong with his oxygen and he blacked out, went straight in.

July 28: 14 P38 (Lockheed Lightnings) of 48 and 49 Squadrons of our new guests 14th pursuit group arrived, having flown their ships overseas.

July 29: The Boche Circus (one Heinkel III, one Me 109 and one Junkers 88) arrived at Atcham and demonstrated. Ringmaster: S/Ldr Wheeler.

August 4: 16 P38s arrive from Ayr, having flown from America with stops including Greenland and Iceland.

December 28: A P39 from USAAC Atcham crashed near Bridgnorth. Pilot killed.

1943

June 23: "One of the USAAF Masters returned from a local flight this morning with numerous bullet holes in his tail – so far nobody will own up." (This item, perhaps some sort of in-joke, is crossed out in the operational records book).

July 5: Atcham aerodrome lighting, so long awaited, was tried out tonight with apparent success.

July 29: A Spitfire from Atcham collided with a 60 OTU Mosquito from High Ercall this afternoon, the latter crashing on some farm buildings near 'W' site. Unfortunately the crews of both aircraft were killed.

Standing from left, two unknowns, Georges Deltour, Emile Plas, Henri Gonay, de Wever, Plisnier, Guillaume and Alain Boussa

On ground, from left, Deltour, Seydel, unknown; on wing, Plisnier, de Wever, Guillaume, unknown, Boussa, unknown

Emile Plas

"Atcham, voiture de Plisnier"

The rough and ready appearance of Atcham is again apparent in this shot of Henri Picard. The control tower is in the distance on the extreme left

Atcham memories

Cliff Marsh was based at RAF High Ercall when he had a phone call from the Air Ministry to go to Atcham to meet the American CO. Taking along his foreman joiner, Archie Healey from Wem, he recalls arriving at the main gate to find the guard was a GI sitting on a folding chair, a carbine across his legs and a Western magazine in his hand.

Mr Marsh was the foreman of the maintenance gang at the airfield and remembers that the RAF supplied the Americans 12 Spitfires because the ship carrying either the fuselages or engines for their American planes – Thunderbolts and Lightnings – was torpedoed.

"Within a month of those being delivered, because of the difference in landing speed and handling of the Spitfire, only three were left serviceable. None of the pilots were seriously hurt," said Mr Marsh, of Copthorne, Shrewsbury.

Once Mr Marsh was rung by the commanding officer – who always used to call him "Works" – and asked to have a look at the new asbestos roof which had been put in one of the flying officers' huts at Number 3 site. He discovered that there were bullet holes where the light fittings should have been.

"They had been to Wellington in the bus and had a good night out, and were a little the worse for drink. When they went to bed the officer nearest the light switch was told to put the lights out. He promptly used his service revolver to shoot them out, with the other chaps cowering in their beds."

The cookhouse and mess rooms were just inside the fence that surrounded Attingham Park. "Lord Berwick's deer were culled by the cookhouse staff. Venison was on the menu for several days before he found out."

And Mr Marsh says the Americans were issued with 50 Hercules cycles because the cookhouse and mess were half a mile off the aerodrome. Not used to the British habit of driving on the left, the roadside was soon strewn with bent cycles.

Maurice Stone, of Madeley, who was a young electrician, remembers being involved in converting the sick quarters after the war. "That was quite a job because there were big hospital wards there. They made about three homes out of each one. The best one was the mortuary which turned into a beautiful bungalow."

Bill Taylor recalled visiting Atcham with the Borough of Wenlock Air Training Corps Squadron when he was about 17.

"I reckon it was about a fortnight before Christmas in 1943. It was a foggy morning," said Mr Taylor, who lived back then in Cherry Tree Hill, Coalbrookdale.

"We were going round the perimeter track to the butts to fire the machine guns and in the fog there were two RAF ambulances on the end of the runway and wreckage around there.

"The Americans taking us round told us that the previous evening a Wellington bomber had been in difficulties and made a forced landing. I think they said there had been a fire on board. As it got to the end of the runway the bomb load exploded.

"It had just made a depression in the runway. There was tarmac and wreckage lying around. I assume the crew perished."

John Comley, of Tividale, Oldbury, recalled visiting with the Air Training Corps when he was 17 in early 1944. "It was a day of intense fog and somehow we finished up in our hired Midland Red bus on the runways. Whether we entered by the main gates or not I do not know. We were welcomed by coffee and donuts, so different to RAF stations where nothing was free and where I suppose that on a Sunday we were a nuisance. At Atcham we were treated as guests and again in complete contrast to RAF stations, allowed to inspect their aircraft at close quarters. The sheer size of the P47 Thunderbolts still remains in the memory.

"Also, we went over a Flying Fortress but here, I must be mistaken, I can only remember seeing an ash tray by the pilot's controls. Afterwards we fired one of their 0.5 inch machine guns on the range and were allowed (I think) to keep a cartridge case. It was a completely different occasion to a visit to the RAF where we were closely monitored and marshalled and I suppose looked upon as cheeky upstarts."

However, even the American relaxed approached had its limits. One of the cadets got into the cockpit of a P47 before the Americans realised what was happening and put them under closer supervision.

The station theatre and, inset, "BQ Squadron peel off" over Atcham. *(Ervin Miller)*

Killed in combat

Among the hundreds of young men to train at Atcham on their way to front line action was Warren R. "Russell" Lobdell. He was there in April and May of 1944, and was then posted to a temporary forward airfield at High Halden in Kent. Just a few weeks later, on June 27, he was killed in action over France at the age of 23.

Lobdell, who was from Baton Rouge, Louisiana, where most of his family still live, would write home often and wisely included his negatives for safe keeping. His words in the last few weeks of his life give a glimpse of what it was like to be a young American officer far from home in a strange English county. In one, presumably referring to Shrewsbury, he wrote: "Have been to town several times in the late evenings, and find things as one would expect. You can have a swell time but, of course, it's quite different from the loud and rowdy parties back home. The people are very nice but, of course, have other things on their mind."

Russell Lobdell's story and military career have been researched by his great nephew, Greg Hackenberg, who has also created a website (www.creativefatcat.com/lobdell) which shares with the public many of the remarkable pictures. The original contact prints had been kept by the family and held in the special collections of the Louisiana State University since Lobdell's death. Mr Hackenberg has scanned and enlarged them, revealing a wealth of detail which had not been observed since they were taken. Among them is Lobdell at Atcham in front of

Russell Lobdell at Atcham with "The Flying Ute". He was killed in action only a few weeks after this picture was taken. *(Greg Hackenberg)*

a P47 dubbed "The Flying Ute" which he described as "the plane I flew quite often after reaching England." Mr Hackenberg says on the website: "I have posted the collection here in order to share the history they record and hopefully learn more about the places and the men depicted in them."

"Poker game in alert room." *(Greg Hackenberg)*

Atcham Thunderbolts claw into the air after take-off, with the Wrekin on the horizon. *(Greg Hackenberg)*

Miller's tale

Major Ervin "Dusty" Miller was already a combat veteran when he was posted to Atcham as Chief Flying Instructor in August 1943. He had a year and a half of operations in Spitfires and Thunderbolts under his belt, first with one of the famous American Eagle squadrons in the RAF, and then with the USAAF.

Major Miller later became station commander, and was in command to close it down as an American base and hand it back to the RAF in March 1945. After the war he continued in the air force and eventually was posted back to England. He settled with his English wife Pat at Bircham, Norfolk, and left the service in about 1955 with the rank of Lieutenant Colonel.

Dusty died on February 21, 2005, at the age of 90 and has left a wonderful legacy, both of memories of his old air base, and a remarkable collection of photographs which were taken while he was there.

Born in Tulsa, Oklahoma, he always wanted to fly, and his hero was Charles Lindberg. He joined the US Navy in 1933 as an avenue of getting into naval aviation. He was a torpedo specialist on a submarine tender, and earned enough to learn to fly privately. Leaving the navy in 1937, he worked as a civil servant in Sacremento, but the outbreak of war provided the opportunity to fly in action, taking advantage of a scheme in 1941 to train up American pilots for service in the RAF – America was not at war at this stage.

Inconveniently he was then drafted into the army, but went on "holiday" to Canada, and crossed over to Britain in September 1941. It was not until about 1943 that the FBI caught up with him. He went into action with 133 Eagle Squadron, which later became 336 Squadron in 4th Fighter Group of the Eighth Air Force. Although not credited with any "kills" he was in continuous combat. He and Pat, from West Kirby, married in August 1942 while he was still in the RAF.

Recalling his time at Atcham, he said: "There was not much there when I arrived – some Thunderbolts, Harvards, a couple of Spits and a P38 or two. It was a training squadron initially and then it was changed to 495th Fighter Training Group in December 1943. That was after I had organised it. We had two squadrons and did a lot of flying. It was pretty hectic.

"The Wrekin was our weather chart –- if we could see

Above: "My Thunderbolt – the only silver job in the UK which I flew to bounce students and formation flights to simulate attacks out of the sun (an RAF identification photograph P47C-2-RE with lengthened fuselage and water injection.)"

it, we would start flying. We had a continuous influx of courses, young chaps from the States training up to go on operational squadrons." Among those trained at Atcham were the future fighter ace "Kid" Hofer.

Major Miller said the Americans had an outstanding reception from local people. "We had parties which brought the girls. We would send trucks out to bring in the nurses and girls from the villages. They were all eager.

"Pat and I had off-base accommodation in Monkmoor Avenue, Shrewsbury, although there was a bunk in the control tower I slept in while on duty. We and our little boy (Paul, who was born at the then Limes Nursing Home in Shrewsbury) lived with a Welsh family, Megan and David Thomas."

Major Miller had his own aircraft, which he says was the only silver P47 Thunderbolt in Europe at the time: "I used to get up in the sun and bounce them (the students). Nobody else flew it. It was a lengthened P47C with water injection, a hot aircraft. They couldn't catch me – good thing, as they were young and eager."

Training was dangerous, with 167 accidents and 35 fatalities in the 495th. "We had a lot of approach and take-off accidents. It was down to the amount of flying being done, and the circumstances. When we started with belly tanks, there were accidents because if the pilot was not alert enough on take-off, with the extra weight the aircraft went off the runway. We found a lot of them were not fully trained and had to go through everything again – formation, instruments, low level.

"We told them to stay away from the Welsh hills because they were deadly, especially in mist. We warned

"Controller, Major Miller; Mrs Pat Miller; Capt. Walt Kis. Briefing before taking Mrs Miller for a ride in a Piper Cub around the Wrekin." (Airman left, unidentified).

them about the Wrekin. We had a couple of terrific chaps who were RAF liaison officers. Sir Richard Leighton was one of them, and there was another chap we called Woody."

Atcham attracted a lot of visitors, and was a convenient stopping off place for ATA pilots and RAF crews because of the excellent meals served in the messes, he said.

"We went back there once, in the 1960s I think. They were just destroying the place. It's sort of heartbreaking. There were gipsies in the officers mess. It was soul destroying. I don't think I would like to go back again." (In fact he was destined to return one last time shortly before his death)

The pictures on the following three pages come from the late Dusty Miller's collection unless otherwise stated.

"Atcham Tower, with: Controller Major Miller, Capt. W.G. Kis."

PERMANENT STAFF   AAF STATION 342
ENGLAND
JUNE 14 1944

An office in the headquarters building.

"Instructors table, officers mess."
Major Miller thinks the girls were from the
American Red Cross.

"The mess hall."

"The Flying Ute." *(Greg Hackenberg*

Cocoa break, late summer 1942. *(Harry A. Marlow)*

"The Officers Club."

Airmen's bar.

The recreation room

"Students' recreation room."

"My office in the control tower with Capt. Kis at his desk (my assistant operations officer)."

The motor pool.

Russell Lobdell, right, captioned this picture: "Sunday refreshment at officers club in England. Sure wish we had one now." *(Greg Hackenberg)*

Station Headquarters building

A shining legacy

Although Atcham closed many years ago, it has left behind an enduring tradition, in the form of a flashing light on top of the Wrekin. The Wrekin beacon was originally an RAF Pundit light erected in wartime to stop aircraft crashing into the 1,335ft hill, one of Shropshire's best-loved landmarks. It also served as a navigation aid. It was put up by the maintenance gang at Atcham. It finally went off forever in 1965 and was later dismantled. Travelling Salopians had come to see it as a friendly light from home and, following a big campaign, a modern-day Wrekin beacon (actually two flashing lights on the Wrekin telecommunications mast) was ceremonially turned on at the stroke of the new millennium.

Cliff Marsh, of Copthorne, Shrewsbury, was working for A M Griffiths of Wolverhampton at Atcham airfield, where he was the foreman of the aerodrome's maintenance gang. In the late autumn of 1942 he was in his workshop and office when the American commanding officer told him he wanted him to go up the Wrekin with him and the Air Ministry clerk of works, Ted Alves, to see about resiting the beacon. About 10 minutes later a Jeep came round and the sergeant driver took the trio to the summit.

"It was the wildest ride I think I have ever had in my life. There were at least four gears he never used. Our backsides were coming up a foot off the rear seat," said Cliff. At the top the colonel quickly pointed out the spot he wanted the beacon to go. A beacon was already on the hill, possibly pre-war, but the American was unhappy with its location. Next morning a six-wheeled lorry turned up at the workshops and took up Cliff and his men – Tom Clarke of Harlescott, Shrewsbury; Harry Shotton of Horsefair, Shrewsbury; Kronje Lewin from Bayston Hill; and Bill Active from Wroxeter.

For the next two or three days, with the lorry going back and forth to take materials, they put in the concrete base and the rag bolts to which the beacon was afterwards fastened. Cliff recalls that the electrician responsible for maintaining the light was Pat Connel of Much Wenlock. Post-war responsibility for the beacon transferred to RAF High Ercall, and then when that closed, to RAF Shawbury.

Mrs Margaret Richardson of Rotherham recalled: "In 1943 I was a WAAF plotter working on the Fighter Sector Ops room at RAF Atcham which was about a mile and a half from Attingham Hall, where we were billeted at this time, and in sight of the Wrekin. We plotted aircraft in the vicinity and the beacon light was operated from the Ops room. There was a large sign on the wall which read 'WREKIN BEACON – ON, WREKIN BEACON – OFF.' It was of great importance.

"The light was always switched off when hostile aircraft were in the sector, as for instance one night in 1943 that I still remember. I was on duty when a warning came through from a nearby station that hostile aircraft were approaching. The WAAF Sergeant switched off the Wrekin beacon – the controller ordered the air raid siren to be sounded in Shrewsbury – and the Corporal of Ops B scrambled our fighters. As it turned out they were few in number that night but they flew directly overhead and could be heard outside by the guard on the gate. That was just one incident, a bit of excitement on a quiet night."

Spring 1944, with the deadly Wrekin looming in the distance. *(Greg Hackenberg)*

And **Diana Summer** of Worcestershire said: "My father was the Air Ministry clerk of works, Ted Alves, who rode in the Jeep with the American commanding officer and Cliff Marsh on that 'wild ride to the summit of the Wrekin' in the late summer of 1942. One of my lifelong claims to fame has been that 'My dad had the light put on the top of the Wrekin!'

"Dad always told us that it had been put there soon after the Americans joined the war and took over Atcham aerodrome from the RAF. He had been clerk of works with the RAF and remained there when the Americans arrived. He said that Americans got there before their aeroplanes were shipped out to them and so used RAF Spitfires to continue their training until they arrived. These were very different from the planes they had trained in initially.

"The pilots were mainly young men with few hours flying experience and several crashed into the Wrekin during night flights. The surrounding Shropshire plain being so flat, one occasionally misjudged the height of the Wrekin as he came into land, with dire consequences. Once the light was installed, it was switched on as they returned and they landed safely."

The first of the many

Atcham was the scene of a small, tragic, and significant part of American military history – the death of the first airman of the Eighth Air Force in the European theatre.

First Lieutenant Al Giacomini, a 24-year-old from Colorado, span in in his unfamiliar Spitfire while approaching the airfield for landing. The accident was on June 29, 1942, only a fortnight after the Americans had taken over the airfield.

He died on the way to hospital. Initially buried in England, his body was disinterred in 1949 when he was buried with full honours at St Anthony's Church, Sterling, Colorado.

Giacomini was a pilot in 308th Fighter Squadron, 31st Fighter Group, USAAF (United States Army Air Force), which was in the process of converting from the P39 Airacobra to the Spitfire.

It was very much a pioneer unit, as evidenced by the visit to Atcham on June 27 by the American ambassador Gil Winant accompanied by two USAAF top brass, General Eaker and General Spaatz.

Giacomini's accident has been researched by Tom Thorne, who has been investigating wartime air crashes in Shropshire. Lt Giacomini took off from Atcham at 12.40pm on a training flight, but for some unknown reason returned to base only ten minutes later.

"As he approached the airfield from the east, with wheels and flaps down for a landing, he made a rather steep turn to line up with the runway and stalled.

"Lt Giacomini immediately gave a good burst of throttle but was sadly unable to regain control and crashed to the ground one mile east of Atcham airfield," says Mr Thorne.

Al Giacomini on a P39

"He holds the unfortunate double distinction of being the first casualty to be suffered by the American Eighth Air Force in Europe and the first resident of Logan County, Colorado, to be killed in any service during the Second World War.

"Al was a fairly experienced pilot with just over 440 hours on all types, although it can be seen on the accident card that he did not have much experience on Spitfires with only three hours on type. This almost certainly contributed to his accidental stalling of the aircraft, although the engineering officer said that there was the possibility of engine trouble. This could not be confirmed."

Alfred William Giacomini, known as Al to his family, was born on January 11, 1918, in Sterling, Colorado. He grew up on the family ranch just outside the town.

"Al's brother and sister are still living in the Sterling area, both in their 90s. Apparently his brother Clarence is still ranching a little at the age of 91! I wrote to the family and was in contact with Patty Trout – Al's niece – who sent the information and photo," added Mr Thorne.

In the Cheshire town of Nantwich a special place of honour goes to an Atcham pilot. His grave is at the spot where his aircraft crashed near the River Weaver.

The inscription tells the story: "Here lies 1st Lt Arthur L. Brown, USAAF, aged 23 years, of New York, who crashed in his Thunderbolt to avoid this town, January 14, 1944."

Lt Leslie Brown was with the 495th Fighter Training Group based at Atcham airfield. His P47 Thunderbolt got into difficulties over the town. Townsfolk believe he stayed at the controls to avoid the stricken plane crashing into the town centre. After the aircraft crashed into a field it was sucked into quicksand and only the tail was ever recovered by the American military, despite rescue efforts to reach the pilot's body using lifting equipment.

In gratitude for the pilot's actions, a local street, Brown Avenue, is named after him and for years Nantwich Brownies maintained his grave. Former Brown Owl Gladys Henshall, who had continued this act of gratitude, died in 2000 at the age of 84. In 2002 a flowering cherry tree was planted near the airman's grave to mark her decades of dedication, and Margaret Brown, one of the original Brownies who had helped Mrs Henshall over the years, continued to tend the grave.

After the war members of Leslie Brown's family came over several times and a memorial service is held at the grave for Remembrance Day.

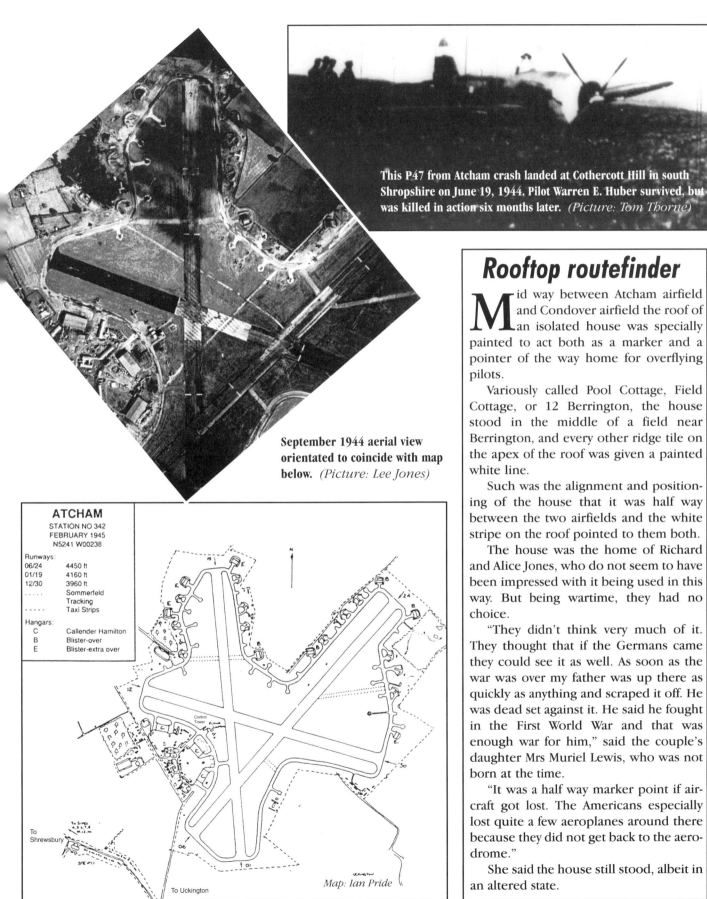

This P47 from Atcham crash landed at Cothercott Hill in south Shropshire on June 19, 1944. Pilot Warren E. Huber survived, but was killed in action six months later. *(Picture: Tom Thorne)*

September 1944 aerial view orientated to coincide with map below. *(Picture: Lee Jones)*

ATCHAM
STATION NO 342
FEBRUARY 1945
N5241 W00238

Runways:
06/24	4450 ft
01/19	4160 ft
12/30	3960 ft
.....	Sommerfeld Tracking
- - - -	Taxi Strips

Hangars:
C	Callender Hamilton
B	Blister-over
E	Blister-extra over

Control Tower

To Shrewsbury

To Uckington

Map: Ian Pride

Rooftop routefinder

Mid way between Atcham airfield and Condover airfield the roof of an isolated house was specially painted to act both as a marker and a pointer of the way home for overflying pilots.

Variously called Pool Cottage, Field Cottage, or 12 Berrington, the house stood in the middle of a field near Berrington, and every other ridge tile on the apex of the roof was given a painted white line.

Such was the alignment and positioning of the house that it was half way between the two airfields and the white stripe on the roof pointed to them both.

The house was the home of Richard and Alice Jones, who do not seem to have been impressed with it being used in this way. But being wartime, they had no choice.

"They didn't think very much of it. They thought that if the Germans came they could see it as well. As soon as the war was over my father was up there as quickly as anything and scraped it off. He was dead set against it. He said he fought in the First World War and that was enough war for him," said the couple's daughter Mrs Muriel Lewis, who was not born at the time.

"It was a half way marker point if aircraft got lost. The Americans especially lost quite a few aeroplanes around there because they did not get back to the aerodrome."

She said the house still stood, albeit in an altered state.

"Hangars behind the tower with Thunderbolts, Harvards, Norseman."

Atcham today

First things first. Shropshire's airfields are almost all in rural locations and the sites are generally owned by farmers and other landowners, so make sure you get permission if you intend to explore them. However, for those who merely intend to make a casual diversion out of curiosity, most of the sites can be made out from public roads and paths.

To get to the site of Atcham airfield, take the old A5 (now called the B5061) between Shrewsbury and Telford. A little over a mile east of Atcham village, take the B4394 road, signposted to Atcham industrial estate. After only a short distance, the road becomes absolutely straight for a stretch of around 500 yards – the road here runs along the edge of the line of the main runway, which has long been dug up.

Atcham industrial estate, off to the left, is on the site of the airfield's headquarters, hangars and technical buildings – the hub of the old air base. It has been developed over the past decade and as a result all, or almost all, the original buildings here have been demolished.

Too late – 83-year-old American veteran Harry A. Marlow, who served at Atcham in 1942, returns for the first time on October 5, 2001, to find that some of the last wartime buildings had been demolished shortly beforehand.

Atcham in 2008. For several hundred yards the B4394 road follows the line of the old main runway. Compare this to the wartime view from a similar spot on page 7.

The windswept landscape that was Bratton airfield.

Bratton

Bratton airfield was created during the war on flat fields north of Wellington with the help of two circus elephants, named Saucy and Salt. They were loaned to help grub out trees and hedges from the original site, then towed sledges piled with the material removed for subsequent disposal.

The pair were kept in farm buildings to the north of the airfield and watered in the canal, which has since disappeared. According to Shropshire airfields historian Flt Lt Ian Pride, one of the handlers apparently lost his job when a well-meaning citizen objected to one of the elephants being made to perform headstands in the road for the benefit of local children.

The 190-acre airfield came into existence in October 1940 and that winter, to stop a glider-borne invasion, dozens of vehicles were obtained from local scrapyards and dispersed all over the site. One scrap car had the keys left in and the Engineering Officer successfully started it and used the vehicle for the duration of his time at Bratton.

When the grass airfield dried out in the spring the vehicles were cleared, but it was very bumpy and rutted. A search of scrapyards produced a steamroller from Bayston Hill which was revived by RAF engineers and driven to Bratton to iron out the bumps.

The airfield was a relief landing ground for RAF Shawbury. Airspeed Oxfords, a twin-engine trainer, were commonly seen at Bratton. Crews for training came from Shawbury in a fleet of Midland Red buses. Ownership transferred to Tern Hill in January 1944 and Miles Masters used the airfield, and there were also Oxfords from the Royal Naval Air Station at Hinstock. At the end of 1944 there were 126 RAF personnel on station strength. The base closed in the summer of 1945.

Today there is a large drainage ditch across the site. All the hangars have long gone, together with almost all the airfield buildings, which did not amount to much in the first place.

The airfield is not far from the modern Shawbirch housing estate. It is likely that few residents, nor many drivers motoring along the A442, realise that they are on the doorstep of one of the county's old wartime airfields.

Saucy and Salt

Mr Perce Jones, of Cardington Drive, Shrewsbury, said: "I was born at Long Lane in the late 1930s and the main field of 'Bratton' was directly opposite our house. Every day from dawn until dusk, and often during the night, the sounds of planes became part of our lives. The aircraft were mainly Oxfords, Hurricanes, and Spitfires. There were possibly others which I don't remember now.

"We had to walk to Longdon-on-Tern School – this would be around 1942-43 – and the planes used to be

Even circus elephants have "joined-up" to help with important work being carried out "Somewhere in Shropshire"! But they still find time during off-duty hours to give the local kiddies a ride.

A report in the Wellington Journal and Shrewsbury News of February 24, 1940, telling of the Bratton elephants. Notice that, due to wartime censorship, information of the location is restricted to saying it is "somewhere in Shropshire".

parked wing tip to wing tip alongside the road, up to Longdon Halt (this railway is now gone). All these planes would be starting up and the noise was deafening.

"We witnessed several crashes, both serious and odd bumps. Two in particular I remember seeing. The first was two aircraft taking-off and colliding. They crashed in flames near to the Gate Inn public house. The second was seeing a single seat aircraft, possibly either a Hurricane or a Spitfire, fail to take-off. It went through the hedge opposite the house called Wayside on the B road from the Gate Inn to Longdon-on-Tern. The plane

came to rest blocking the road. Instead of going to school, we went to see the crash.

"The pilot, unhurt, climbed out and as we got near told us to 'go away' (that was the gist of it). He then kicked the tail of the plane, climbed back through the hole in the hedge and walked off across the airfield."

Perce went on: "My schoolmates from those years will, I am sure, remember also being given rides in the rear of the Oxford planes when they were being moved around. The sentry posts dotted around the perimeter of the airfield provided play places for us after the war. The brickwork of only one sentry post remains today.

"All the buildings and hangars have gone. Several of the buildings were used by families to live in after the war when housing was scarce.

"I can confirm that elephants were used to try and clear the felled trees when the airfield was created. My mother, who is 91, remembers the event very well. She believes they came possibly from Dudley Zoo. But they were no use for the job. I understand that once they had cut the wood down in the middle of the airfield the elephants refused to lift it"

And **Brian Hollis** said: "They were Salt and Saucy and were housed at the big house where the guardroom was, just adjoining the airfield. It was a farm and there was a big tall building adjoining the house. They would take the elephants down the road past what used to be our garage at Long Lane. They would stop for a biscuit every morning and would not go past the garage until they had one. It was me who used to give them the biscuit.

"They would be taken to a little brook just beyond our garage to wash them and for them to have a drink." Mr Hollis, of Ditton Priors, also remembers there being concert parties at Bratton.

"I remember Douglas Cardew Robinson, a comedian. His catchphrase was Cardew, the Cad of the School. He used to dress up as a schoolboy and tell jokes about school." The only aircraft he recalls at the base were Airspeed Oxfords. "I used to have to walk past the drome to go to school. I had my ears blasted every morning with

12 Airspeed Oxfords revving up."

Brian Bywater, of Long Lane, was part of the construction team which built the airfield. "The contractor was R.M. Douglas. It was my first job after leaving school and I was a general helper. It was all fields, brooks, trees and hedges and it was all flattened out. Usually they use tractors, but they used elephants, which is amazing and very unusual.

"The front of the time office where we signed on still stands. They didn't have a clock in those days and you signed when you started to work. It was the first building built there.

"I once saw an aircraft cut out over the airfield and the chap jumped out. His parachute opened – I never thought it would. We all thought he had had it and he hit the deck, but he was all right. The first thing he wanted was a cigarette. The plane crashed on the landing field and burst into flames. It was a Spitfire, or perhaps a Hurricane. There was live ammunition on it and suddenly the bullets started going off and flying around."

Mr Bywater also vaguely recalls sections of railway tracks being laid vertically in the

Remnants of the few surviving buildings at Bratton. These are at the northern part of the airfield (pictured in early 1999, still there in 2008, albeit somewhat masked by new development at the site).

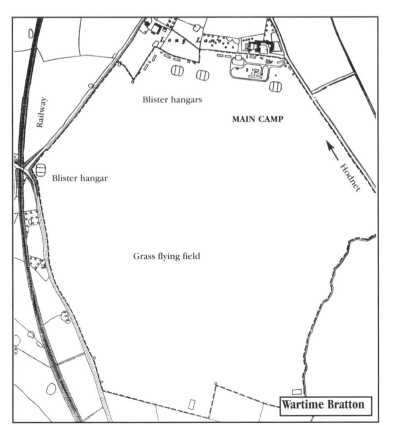

landing field at one stage to deter a glider-borne invasion.

Tommy Jones, of West View, Bratton, said: "I was living at Walcot in those days and remember it because it was a training and emergency landing field, mostly for Shawbury and Tern Hill and other airfields around about. As regards it being built, it didn't take a lot of doing because they were more or less prefab buildings. The ground was levelled and it was just a metal runway put over the top of it. That was still there long after it was used as an airfield.

"Aircraft could only take-off in one direction or the opposite direction, at 90 degrees to the A442, so if there was a north or south wind it was a bit difficult. It was an east-west runway. They couldn't go the other way because of the houses and electrical cables.

"There was a hangar this end, where there used to be Longdon Halt. All it was was a dome of metal. There were no planes actually based there. It was used for circuits and bumps all day, and then at the end of the day the planes would return to the airfield they had come from. It was also used sometimes as a crash drome.

"After the war the land returned to agriculture but the buildings were used for living in for a while. The concrete huts were there for ages."

A rather undignified end for Spitfire P9446 of No. 57 OTU Hawarden after it made a forced landing at Bratton on December 7, 1941. The pilot escaped with minor injuries. *Picture courtesy of The RAF Museum.*

Buckstead and Firkin 2

Reg Howard, of Eaton Constantine, was among navy officers who flew at Bratton in 1944 before moving to the navy airfield at Hinstock. "At Bratton the local pub was called the Bucks Head and they used that as the station call sign. They changed it slightly. It didn't sound good on R/T, so they called it Buckstead. All the pilots were named after beer barrels. My unfortunate one was Firkin 2."

His instructor Lt Tony Law, allegedly a relative of the former prime minister Bonar Law, had a big black and white sheep dog which the airmen called Panda which would have flights in the Oxford aircraft. "It became incorporated in the R/T vocabulary. When you landed you said 'pancake, request panda', which meant you wanted transport."

Mr Howard, a Sub Lieutenant at the time, went there in about March 1944, training up to be an instructor. "My recollection is that there were more Lieutenant Commanders than anyone else. There were only a hand-ful of Sub Lts like myself. The Captain was an RNVR officer which was most unusual. He was Captain Jonny Pugh, who was ex-Jersey Airways. The radio officer was Philip Moss."

When he had been posted to the station, he had protested as it was away from the action. "The CO said 'don't do that, you are going to learn how to fly twin-engine aircraft. Not many people in the Fleet Air Arm are able to do so. They're bringing in the Mosquito (i.e. the planned naval version). Go there and be in the instructing lark.'

"That was very much as it was in wartime. There was a rumour that the CO at the time was trying to get instructors medals because he felt it was just as hazardous as being in the front line, but he didn't succeed.

"The officers mess was at Hinstock Hall, and we would go daily from there to wherever we were flying from, which initially was always Bratton, but it slowly evolved to include Hinstock as well."

Naval airmen relax against an air raid shelter at RAF Bratton in 1944. This photograph from Mr Howard's collection is an extremely rare view from an airfield of which hardly any wartime photos have surfaced.

Bratton today

Take the A442 road heading north from Wellington towards Hodnet. About half a mile after you leave the modern housing behind, the fields on the left open out into a large expanse of agricultural land, bisected by a post-war drainage ditch. This was the flying field.

A little further on a turnoff to the left leads to the site of the airfield accommodation, dining hall, and so on – all gone and now in business use. Drive a little further along the main road and you come to the Bucks Head, the airfield's "local".

A left turning here along the minor road towards Longdon-on-Tern offers this view (above) over the flying field, with one of the airfield's brick defence posts still surviving.

There is no flying at Bratton these days, but things might have been very different. In the early 1990s developers came up with the revolutionary Skypark plan. In the first scheme of

its type in Europe, 65 executive homes with garages and hangars for their private planes would have been built.

The local council was keen on the plan. But it never got off the ground.

A government inspector threw the idea out. It was sunk in a sea of protests from residents nearby, worried about safety and noise.

Bridleway Gate

Bridleway Gate must be among Shropshire's more unexpected airfields – because it is by no means flat. It lies in fields north of Preston Brockhurst, bounded to the east by the busy A49, and on the west by the B5063 Wem road.

Today virtually nothing is left. A hedge runs across the old airfield site and council houses have been built alongside the A49 where the main camp once stood.

During its short wartime life Bridleway Gate, which was named after the farm from which the land was requisitioned, was a relief landing ground for nearby RAF Shawbury. There were temporary hangars, and planes would be hidden under trees in woods to the north of the site.

According to Shropshire airfields historian Flt Lt Ian Pride, it opened in January 1941 but became waterlogged and remained unusable until April and on frequent occasions thereafter. Its grass runways were used by Airspeed Oxford aircraft, twin-engined trainers, with circuits being flown at 700ft to avoid the 1,000ft circuit at Shawbury two miles away.

With high ground to the east, the occupants of Rock Hall, a now demolished property just over the road to the south east of the airfield, were given a light to put in a bedroom window to make night flying safer.

Bridleway Gate was hardly used by aircraft after March 1943 and closed for flying in January 1944. It was then used as a massive fuel depot for storing jerry cans and five-gallon drums for the planned invasion. By March 1944 there were 327,502 cans on site.

Flt Lt Pride says that from May 1944 the airfield was used almost daily for parachute and container dropping exercises, mounted from Tilstock airfield near Whitchurch, and these continued for the next 18 months. The station strength at Bridleway Gate was 124 at the end of 1944.

The last known aircraft movement was a Wellington which force landed in April 1945, departing a few days later.

Towards the end of the war the flying control area alongside the Wem road was used as an Italian POW camp. The main camp buildings by the A49 were quickly occupied by squatters after the war.

Post-war the airfield site itself was quickly reclaimed for agriculture.

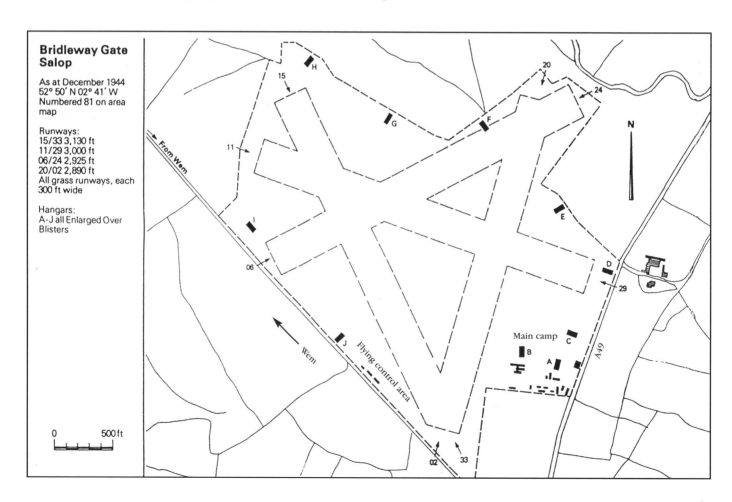

**Bridleway Gate
Salop**

As at December 1944
52° 50′ N 02° 41′ W
Numbered 81 on area
map

Runways:
15/33 3,130 ft
11/29 3,000 ft
06/24 2,925 ft
20/02 2,890 ft
All grass runways, each
300 ft wide

Hangars:
A-J all Enlarged Over
Blisters

0   500 ft

Living in the flightpath

Stan Langdon, who lived on the doorstep of Bridleway Gate airfield as a child, remembers some near misses as the aircraft raced down the runway and just cleared the top of his home. And, with rising ground to the east of the airfield, the RAF had an ingenious solution to make night flying safer – they gave his parents a lamp and asked them to hang it in a bedroom window.

When flying stopped, there was new cause for people living nearby to worry. The airfield became a massive open-air dump storing fuel for D-Day. Mr Langdon, who now lives at Salisbury Road, Market Drayton, lived at the time at a gamekeeper's cottage called Rock Hall, literally just across the A49 from the airfield on its south eastern edge. His father Arthur was a gamekeeper for Sir Gerald Corbet's estate. The cottage was demolished some years ago.

"I can remember all the diggers and caterpillars and you name it ripping out the hedges and trees to make a huge 200-acre grass airfield in the spring of 1940. What was so disappointing for me as a kid of eight is that we had a pond where we used to fish and that was drained and filled in.

"It was not a flat field by any means. If the aircraft were using the flightpath from the Springs woods they sort of raced downhill to get airborne. Our home was so close that there were times when we thought we had 'bought our lot'. The aircraft just cleared the top of our house. Aircraft taking off from north to south found themselves getting lower and lower as they raced to get airborne, and that's why we seemed to have had a few narrow misses.

"We got to know one or two of the pilots and they always laughed and said: 'We will be in for tea yet!' The commanding officer arranged it for us to display some kind of warning light when they were night flying, which they supplied. It was a paraffin lamp, an old hurricane lamp, and it was in the end bedroom window – it was a spare bedroom.

"They used part of the Springs, a huge wood, to draw the planes underneath the trees to hide them from the Jerries. Another thing I always remember as a boy is that all the village kids used to go to the camp to the cinema. It was our weekly spot and we used to go and enjoy these films. It was actually the dining room, and they put a few chairs across, put up a screen, and that was it. There are council houses where the main camp was now.

"Then there was the flying wing by the Wem road which is where the pilots had their meals. They were actually based at RAF Shawbury and were taken there night and morning for flying duties. They would be hanging out of the back of the lorries singing and waving.

"There must have been roughly 20 or 30 buildings on the main camp (alongside the A49). They were all wooden shacks, really. Most of them were billets for the ground crew. There was a cook house and then this big dining hall. All the locals used to go.

"They used to fly Oxfords. Locals called them flying coffins. They were yellowish. There was never a serious crash. We used to get the odd bellyflop, one would come down and forget to put the wheels down and that sort of thing. After two or three years the aircraft disappeared and it became a petrol storage dump. Next thing we knew, from the area of the flying wing to the east, there were rows and rows, down to the bottom, of huge mounds of jerry cans. Each mound would be seven or eight feet high, and I would say 100 yards long.

"They covered them with camouflage netting. We were dead scared of it blowing up. Towards the end of the war the flying field was used to practise parachute dropping, flying from Sleap airfield I think. They put a marker on the field and they had to drop the canister close to that marker.

"About the time the fuel went the flying headquarters became an Italian prisoner of war camp. There were about a dozen huts there which were converted into billets. The Italians would work on local farms in the day and at weekends, believe it or not, they used to walk around in pairs on the roads. They had a uniform with all different patches on them; bright yellow-green, so you knew they were prisoners of war.

Stan Langdon in 1999 with a map he drew of Bridleway Gate.

Council houses stand on the site of the main camp of the old airfield. Hardly anything remains to give a clue that this area close to the busy A49 was once part of a wartime air base.

"They could see we kept chickens and ducks and would barter with my mother for chickens and fresh eggs, bartering with things they had from their kitchen, like some sugar or tea which we couldn't get because it was rationed.

"The main camp, as war ended, was taken over by squatters."

Mr Langdon played his own part in the site's history when, after the war, he ploughed the field to return it to agriculture for the farmer, a Mr Phillips of Bridleway Gate Farm, from whom the land had been requisitioned.

John Vaux, who lives at Herne Bay, Kent, was stationed at RAF Shawbury from 1940 to the end of 1941, attached to a new section called Ground Gunners, later to become the RAF Regiment, and one of his duties was the defence of the station and areas round about – such as Shawbury's relief landing ground at Bridleway Gate – from airborne invasion.

"Exactly what six trucks converted into armoured cars ("Armadillos") and provided with a radio, Lewis gun, some hand grenades and a gunner could do in protecting the station from invasion is uncertain. It is true we had a radio – when it worked – a tent out at Bridleway Gate and a tele-phone, so I suppose we could at least inform RT control at HQ of an invasion – briefly!

"Our main concern was the relief landing ground at Bridleway Gate. It was once just large fields but the hedges had been bulldozed away and a couple of huts provided and one Armadillo. Here under training pilots flew twin-engined Oxfords to improve their landing skills.

"Having one morning observed six crashes in about two hours on a windy day at Bridleway Gate I came to the conclusion their landing techniques did need improving. One young chap landed with his wheels up and then tried to go round again with only half his props. With his engines making an extraordinary noise he just missed the NAAFI van and plonked himself down on top of a hedge on the Wem road. He was not hurt.

"One day our Armadillo was detailed to go to Bridleway Gate for a 24-hour duty. There were no Oxfords that day as the weather was too bad for flying, so the landing ground was empty except for the dark shape of a Wellington that had made an emergency landing the day before. Once evening Stand To was over we set about making ourselves some sort of meal before setting out to patrol the airfield. It was cold with a ground frost.

"The air raid sirens began to wail; loud from Wem, less so from Shawbury and very faint from Shrewsbury. The moan slowly faded away and then came the familiar droning as the first wave of enemy bombers flew overhead going north. We stopped and gazed up at the star-filled sky and then one of the patrol pointed at the Wellington. 'Hey! What's that light down there?'

"A faint light could be seen from the big aircraft but as we moved it vanished. Anyone there had no right to be within half a mile of the airfield, let alone the bomber. There was no help for it, we had to go down a slope and out to the aircraft and investigate, in the dark, for to show torchlight in the middle of an air raid was not sensible.

"But in spite of the raid it was still very dark indeed when we got to the bomber and there was no sign of any light but a sudden movement in the nearby woods made us all think someone had heard us coming and run into the woods, so we set off in pursuit. To struggle through a thick wood in pitch darkness carrying respirators, rifles, and ammunition was a sure recipe for disaster, which soon came when we slipped 15 feet down an unseen edge to plunge into a muddy ditch of some kind.

"Much bruised and with a considerable number of scratches and some bad language we struggled out of the ditch or stream and made our way back to the airfield. By now the raid was at its peak, wave after wave of bombers were going over as the searchlights swept the sky and the anti-aircraft was quite spectacular. Continuous flashes low down indicated more bombs and a dull red glow began to show to the north.

"As we paused to stare we became aware of an aircraft approaching very low and then a German bomber appeared at barely 300ft with its port engine on fire. The flames clearly lit up the black cross on its side and the curved shape of the wings. It was a Heinkel III and was just maintaining height. Then it began a slow turn to starboard and vanished behind

some trees, and a few moments later a big orange mushroom of flame shot up above the trees followed by a dull boom. We had no means of knowing if the crew were still in the doomed machine or had been able to bale out, perhaps not far away.

"We now moved along a narrow lane running beside the woods and suddenly we heard distant voices calling and they were not speaking English. We stopped and hid behind a holly bush – very prickly – until five men in unfamiliar uniforms appeared and we jumped out and bellowed 'Halt!' and shoved our rifles towards them.

"They stopped in great alarm but quite understood the motions we made with our rifles. We marched them back to our 'base' where a phone call to HQ got a rather grumpy reply. It was 0300 hours.

"We were told a detail of soldiers would come out and pick the five men up. In an hour a truck arrived with seven soldiers and they all departed.

"We later heard they were Free Polish Air Force officers who had been for a drink in Wem and after that had got hopelessly lost. They were returned to their

A view of the old airfield site from near the A49. Inset: Mr Vaux's cartoon of an "Armadillo" in action.

unit with a very strong recommendation that they did not in future wander about a foreign country at war, in the dark, not able to speak the language and in the middle of an air raid.

"However, we still had not solved the problem of the light in the Wellington bomber. Finally we all reached the aircraft and decided that whoever was showing the light must still be on board, so we would go in and catch him. We carefully made our way into the aircraft and this time

did use the torch. The mystery was solved. The glow of the luminous instrument panel had been reflected by the curved perspex windows and in some way focussed into a narrow beam of light which disappeared as soon as you moved away from the beam. Simple really."

Sketches below by John Vaux

The Blizzard Bridleway Gate Jan 1941. We were supposed to be on duty for 24 hours it looked out to be 96 hours! We lived on beans and coffee mainly!

Oxford does a 'wheels up' landing at Bridleway Gate with both props broken it bounced and crashed into a hedge on the Wem road The pupil pilot was not hurt fortunately it missed the NAAFI van! Just!

1944

January 15: No 245 MU formed as an RAF detachment from HQ No 42 Group at Bridleway Gate (an unused satellite to RAF station Shawbury) as a packed fuel unit.

January 17: First trainload of packed spirit arrived and was offloaded. 18,000 jerricans.

February 29: Stock: jerricans 327,512; 5-gallon USA drums 10,381; 4-gallon lub oil 14,526.

May 2: Advice rcvd from HQ maintenance command dated May 2, 1944, that approval was given for RAF Tilstock to use the airfield for parachute container dropping exercises.

May 6: 1400. The first parachute container dropping exercises

commenced.

June 5: A photograph was taken of the unit personnel. Although the weather was cold, the result was good. (Parachute container dropping exercises continued into 1945).

1945

November: C&M party, Preston Brockhurst. "Parachute container exercises continued when weather permitted by detachment from RAF Tilstock and Sleap."

"As a decision is expected daily on the formal disposal of the site, and taking also into consideration that the unit is being run by a skeleton staff, no concrete arrangements can be made for the Christmas break period."

The staff of 245 Maintenance Unit at Bridleway Gate airfield on June 5, 1944. They are, back row, from left: Corporal F. Marrow (? name difficult to read), AC2 J. O'Neill, AC1 A. Dolton, LAC A. Deacon, LAC F.L. Derlin, LAC R. Lowe, Cpl J. Price, Cpl R. Evans.
Middle row, from left: LAC S. Hayward, Cpl C. Tothill, LAC A. Rosier (or maybe Rosin), AC2 R. Watt, AC2 D. McLaren, AC2 A. McGrath, AC2 M. Slattery, AC2 P.A. Maguire, LAC J. Thom.
Front, from left: AC2 H. Gregory, AC1 R.J. Parkes, Sgt F.L. Pamucker (?), F/O J.P. Gallagher, W/O E.A. Smith, LAC H. Roberts, AC1 W. Rocke (or Roche), Cpl Dickie (no initial given). *(National Archives)*

Bridleway Gate today

Take the A49 road north of Shrewsbury. Shortly after the village of Preston Brockhurst the B5063 road towards Wem forks off to the left. The airfield was bounded by these two roads and the woods to the north. The main camp area was next to the A49, where a clutch of council houses now stand.

The old flying field is now completely given over to agriculture and is crossed by a hedge, and is not even particularly flat, so some imagination is needed to conjure up images of this as an active airfield. No wartime buildings survive.

View from the Wem road looking across the flying area.

Brockton

Using all the techniques of camouflage and disguise, Brockton airfield was hidden away in the countryside so effectively that this "secret" wartime airfield remains pretty much a secret for many people.

Yet it is right on the doorstep of modern Telford, and in the shadow of the village of Kemberton. The airfield buildings were deliberately designed to look distinctly unwarlike in an effort to fool any roaming Luftwaffe raiders.

The canteen and watch office are today cosy bungalows. An unremarkable barn-like building a short distance behind the Masons Arms, which was very much the airfield's "local", is in fact a surviving hangar.

There were two runways of grass, overlaid with wire mesh, some of which can still be seen reinforcing hedges and fences in the area. The longer runway ran north west-south east and was about 3,300ft.

And it was not just tiddly planes which landed at Brockton, which was known to locals as "the landing ground" or "the strip". Whitley and Wellington bombers, together with the legendary Spitfire, were among types here. Special hides were built to conceal the aircraft and ash was used to give the impression hedges ran across the runways. Cattle grazed within fenced areas to make the elaborate deception even more convincing.

Brockton was a satellite landing ground to RAF Cosford, designated 30 SLG. Its role was essentially to look after and store aircraft from the parent base. It came into being on June 30, 1941, and is thought to have closed in about 1945, reverting once more to anonymous fields.

Brockton memories

Jim Reeve cleared the way for the first aircraft to land at Brockton airfield. Mr Reeve was a Mancunian working at the time at RAF Cosford as a civilian engine fitter. He and his friend, the late Jack Davies who used to keep a cycle shop in Newport, arrived by motorbike at their new base at Brockton to find it was just a rough field.

"There was somebody already there giving orders and we were asked to go up and down this big field and pick up any obstructions such as tree branches," said Mr Reeve.

While they were doing so a Spitfire from Cosford flown by a Pilot Officer Francis appeared and came in to land, the uneven ground causing its wings to rock. "I thought it was going to knock a wing tip. It came to a stop and that was the first plane to land at Brockton," said Mr Reeve, who does not remember the date.

"He took off again and after that more people started to come over. We had the grass cut and rolls of very strong square mesh were laid on the ground."

Several makeshift hangars were erected – wire mesh over steel frames, and covered in artificial grass, camouflaging the precious planes. "We had Whitleys mainly – funny old two-engined bombers – together with Spitfires now and again. Blenheims came later and there were also Beauforts and Wellingtons. There were Ansons, Oxfords, and we had a Beaufighter," said Mr Reeve.

A pilot would fly over from Cosford in an Anson every so often to test-fly the planes. "I often went up with them. They used to ask the fitter or armourer or wireless op to go up with them, to have faith in their work I suppose."

Mr Reeve said the Brockton field, where he never saw an accident, was quite busy. It had two runways, arranged in an L shape. "Sometimes we got Whitleys coming in from a factory. I used to stand outside the hangar and you could see them in the distance coming in. We used to have as many as five or six at once. Then another plane would come in called a ferry plane to take all the pilots back to Cosford."

His wife Eda Reeve (then Miss Eda Stephens) lived in Mill Lane, Kemberton, and could see planes landing at close quarters.

"They used to come over the edge of our garden and you could wave to the pilots. We got to know them. Some of the pilots lodged at Kemberton Hall and at the Rectory, and at the Quarters," she said.

Eda first met Jim when she went with her sister Margaret, who worked in the canteen at RAF Cosford, to a 9 Maintenance Unit dance in Albrighton. Eda remembers that when Margaret married at Kemberton Church, Brockton's commanding officer, an RAF man named Gibbs, returned unexpectedly to find all the airfield's

Jim and Eda Reeve in wartime.

A unique picture of the entire Brockton airfield staff, probably taken early in the airfield's life. It comes from Mr and Mrs Jim Reeve, of Shifnal, who identify the staff where known as: **Back row**: extreme left, George Ford, transport and standby ambulance driver; fourth left, Harry Darlington, who lived near Newport and was a rigger; sixth from right, Charlie Fennell, electrician from Market Drayton; then George Hughes, fitter from Newport; Jack Davies, from Newport; and third from right, Bill Doody, a radio operator from Wellington. **Third row**: left, Harry Edkins, a labourer; second left "Bill", a labourer who kept the Pheasant pub in Madeley; sixth from left, Ted Cant, a Londoner, who was an engine fitter; eighth from right, Tom Latimer from the South Coast, an electrician; next is Billy Price, deputy to the foreman; then Dave Morley, a Londoner who lived in Albrighton; third from right is Ted Hadley, from Madeley; then Jim Reeve; and, at the end of the row, George Enfield. **Second row**: third from left (in light jacket), Harry Wass, from Kemberton; fifth along, Bill Bowen, the foreman; next to him, centre of row, "Gibbs", the commanding officer; second from right, Don Crampton, who lodged in Shifnal. **Front row**: second from left, "Taffy", an armourer; second from right, Jimmy Iredale or Airdale, who lodged in Wolverhampton; extreme right, Dicky Howard, from Shifnal, who drove the Bedford trucks backwards and forwards from Cosford carrying supplies.

mechanics and fitters outside the church when they should have been at work!

Her father invited him in to toast the bride, and after the CO had cut himself a slice of ham – meat was scarce – nothing more was said about the matter. Jim served at Brockton until about 1945 when he transferred to Silloth in Cumbria. He and Eda married in 1948.

Norman Angell from Shifnal was a child at the time of the strip's heyday: "I can remember Brockton from when I was at Kemberton School during the war. It was always known as 'the landing ground'.

"The main recollection I have is of the Whitley bombers which towed Horsa gliders.

"The gliders would release from the tow and glide in to Cosford and then the Whitleys would come over Brockton and release the tow ropes which would drop to the ground and be taken back to Cosford by lorry.

"We used to go to the Masons Arms in Kemberton to have our hair cut on a Sunday afternoon and you could see the planes on the airfield from the back of the pub, and also when you looked from the main Shifnal to Bridgnorth road.

"At the end of the war some of the glider bodies were sold – just the fuselage – and they made wonderful storage sheds. My grandfather bought one and my uncle and father each had part of it. We had a section of it in our garden in Kemberton which doubled as a shed and a playhouse.

"When we left my father sold it to a farmer at Brockton."

Vic Jackson, of Dawley, said: "I went to Brockton in 1939 after the war started. They set us to work cleaning the place up. There was a firm there called Currell, Lewis & Martin – I don't know the spelling – which came from Wolverhampton. We had a little truck and loaded all the rubbish like old cars, and bikes, which had been dumped there over time, and buried all the rubbish in a field alongside the road to Beckbury.

"I was a labourer and we put the bombers away. We had Whitleys and Wellingtons and we had to back them into the trees and put big concrete weights on them to stop them blowing away, and put a few branches on the front so you couldn't tell they were there.

"Then there came two steam wagons with a roller on and they went each side of the runway and rolled that flat. One day a Spitfire came in, some say it was a Dutchman, and he missed the wire which was on the roller running from one steam wagon to the other.

"There were soldiers with guns there in little dugouts all around the runway. I was there from 1939 to 1940. I used to walk from Dawley to be down there at 7.30am and then walk back at night. I was only a young lad then. I left school in 1938 at the age of 15.

"It was used as a storage place and they would come in to fly the planes away. One girl who used to ferry planes took off in a plane to deliver it somewhere and was never seen again.

"When they fetched the planes out they used to go down the bank onto the runway and they would leave tyre marks. They had a piece of wood like a railway sleeper with a handle on it and after every plane took off I had to use it to stamp out the tyre marks on the ground so the Germans couldn't see them."

A place called home

One of the old airfield buildings became home to Bill and Frances Turner. Mr Turner did not know it was an airfield building until he went into the local shop and they said: "You're the people who have taken over the house on the strip."

Bill served in the wartime RAF as a bomb aimer on Whitleys and Halifaxes. He said in 1998: "It was surprising and rather pleasing in a way to know I'm now living in an old RAF building."

Mrs Margaret Chatham of Kemberton remembered of the airfield: "They used to have the dog handlers at Brockton Grange and the day we moved in during February 1944, they moved out. Then they put a prefab bungalow for them in the field near the house, with a Nissen hut right across the front drive of Brockton Grange."

Mrs Chatham moved in to Brockton Grange with her husband and daughter. But the family were not allowed to do any decorating in their new home until the Air Ministry had assessed the damage from its military occupation for compensation purposes. Mrs Chatham said the airfield was quite busy and the planes were stored under mesh camouflage.

Bill Turner outside his home – the old Brockton airfield office – in 1998..

War diary

1941

June 30: Recorded as being partly available for use.

July 2: Airfield officially opened. Initially decided to use it for storage and preparation of Wellingtons, Whitleys and Blenheims, but soon after opening it was decided that other types could be added.

1942

January/February: Receipt and dispatch of aircraft held up due to snow and wet patches on the north-south landing strip.

May 31: In addition to Wellingtons and Whitleys, Spitfires were now regularly coming in and out. Two camouflage hedges constructed across the landing strip.

June: Output of operational aircraft during the month increased, a total of 28 being dispatched during the period. Site contractors completed the work of creating dummy hedges by painting across the landing strips, and the results from the air were reported by unit pilots to be entirely satisfactory. The perimeter of the greater part of the satellite was staked off to permit the grazing of cattle and this resulted in a considerable improvement of the site from a camouflage point of view. A day patrol in the area was arranged in addition to the night patrols.

August 31: Work proceeded normally and smoothly, 17 aircraft being dispatched during the month. The satellite constructed a guard dog compound out of its own resources, which was considered by the commanding officer to be most satisfactory. Materials used included wooden posts, manufactured on site, and steel wool (sic). Satellite maintenance gang carried out the work.

October 31: Numbers of aircraft available were small and the month was chiefly notable for the arrival of representatives of Messrs Callenders, the firm undertaking the work of covering the steel aircraft hides.

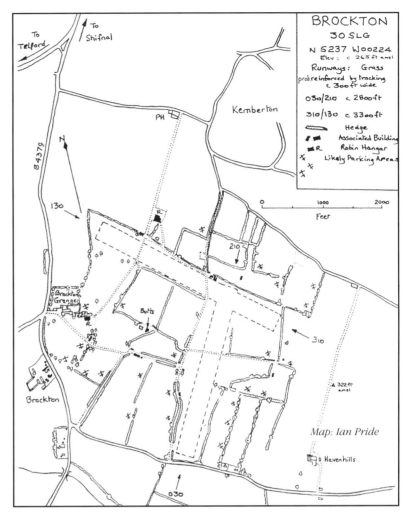

Map: Ian Pride

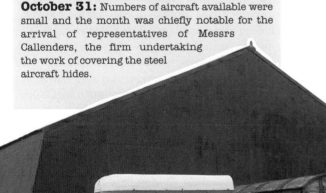

Brockton today

Despite being hidden deep in the countryside, and the deliberately temporary nature of the airfield, a surprising amount of clues – for those who know what to look for – remain of the wartime use.

Brockton village is just south east of Telford, not far from the Halesfield industrial estate. Drive along the B4379 through the village and just south of it turn left, eastwards towards Ryton. Look through any of the large gaps in the hedge on the left and you have an overview of the airfield site. In the distance you will see, in the shadow of the village of Kemberton, a rare survivor in the shape of a Robin hangar, which is now a riding stables. Shooting butts and the shell of an old airfield building are also visible, but the airfield administration buildings (now homes) are screened by trees.

For those lucky enough to possess a horse, there is a bridleway which crosses the site.

This Super Robin hangar near the village of Kemberton is a rare survivor of its type.

"H.Q. No.5 P.A.F.U. RAF Tern Hill, Salop; 'A' Flight, Chetwynd, near Newport, Salop. Jan 1944. WJB front row, extreme right, kneeling." WJB was the late William J. Bennett, from Shrewsbury, a Leading Aircraftsman airframes fitter at wartime Chetwynd. The aircraft on which they are posing is a Hawker Hurricane. *(Selwyn Bennett)*

Chetwynd

Small and rudimentary, the airfield of Chetwynd took a steady toll of young lives during the war. It was the little baby of RAF Tern Hill, as it was to relieve pressure on that big and busy air base that some planes and pilots in training were switched to the newly-created grass airfield which became operational as a relief landing ground on September 13, 1941.

Its role was an important one, that of training fighter pilots. And despite all the disadvantages of the site, which quickly became known to the students back then – an often soggy, undulating landing area with woefully short runways – it is today, over 60 years later, one of Shropshire's few surviving military airfields still in use.

Helicopters from RAF Shawbury regularly use Chetwynd for training on weekdays and there are occasional visits by bigger stuff, like the four-engined Hercules transport plane which landed there and got bogged down in soft ground in

August 1999. Wartime veterans could have warned the pilot to be careful. It was five days before it could fly out again after a major rescue operation which drew crowds.

RAF Chetwynd's training role continued throughout the war, the principal aircraft being the Miles Master trainer, but also some Hurricanes, and with other types dropping in. Accommodation was limited, with a handful of huts for pilots and ground staff, workshops, and a few small hangars.

Night flying was a feature of the courses, and from July 1942 a successful innovation was introduced which allowed this to be done in daytime as well. The runways were marked out with a "sodium flarepath" – presumably high intensity sodium lights – and the student pilots wore shaded goggles or screens to turn day into night.

Comings and goings by air and by road from Tern Hill were frequent. Chetwynd was from time to time unserviceable because of the weather, and on at least one occasion the unit moved more or less en bloc to another airfield (RAF Molesworth in this case) to complete the training on its concrete, all-weather runways.

Training was dangerous. In one particularly bad month, October 1941, three Chetwynd pilots were killed in crashes near the airfield, with a further fatality at Puleston Common in November. Within a few weeks in training, and before seeing any combat, about one in 10 of this particular course had been killed.

The chief flying instructor of the training school – the 5 (Pilot) Advanced Flying Unit – was one high profile casualty. Wing Commander A.W.M. Finny died in January 1943 during spin training. His pupil managed to bale out. It is not clear from records if the wing commander was flying from Tern Hill or Chetwynd at the time of this incident.

Post-war, Chetwynd continued as Tern Hill's little baby, and planes such as Tiger Moths, Harvards, Prentices, and Provosts, were regularly seen here.

With the closure of Tern Hill as an RAF station in 1976, it is RAF Shawbury which is now Chetwynd's parent station, and its helicopters are a common sight at this sparse and barren wartime airfield which continues to play a valuable role in training pilots for the armed services into the 21st century.

War diary

1941

September 13: Flying commenced, as an RLG to Tern Hill. One flight engaged in day flying.

October 17: Master W8562 crashed at Chetwynd RLG while night flying. The pilot, LAC W.C. Vocking, a pupil on 66 course, killed.

October 23: Master W8569 crashed near Chetwynd. The pilot, LAC H.R. Johnson of 66 course, killed.

October 29: Master N7450 crashed near Chetwynd, the pilot, LAC B.N. Lee, of 66 course, being killed.

November 26: Hurricane P3607 crashed at Puleston Common, near Chetwynd, at 1320 hours and LAC J.B. Price, a pupil of 66 Course, received injuries from which he died at 1615 hours the same day.

December 13: 66 Course completed flying training and passed out.

December summary: Progress was good for the first half of the month, but was slow during the latter half owing to the wet and muddy ground.

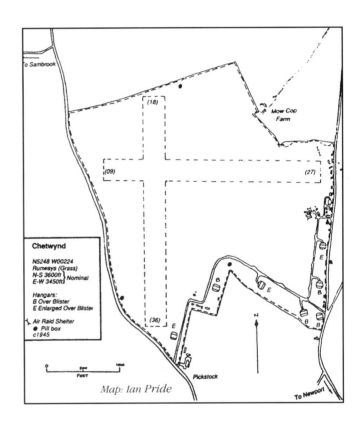

Map: Ian Pride

'A wretched place'

In 1941 Howell Jones was among the first group of pilots trained at the spartan Chetwynd airfield. "We were a group of fighter pilots who did the initial training at RAF Sealand. We had to go to Tern Hill first because the field was not fit for flying.

"It was a rather wretched field to fly on at Chetwynd. It had wet patches on it. There was soft ground and I was one of those who got stuck. I had just landed in a Miles Master, and was taxiing towards the dispersal. The one wheel sank in the ground.

"Chetwynd became a satellite for Tern Hill. We left Tern Hill and we moved down there about half way through the course, because the accommodation was not ready. We eventually stayed there and slept overnight. The facilities were very poor. There was nothing at all, really, just Nissen huts. We managed, but it was a bit rudimentary. We were there for about a month, for the latter part of the course. We continued training until we got our wings. Then of course the Japs raided Pearl Harbor the last week we were there. That put the cat among the pigeons. There was no wings parade for us. We just had to go up to the stores counter at Tern Hill and get all our wings and stripes from over the counter.

"I can't think who the commander was at Chetwynd offhand. He was a Group Captain. He made an entry in my logbook following my taxiing into this soft ground. It reads something like this in red ink: 'Taxied into unmarked soft area. No blame on pilot'.

"We were considered a Flight. There were about a dozen or 15 aircraft at Chetwynd, Masters and Hurricanes. I enjoyed my time there very much. It was a bit hairy sometimes, harem scarem. We had to do night flying there. They put the flarepath away from the soft patches. I lost my best friend there. I was flying with him in the early part of the night, and after I had done my stint I went back to the billet and went to bed, and he took over from me. He crashed quite

near to the airfield on night solo.

"The instructor would take us round once or twice to see we were all right, and then we were considered capable of flying at night. Some took to it quite easily. This pal of mine, Johnson – I can't remember his first name but we called him Johnny

Johnson – obviously lost his bearings. I woke up in the morning and his bed had been taken from the hut, and that was that. That was the end of him. We lost three pilots. One took off in coarse pitch, one got lost on night flying, and another pilot did the same.

"Newport was not far away and it provided two nights a week for our evening recreation, which was mainly dancing. The girls of Newport were only too happy to share an evening's dancing with us in a dance hall at the north end of the town."

The pilots on the course were from all over Britain and the world, but Leading Aircraftsman Jones, as he was then, was from not far away, at Llandrindod Wells. He served with 5 SFTS at Tern Hill from August 8, 1941, to October 12, 1941, and then at Chetwynd from October 12, 1941, to December 12, 1941 (flying logbook, left). Later he went on to operational flying with 261 Squadron in the Far East. He left the RAF with the rank of Flight Lieutenant in 1946 and became a farmer.

Mr Jones (pictured during his RAF service above) made a sentimental return to Chetwynd airfield in 1999 when an RAF Hercules got bogged down there, and noted wryly that it got bogged down in exactly the same spot as he had got bogged down in his Miles Master almost 60 years previously.

Snippets of Chetwynd life

Tom Gatward, of Fishers Lock, Newport, was a leading aircraftsman who was initially stationed at RAF Tern Hill but was soon moved in 1941 to RAF Chetwynd, which was still not complete. "When we got there we had to pitch tents. We were in tents for about a month or more before they completed the Nissen huts, which we then moved into.

"The flying was on the other side of the airfield and we had to walk across the airfield to get our lunch and meals. The cookhouse was on one side, and we were on the other side, by the road which runs from Pickstock to Sambrook. We had four or five Nissen huts there."

Mr Gatward, an instrument maker hailing originally from Royston, Hertfordshire, said while they were at Chetwynd they would be sent to air stations far and wide,

including Bassingbourn and Molesworth, for several weeks at a time, before returning to Chetwynd.

"We were stationed there permanently, and the aircrew used to come in from Tern Hill by bus. Some were stationed by the billets by the cookhouse. Some came down each day, some were on refresher courses, some were training. We had Miles Masters and a couple of Hurricanes, and a couple of Spitfires on refresher courses from fellows who had been on general ops. We had a Tiger Moth there. We had to anchor it down every night otherwise the wind would blow it over.

"For night flying we used paraffin flares. All of a sudden this huge aircraft appeared and tried to land. It was a Wellington and landed on our flarepath. It could not pull up in the length of the field and so it went over the road, across the Sambrook road, into a potato field and stopped just short of the Meese. All the fuselage was piled up with potatoes. I think they were Free Frenchmen. They asked: 'Where are we? Are we in France?' We said: 'No, you're not – you're in Shropshire.' They were from a base in Yorkshire and were loaded with incendiaries and were supposed to be on an incendiary raid to Germany. I was on duty and we went there and rushed across. They were all right.

"There were some pilots from Seighford who came over and dropped a challenge to our men. They were on refresher courses in Hurricanes and it was for a dogfight. In the ensuing dogfight they collided and both crashed. We had to jump into the fire tender and rush down. It was awful, terrible. The Chetwynd plane crashed up Stafford Road, Newport.

"We watched two flying planes over Chetwynd Firs dog-fighting. I don't know where they came from. One crashed at Standford Bridge, and the other at (Hincks plantation) Lilleshall. The first aircraft was spinning down gently and the

Still rudimentary – but still in use. Chetwynd's flying control today.

bloke was in his parachute and it caught on the tail. He was swinging about underneath it. It crashed and apparently he was all right until the tail end fell on him."

Recalling how Chetwynd's infamous soft ground sometimes meant it was left idle for weeks on end, he said: "We would be gone six or seven weeks or perhaps a couple of months and then when we arrived back they would say 'We thought we got rid of you'.

"One thing they tried to put over on us was the story about Madame Piggott, the ghost of Chetwynd, who used years ago to walk down the road with chains. When we used to go for a drink in the pubs the old hands would say 'Look out for Madame Piggott when you go back'.

"The commander was Flt Lt Agabeg (nicknamed Aggy). He was half Indian. He called himself the Camp Commandant, not just the camp commander. He was a really nice bloke."

Mr Gatward, who left Chetwynd some time in the second half of 1943, recalls: "There was one hangar, right at the top corner where the cookhouse was. There was not much work done there. Most of the work was done on the field, outside. If there were any major repairs to do, they were taken back to Tern Hill.

"We used to run a football team there and play surrounding teams, like the navy at Childs Ercall. I was made captain. I played left half. We won our league easily. There were some good players in that team. Eddie Holmes was on the Arsenal books, and Jock Swan was on the Celtic books. They were based at Chetwynd with the RAF. We hadn't got a goalkeeper, that was the trouble. We used to talk somebody into playing in goal."

LAC Gatward was posted from Chetwynd to serve with Coastal Command at Lizard Point, Cornwall.

1942

January 1942 summary: E and F Flights, 68 course, detached to RLG Chetwynd from Tern Hill. Progress was however negligible owing to bad weather and consequent bad state of the landing ground.

April 13: 5 Service Flying Training School became 5 (Pilot) Advanced Flying Unit.

April 24: Flying instruction recommenced at Chetwynd RLG.

May 1942 summary: Chetwynd aerodrome almost unserviceable since 25.5.42 owing to partial waterlogged condition of the ground.

July 25: "Day-night flying" using sodium flarepath started. Pupils took off from Tern Hill to carry out the day-night flying exercise at Chetwynd. "Day-night flying is rapidly proving its value as a training feature in that an increasing number of pupils are flying solo at night after only one dual night landing."

September 9: Master crashed and burned at Chetwynd 0300 hours. Site one and a half miles east. Results fatal to both crew. Apparently overshot flarepath and turned too low, hitting a tree. Flying Officer Wright was able to reach the site in a few minutes by motorcycle, the ambulance and fire tender being already there.

Barnstorming antics

The open-ended blister hangars at RAF Chetwynd seem to have been too much of a temptation for some daredevil pilots. **Tom Jervis**, who lived at the time in the last house in adjoining Pickstock, says that on two occasions aircraft actually flew through them. Although he didn't personally see this happen, he says others told him about it.

"One of the pilots, and I can't remember names, decided to fly through the hangar just up off the road from our place. He must have done it. A couple of people, who I suppose were mechanics, told me that so-and-so had flown through that hangar. That was in a Master. Then another pilot said he was going to do it in a Hurricane, and he did. I heard the whoosh as it flew through. They both got away with it."

In another incident he recalls a crash involving a Wellington bomber. "I was coming along on my bike the night that Wellington came across. It was about 400 yards away. I think he must have been lost. He circled the aerodrome several times, and then overshot and it crashed across the road in front of me. I was 18 and had been working out at Ellerton Wood doing some fencing. This was about quarter past seven in the evening. It was dark. It must have been the spring, and was in 1942.

"There was a lot of noise and clatter. I did not stop. I could see the Jeeps were all coming straight down the field. I thought they did not need me in the way. I think the crew weren't too bad. It landed between Nicklin's field and Thomas Wheat's field. It was well guarded when I went back. I had to cycle by to get to work the next morning.

"I can tell you some things about the airfield. One

Master was landing when another plane crossed his path. The instructor took control and pulled the plane up and got it off the ground. At the far end of where they did the runway was a windsock and he had not got quite high enough to miss it. The end of the wing caught it and swung him straight round. This was practically in front of our place, and back towards the road. There was a little tiny holly bush and he clipped the top of that. I'm afraid it set on fire and they were burned. They came and foamed that fire. I know for a fact that not even weeds grew for 11 years after that."

George Nicklin, of Showell Mill farm, was too young to have clear memories of the wartime period, but there are tales which his late father Reg told him which lend support to the story that pilots flew through the hangars. "My dad came out with the tale that just after it was built they used to dare one another to fly under the hangars, which were open-ended. It was a dare for packets of fags.

"My dad could remember the airfield being made. There were one or two big, natural, pitholes, which they filled. The talk goes that there was one place where the horse and cart had backed into the pithole and they had to cut the horse out and get the horse away, but the cart disappeared in

A general view over the site.

the hole.

"Another thing my dad said was that if you ever wanted a bag of grass seeds, you could get as much as you wanted when they were doing the reseeding when they originally made it. The first thing I can remember about it is that all the trees on our ground which belonged to the Chetwynd estate were cut down. I can remember playing on them as kids. They lay there for years and years before anybody did anything about them because there were no such things as chain saws – they were all cross cut saws. I think at the end of the war they put obstacles on it to stop enemy aircraft from landing on the field.

"This plane came down right in between the wheat and potato field. It filled the back of the aeroplane with potatoes. It had no end of little bombs in it. My dad went

up there and he got threatened with a gun, and warned he would be shot."

Geoff Abel, from Wellington, had a brief acquaintance with Chetwynd airfield in 1942. "I was trained in Canada and we returned in April and spent two weeks at Tern Hill. We were trained in Harvards, which were American, and so when we returned we were sent to Tern Hill to convert to Miles Masters, which was a typical British aircraft.

"We used to fly to this satellite aerodrome, and do circuits and bumps. There was just a landing strip and the rest of it was a field. On the left of this strip there was a Nissen hut which had a stove. We sat around the stove if it was bad weather and flew back to Tern Hill at night."

Afterwards he went to RAF Aston Down where he converted to Spitfires.

Chetwynd today

Take the A41 road northwards out of Newport. Beyond Chetwynd church (on the left), take the minor road to the right, to Puleston. At Puleston, take the second turn to the left, and follow this country road for about a mile. Chetwynd airfield becomes visible on the left. There are one or two buildings and signs, but it is sparser than ever.

Chetwynd airfield is an active airfield in the ownership of the Ministry of Defence. Although no aircraft are based there, it is in regular use by visiting helicopters from RAF Shawbury for training.

RAF Chetwynd's notoriously soggy surface captured a modern victim in the shape of a giant C130 Hercules which became bogged down in August 1999. It had been practising landing and taking off from a small airfield, but recent heavy rain had made Chetwynd even more treacherous than normal. It was stranded for five days and Bank Holiday crowds of hundreds of people turned out to watch it fly off back to its base at RAF Lyneham.

Condover

RAF Condover spent the wartime years dedicated to the unspectacular but vital task of training, although the occasional visit from heavy bombers livened things up from time to time. In fact it has been described as a bit of a white elephant because, although not a small airfield, it was relatively underused. Today the derelict control tower, with the words "Flying Control" still faintly visible on it, is like a ghost to remind us of those years.

The three concrete runways have long disappeared, yet quite a few of the wartime buildings survive, some of which are used in an industrial estate. And horses from Berriewood Farm canter here and there.

For people who are accustomed to today's billiard-table flat airports, the undulating nature of the site is a surprise. The runway running north-south in particular has a pronounced concavity. Condover was originally planned as a satellite to RAF Atcham and the first visitor was the commanding officer at Atcham, who arrived in a Miles Magister on October 17, 1941, to inspect progress. Condover officially opened on August 21, 1942, but under the auspices of RAF Shawbury which used it for its Oxfords. Pupils were introduced to navigation and cross country flying and there was also night flying.

There were, from time to time, unexpected visitors. A Pathfinder Lancaster on "ops" made an emergency landing. The Oxfords moved out in January 1944 and Miles Masters from Tern Hill arrived, but after only three months flying stopped for runway repairs. By the end of 1944 there were 661 RAF and 98 WAAF personnel at the station.

In January 1945 Harvards, a particularly noisy single-engined trainer, arrived and tore around the countryside, but in June the aircraft left and the RAF Condover story was essentially over.

A very rare picture from the papers of the late William J. Bennett of Shrewsbury. His original caption, reading from left, was: "Condover, March 1945, Cpl Whitehead, Sgt (?) Savile (or Savill), Joe Bannister, self, A/C Roberts." The aircraft is a Harvard. *(Selwyn Bennett)*

'Avro' Anson's war

Mrs **Margaret Edwards** of Shrewsbury was based at RAF Condover for about 18 months as a driver in the WAAF. "It was the happiest place you could be. It was like a family," said Mrs Edwards, who had joined up as a teenager around 1940.

Her maiden name of Anson immediately gave rise to a nickname which stuck – "Avro" Anson.

"People who knew me then still call me Avro," said Mrs Edwards, who arrived at Condover from RAF Shawbury about the beginning of 1942.

"They were flying Miles Masters. It was a training station and a very small place at the time." She was billeted in a Nissen hut but was lucky because in her free time she was able to get to her home, which was close by at North Hermitage, Shrewsbury.

"We used to go to the Fox Inn at Ryton. Rather! That was our pub. We had some marvellous times there, sneaking back after 12. It was a happy site and we had some nice people round us. We had Mrs Evans at The Cottage, which was next to the MT (motor transport) section. She was good to us. We called her Ma and she used to look after us if we had any troubles.

"We weren't supposed to climb the fence and go to her cottage, but we knew she was always there for us. She was a marvellous person."

Her duties as a driver were varied, ranging from fetching officers from the railway station, to driving round the airfield to put down flarepath lights, driving an ambulance to crash sites, and taking German and Italian prisoners of war to their work on farms in a Dodge tipper.

"When you went in in the morning you looked on the board and whatever was on the board, you did. Sometimes you were on flarepath duty. We didn't have runway lights at Condover and had to take out lanterns. If that was your job you picked up a Bantam Carrier, a low loading vehicle, fetched the engineer who sat with you and had to put these lights all along the runway. If the wind changed you had to get the man again and fetch them in.

"I went to several air crashes from Condover. There was one I went to in which I was first on the scene. A Canadian on his first solo, in a Master I think, had flown into The Lawley (a nearby hill). He was too low and was killed outright. I was on ambulance duty that night.

"We had a Lancaster come in one day. The airfield was not nearly big enough for a Lancaster. It had dropped its bombs

out at sea and when it started to come in it was so huge that I thought that it was never going to get in. It didn't, and went round again, and the next time it came in.

"I was sent out to take the crew to the officers mess. When I got there one of them said to me 'would you like to have a look in our ship?' I'm not sure whether the crew were Canadian. I got in and it was terribly hot and stuffy. I have never forgotten that feeling. They gave me some chocolate which all the girls tried to get off me."

For recreation they could go to the Naafi or to the hall nearby on camp, where there were dances. And she would drive a camouflaged bus to Shrewsbury, parking at a pub in Smithfield Road and dropping off people from the base for a night out, although she preferred herself to take the opportunity to visit her mother at home before driving the group, some of whom would by now be the worse for drink, back to base.

It was an incident while taking a walk from home which had inspired her to become a driver in the first place.

"I went for a walk when I was about 17 and walked over the golf course and got to a stile where there were all these 30 cwt Fordsons lined up. These girls got out and were eating these rations, which were put in a white linen bag in those days. I talked to some and thought 'this is the life for me.' My mother wanted me to go into nursing."

Mrs Edwards (seen inset in about 1942) served at Heaton Park after her time at Condover. She went on to organise the annual reunion for people who served at RAF Shawbury and RAF Condover during the war.

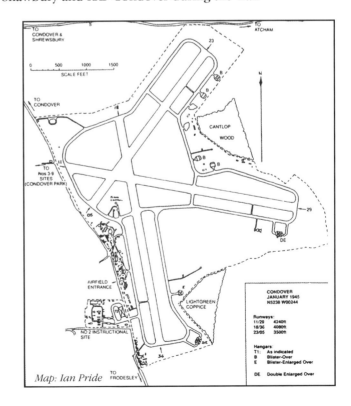

Map: Ian Pride

A parkland airfield

The service personnel who trained at Condover came from all over the world, and were able to enjoy the benefits of living in what was virtually a parkland setting. One Condover pensioner recalled: "We had all the British colonials – South African officers, Canadians, Australians, and even someone from the Falklands. I remember my mother coming in and saying 'where's the world atlas? I must find the Falklands as I've just been talking to an airman who volunteered and came from the Falklands.'"

The pensioner, who asked not to be named, remembers visiting the airfield to go to a dinner dance in the officers mess.

"They all lived in this wonderful forest which was part of the original Condover estate. They built a concrete road which went into the trees and that was where all the airmen slept and ate. There was a women's quarters too. All the trees have been chopped down now and it's very difficult for anyone to envisage what it was like."

As a teenager, **George Jones** would surreptitiously have a look round parked aircraft at Condover airfield. "Sometimes planes would be parked right down by some of our ground and you could more or less go in and have a look as long as nobody was about. I did, and so did one or two others. They were things like Oxfords and Harvards," he said.

"We were living at Cantlop Farm and they took some of our ground off us for the aerodrome. They knocked two of our farm cottages down and slapped the runway right in the middle of them and built us two pre-fabs by the farm. The aerodrome was for training pilots. They had these Oxfords and Harvards, although we would get one or two odd big ones coming down there, like Lancasters, and I think we had a Flying Fortress down once, when they got lost.

"Sometimes they couldn't land at Atcham because of fog. They used to come and land at Condover because it was higher up. The accommodation was in Condover Park. That's all built up now, with big new houses."

Mr Jones, from Shrewsbury, was just 14 when the war broke out and worked on his father Alfred's farm before being called up into the Army at 18.

John Cartwright, who at the time lived at Home Farm, Condover, said: "I used to go with my dad to take milk there. We had the churns in the back of the car. I remember the old red and white gates and the bar that came up and down and let you in. My dad had to go and fetch the money – they never paid very quickly. I was born in 1942 so would not have been very old."

Mr Cartwright, of Ryton Farm, Ryton, added: "There was a crash outside this farm. We have holiday cottages and two or three years ago somebody stayed here who was the person who pulled the dead crewman from the plane which crashed at the back of the buildings here.

"I was looking at the old control tower only this morning. It's a wonder that nobody has put a preservation order on it."

Another wartime memory concerns an RAF serviceman who was killed in a fight which took place outside the Fox pub at Ryton.

Condover's derelict control tower, on which the words 'Flying Control' can still be made out. The airfield, including the control tower, were put up for sale in seven lots in 2007.

Warriors who did not return

Gordon Piprell was one of the hundreds, or perhaps thousands, of young warriors who honed their craft at RAF Condover. Some of the flying students would die in training crashes – the nearby Stretton hills were a particular hazard. Others, like Piprell himself, would lose their lives during "ops". Their sacrifice explains why old airfields like Condover hold such a special place in the hearts of surviving aircrews and their relatives.

In the late 1990s Glyn Rowlands of Bala made a trip to Condover to take some pictures at the special request of Gordon's brother, Mr Gerry Piprell, from Saskatchewan, Canada. Gordon had been on a navigation course at Condover from October 1943 to January 1944. Afterwards he went to RAF Ludford Magna, near Market Rasen, and was promoted to Flying Officer, piloting Lancaster bombers on raids.

"Sadly his aircraft was hit. He stayed at the controls and managed to avoid a small village in Sweden before the Lancaster crashed, killing him. To perpetuate his memory and bravery, the folks at home named a lake after him on the periphery of Narrow Hills Provincial Park on Route 913 north of Prince Albert, in Saskatchewan," said Mr Rowlands, whose daughter Rhian married Gerry's brother's son.

A Sergeant Cunningham was the only survivor of the crew, whose average age was 20. He told how the plane had been attacked by an enemy fighter near the Swedish coast. The plane came down in water and the victims are buried in Sweden. Over 3,000 people attended the funeral.

"Gerry recalls his parents subsequently receiving several letters from local Swedish residents describing the bravery of aircrews trying to steer their stricken aircraft away from built-up areas into the sea," said Mr Rowlands.

Condover today

In the village of Condover, take the minor road which is signposted to Frodeseley. Follow the road for about a mile, and it rises up to higher ground. As you continue, the airfield is on the left. A number of buildings survive including the control tower. Much of the site was used until recently by the horses of Berriewood Farm but the entire airfield site and control tower were put up for sale in 2007. A short distance further on more airfield buildings survive in good condition on the right, where they form a small industrial estate.

Gordon Piprell in a photo believed to have been taken at Condover in October 1943. *(Glyn Rowlands)*

Horses graze among the old airfield buildings.

Looking south from the mid point of the old north-south runway.

Cosford

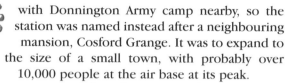

RAF Cosford is a major RAF station which is continuing to play an important role in the 21st century. It is one of the "winners" of the peace dividend following the ending of the Cold War, as much technical training is now consolidated at the sprawling complex. Down the years it has encompassed the roles of factory, workshop, and training centre – all ground-based roles. The actual flying field is small, even by Second World War standards.

The RAF Cosford story began in the summer of 1938 when the first of many young trainees arrived at the then gleaming new station. But flying had come to Cosford three years earlier, when Alan Cobham brought his National Aviation Day Display on September 6, 1935, flying from a field on the other side of the Shifnal road from the later airfield, at the bottom of Kennel Bank.

The air base was built as part of the RAF's big expansion plan as storm clouds gathered in the late 1930s and it was originally planned to be called RAF Donington, after the nearby village.

It was feared however that there might be confusion with Donnington Army camp nearby, so the station was named instead after a neighbouring mansion, Cosford Grange. It was to expand to the size of a small town, with probably over 10,000 people at the air base at its peak.

It combined a variety of roles. One of the main parts was 9 Maintenance Unit which received, stored and prepared such aircraft as Spitfires, Battles, Blenheims and Ansons.

Cosford has special connections with Spitfires. Not only were they a familiar sight at the wartime base, but it also had a Spitfire assembly plant, a branch of the main factory at Castle Bromwich.

The famed record-breaking pre-war pilot Alex Henshaw was, as chief pilot at Castle Bromwich, a regular visitor and was nearly killed in a return flight from Cosford in July 1942 when his Spitfire's engine stopped and he crashed into a house in Willenhall.

The Castle Bromwich plant and dispersal factories at Cosford and Desford made 11,694 Spitfires between 1940 and 1946. Satellite landing grounds were set up at Weston Park and Brockton, near Kemberton.

The King and Queen visited in 1940 and the following year it came under attack from the Luftwaffe. Incendiary bombs were dropped and promptly extinguished. Two high explosive bombs narrowly missed an 'E'-type hangar on 'B' site. In November 1941 a Spitfire from Tern Hill crashed on the 3,600ft runway then being built. The pilot was not hurt.

Large numbers of Horsa and Hotspur gliders were assembled at Cosford for the invasion of Europe.

Somebody had to fly the hundreds of aircraft to and from the base, and a ferry pilot pool was formed which in 1943 became an all-woman ferry pilot pool, commanded by Mrs Marion Wilberforce.

At war's end RAF Cosford became the gateway to home for thousands of returning British prisoners of war, who were processed through the base.

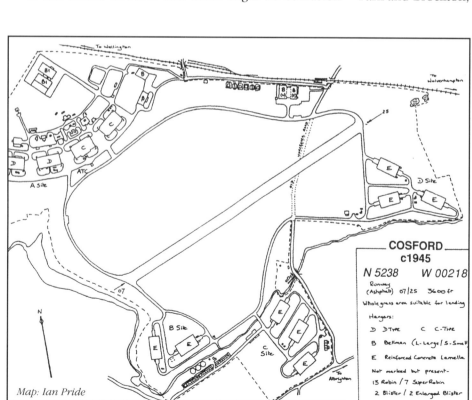

Map: Ian Pride

A June 1940 view of Cosford, before the runway was built, showing how the hangars were camouflaged and fake hedges were painted over the flying field. *(RAF Cosford)*

Aircrew or trainees get a close look at a Spitfire cockpit. *(RAF Cosford)*

aff and workers with a Horsa glider assembled at Cosford in July 1945.

Bombs on Cosford

The father of **Don Underwood**, of Stirchley, Telford, worked at Cosford from 1938 until 1965. He should have retired at 60 but he asked to stay on until he was 65. Don himself recalls some of the stirring events there.

"Some of the things I clearly remember about Cosford are the visit by the present Queen's parents in 1940. I also remember the bombing raid on the air base. In addition to bombs near hangars on the Wolverhampton Road area of Albrighton, there were two bombs dropped near Albrighton Vicarage, also some incendiary bombs in the High Street and on some unoccupied houses in Patshull Road. Fortunately I don't think there were any casualties.

"In another sad incident I was standing near a neighbour's front door and heard the familiar sound of a Spitfire. Suddenly the engine began to splutter. I could see the plane flying upside down until suddenly the engine cut out and it dropped like a stone. I thought it was going to crash in the middle of Albrighton. I jumped on my cycle and rode up to Donington Church and looking across the field I could see some of the trees had branches stripped off.

"I ran across and looked over the wall and saw the smashed-up Spitfire with just a wisp of smoke coming from it. Suddenly a voice shouted 'Come away from there'. I looked behind and coming across the field was our local policeman, at that time, Constable Jack Leighton. He gave me a good telling off and told me not to say anything to anyone. I don't know whether the pilot baled out before the plane hit the ground. I hope so.

"I also remember the RAF authorities building a track across the A464, at the bottom of the Kennel Bank, towards Beckbury. At intervals were small wooden buildings, painted to look like farm cottages with painted windows and doors to fool the enemy. In each of these buildings was a small plane that had folding wings. I found out after the war that these small planes were called Lysanders and they were used mainly by the SOE in France."

Cosford had a large cinema and any relatives of employees had a pass to go and see any of the films, added Mr Underwood.

War diary

1937
August: Building work started.

1938
July 15: An RAF contingent, commanded by Squadron Leader A.L. Franks, took possession.

1939
March 15: No 9 Maintenance Unit opened at Cosford to function as an aircraft storage unit.
March 24: First aircraft received – an Anson.

1940
February 4: A warning received by signal that sabotage activities by the IRA were anticipated throughout the country. Warder patrols were accordingly increased and other necessary precautions taken.
September 4: 1500. A fire of a small nature broke out on the grass top of one of D site hangars. Prompt action quickly subdued the outbreak.

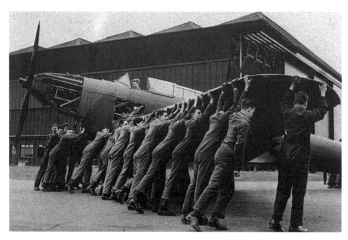

Trainees wheel a Fairey Battle into a hangar after practising aerodrome procedures. *(RAF Cosford)*

Civilian women technical workers, 1942-43. *(RAF Cosford)*

A mass landing of Horsa gliders in 1944. *(RAF Cosford)*

Wartime trainees learn repair procedures on a Hurricane. *(RAF Cosford)*

1941

March 11: Incendiary bombs were dropped by enemy aircraft on the flying ground and were promptly extinguished by unit "other" personnel. Two H.E. bombs narrowly missed an E-type hangar on B site, causing damage to a considerable portion of an end wall. Two other H.E. bombs dropped in open country damaged access roads to dispersed aircraft. Apart from two Lysander aircraft in E type hangar, no other damage was sustained, and there were no casualties or injuries to personnel.

November 9: A Spitfire from Tern Hill crashed on new runway under construction. The pilot was uninjured.

1942

July 30: The first Horsa glider produced by the unit was towed away by a Halifax aircraft.

A key player

RAF Cosford has grown to become the biggest ground training station in the whole of the RAF. And the youngsters who today pass through its gates are following in the footsteps of tens of thousands of trainees before them who have learnt their trade at Cosford, which now takes the title DCAE (Defence College of Aeronautical Engineering).

In both war and peace, its role has been inestimable, turning out the trained airmen and women on which the service depends.

The 3,600ft paved runway, which replaced the original grass landing area, is far too short to operate modern high performance jets safely. Nevertheless flying does take place, with three flying units.

The University of Birmingham Air Squadron flies Bulldog trainers, giving flying training to students at Midlands universities doing degrees and on RAF scholarships.

Number Eight Air Experience Flight, also flying Bulldogs, gives air experience to Air Training Corps and Combined Cadet Force cadets, while the excitingly named 633 Squadron of the ATC flies self-launched gliders – gliders with an engine.

It is also home to Wrekin Gliding Club. Jet Provosts which can often be seen taxiing do not actually fly, as they are used to train ground handling and runway procedures.

RAF Cosford provides training for all aircraft-related engineering trades, trains the RAF's PE instructors and has a school of photography for all three services.

Today it is also home to the Shropshire air ambulance helicopter to which so many people are indebted, and historically was home of a major hospital which served both public and service personnel. Despite protests it was closed on December 31, 1977.

The future of Cosford itself is uncertain following its failure to win the contract to become a defence training super centre, losing out in the "beauty contest" to St Athan in South Wales. There has been talk of it becoming an Army "super garrison", but no definitive announcement has yet been made.

The RAF Museum

Sitting cheek by jowl with the air base at Cosford, and using some of its old hangars, is the Royal Air Force Museum, boasting the biggest single display of its type in Britain.

It is now one of Britain's premier aviation heritage centres, with its status further enhanced by the 2007 royal opening of the National Cold War Exhibition.

Its collection of historic aircraft, missiles, engines and vehicles has gained an international reputation. It is continuing to expand, and the complex now includes a centre at which old aircraft are expertly restored. The museum includes an aviation heritage centre, with art galleries, and conference, banqueting and archive facilities.

Cosford's pre-war control tower is a museum piece in itself. It is the last remaining fort-type control tower which is in full use in the RAF. It is not a listed building, and is small and therefore cramped, nor does it have radar. Nevertheless it copes with over 20,000 air movements a year. Its QGH recovery equipment is an old fashioned way of bringing down aircraft safely through cloud. The balcony provides a grandstand view and on the ground floor an array of flower boxes makes it one of the more florally colourful buildings in RAF service.

This Vulcan was one of the biggest aircraft ever to land on Cosford's runway. After two test approaches the Falklands veteran touched down in January 1983 to go into retirement at the museum. Then it got bogged down in the mud as it was being towed across the station.

Cosford today

The huge base straddles the A41 road just north of Albrighton, near Wolverhampton. A railway passes by the airfield itself and there is even a little station. However, the best way to view Cosford is to visit it – the RAF Museum which occupies much of the airfield site is now one of the best museums of its type in the world and is continuing to expand. And the best thing of all about it is that admission is free. There is also an annual air show which attracts massive crowds.

Cosford is an active airfield but the aircraft tend to be of the lighter type as the runway is uncomfortably short by modern-day standards – jets can just about land, but cannot then take-off again safely.

A modern view of Cosford airfield from the air.

The hub of the old RAF High Ercall complex remains in good condition but is awaiting a new role in the 21st century.

High Ercall

Of all Shropshire's airfields, RAF High Ercall has perhaps the most varied and interesting history. While most of the county's wartime airfields were engaged in training, High Ercall was, during the Blitz, a front line nightfighter station. Five Luftwaffe bombers were claimed shot down by High Ercall's Beaufighters – four of them by a squadron led by Wing Commander Max Aitken, the son of Lord Beaverbrook, who was the Minister of Aircraft Production.

It was not all one way. On March 7, 1941, a German raider bombed and shot up the aerodrome, with little damage and no casualties. And on another occasion a Beaufighter which crashed at Poynton Green, near High Ercall, was found to have bullet holes in it.

Throughout its wartime life – and beyond – there was a major unit at High Ercall, 29 Maintenance Unit, employing hundreds of local civilians, which repaired, modified, checked, tested and stored aircraft. But while 29 MU was the stable "core", there were many comings and goings in what was a huge airfield complex which was home to various units.

Spitfires. Hurricanes. Typhoons. American fighters. Lancasters returning from raids popping in because of bad weather at their home bases. A bizarre-in-retrospect unit, codenamed Turbinlite, in which a Havoc light bomber was in effect turned into a flying torch. Mosquitos training crews for operations in Europe. An aircraft packing unit (222 MU) which sent off packed planes to various theatres of war. All were at High Ercall – and more.

The King and Queen visited. And after the war, the airfield and fields around it were crammed with an astonishing number of surplus warplanes – over 1,700, including many four-engined bombers – for storage or breaking up. In other words, High Ercall airfield was home at that time to more planes than the whole of the current RAF. Some were sold. You could buy an Airspeed Oxford for 1/6d (8p).

On a lighter note, the wartime air station was proud of its gardening prowess, the ground being said to be some of the best in Britain for growing root vegetables like carrots and turnips.

Former staff at the civilian unit, 29 MU, say the last planes left there in February 1957, and then vehicles were kept there. 29 MU finally closed in February 1962. The site was sold by the Ministry of Defence in 1968 and became a road transport industry training centre called MOTEC. Its successor Centrex failed in 1998 and the main buildings await a new role. It was in the news recently amid a rumour that the site would become an accommodation centre for asylum seekers. It caused uproar, and the scheme came to nothing.

High Ercall's three runways have been ripped up but the hangars are still used for warehousing.

Incidentally there is a story that, while at High Ercall, Max Aitken flew his Beaufighter under the Iron Bridge, although common sense suggests this would be near-suicidal. A spokeswoman for Sir Max's widow, Lady Aitken, said: "She has heard this story and thinks the best way to find out would be to look in his logbook at the RAF Museum, Hendon."

However, the RAF Museum could find nothing to authenticate the tale.

Flying Officer Dennis Moore, left, with pilot Flying Officer John Ayre at 60 OTU High Ercall in front of their Mosquito Mk VI, September 1944. *(Dennis Moore)*

War diary

1940

October 1: Opening of 29 Maintenance Unit as civilian-manned aircraft storage and maintenance unit.
November 22: Two Mohawks delivered by air.
December 29: Four Harvard Is arrive. N7084 crashed on landing.

1941

March 7, pm: "An attack during poor visibility and low cloud was made by an enemy plane, believed to be a Ju88. Four 500lb H.E. bombs and four 1 kilo incendiary bombs were dropped. Hangars and personnel were machinegunned. Minor damage was caused to buildings. There were no casualties. Fire was opened on enemy by station defence M.G. posts."
April 23: A Flight of 68 Squadron arrived.
May 30: Air Commodore HRH Prince Bernhard of the Netherlands visited.
May monthly summary: Re-equipment of 68 Sqn with Beaufighters instead of Blenheims began.
June 16/17: "One Beaufighter I, Flt Lt D.S. Pain, AFC, A Flt, No 68 Sqn (pilot) and F/O Davies, 68 Sqn, A.I. Instructor (operator) engaged and destroyed a Heinkel III, this being the first successful interception made from this station." The aircraft came down at Timsbury, S.W. of Bath. The pilot bailed out but four crew were killed.
June 21: An ENSA unit provided the first entertainment on the station with a mobile cinema and impromptu concert in the airmen's dining hall.
September 19: Station cinema opened. Proceeds of first performance, totalling £14, handed over to the RAF Benevolent Fund.
October 11: "House-warming party" in officers mess.

Mosquito memories

Dennis Moore, of Wolverhampton, trained at High Ercall from October 13 to December 5, 1944, with 60 OTU, during which time he crammed in 66 hours flying time.

"My pilot was Flying Officer John Ayre, and in fact I flew with him continually for the rest of the war.

"High Ercall had some very nice permanent buildings, but the crews mainly were situated around the airfield in any old hut that had a roof which would keep you dry and warm. Part of the idea was of course to condition us for conditions we were expected to face on the continent. So conditions at High Ercall for the crews were not that brilliant."

The planes they flew at High Ercall were the Mark VI Mosquito, which had eight guns but could also carry bombs internally.

Their training at High Ercall was virtually all at night, and aimed to prepare them for operational flying, in which their role would be interdiction missions.

"Our watering hole was the Tayleur Arms at Longdon-on-Tern. At the base, the officers mess had a fairly good amount of liquor stored away which we carried with us when we left the United Kingdom and went to the continent.

"We spent a lot of the time on the camp. With our nights being 'days', we were asleep most of the daytime and working at night. It was a bit of a cock-eyed day we had."

Mr Moore, who was at the time a Flying Officer and a navigator, does not recall there being a particularly high accident rate at High Ercall.

"It was a little higher in Canada, when we were first introduced to the Mosquito. However, I do remember, strangely enough, one or two ground accidents at High Ercall while people were taxiing. You would taxi around the perimeter which was marked by very faint blue lights and you could hit obstructions and various things. That did happen."

For lost pilots, there was a system called Sandra in which four searchlights at the base would form a cone of light to mark the airfield.

"We could not have done without being at High Ercall, for the simple reason that navigating in this country with the blackout was very different to navigating in Canada where quite frankly you could see where you were going," said Mr Moore, who left High Ercall to join 21 Squadron at Thorney Island and fly on operations.

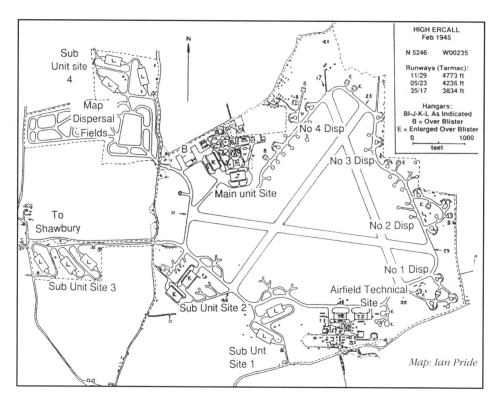

Map: Ian Pride

1941	1942

1941

October 12: A Beaufighter I of 68 Sqn, Pilot Officer Mansfeld and A.I. Operator Sgt Janacek (Czech) while on patrol from Valley contacted five e/a of which two were destroyed and one damaged (They were Ju88s).

October 16: No 46 SLG opened (at Brinklow).

October 22: A Beaufighter I, P/O W.D. Winward, A.I. operator Sgt C.K. Wood, of 68 Sqn, made contact with a Ju88 which was shot down into the sea.

October 22: A Beaufighter no R2099, pilot F/O J. Kloboucnik (Czech), A.I. operator Sgt Klvacek (Czech) suffered the first flying battle casualty of the station while on operational patrol from Valley.

The pilot requested permission to land at High Ercall at 2249 and again at 2255 but this was refused as the runway was temporarily obstructed by aircraft which could not taxi. At 2303 the pilot last contacted RAF Stn Atcham, but High Ercall was unable to get him again. An enemy aircraft was reported in the vicinity at this time and bullet marks were found on the wreckage of the Beaufighter which crashed at a point about 1 mile south west of High Ercall, at Poynton Green.

October 25: One Ju88 damaged was claimed by a Beaufighter I of 68 Sqn, pilot W/O Welch, A.I. operator P/O Bennett (in Crewe area). "Black smoke was seen to come from the port centre section of the e/a which disappeared in a steep dive to port"

November 19: The first "dining-in night" was held in the officers' mess...Wing Commander Max Aitken, DFC, commanding No 68 Sqn, was (among) those present.

December 10: AC2 Davies was killed through stumbling while removing a chock and falling into the propeller.

1942

January 19: Performance of the comedy 'The Late Christopher Bean' was given in the airmen's dining hall. The occasion marked the first performance of the station orchestra which played during the interval and before the rise of the curtain.

January 22: Wing Commander Max Aitken DFC assumed temporary command of the station.

February 13: District Court Martial to try Sgt Monk for publishing an article in the "News review" relating to the issue of spears (sic) to airmen. He was charged with conduct to the prejudice of good order and discipline. (outcome not recorded!).

February 26: Squadron beat up Crewe. All airborne in 3 mins 20 secs.

March 8: 68 Sqn move to Coltishall, 15 Beaufighters and three Blenheims.

March 8: 255 Sqn arrived, W/Cdr Kelly, 11 Beaufighters and one Blenheim. One Beaufighter ran off the runway and got bogged.

March 14: 0300hrs a Wellington, Sqn Ldr Bingham Hall, and crew of five landed after operational flight over Cologne. All OK and given breakfast at the officers mess.

May 4: No 222 MU aircraft packing depot formed.

May 19: P39 crash landed by No 1 runway.

June 6: 255 Sqn flew to Honiley. Two new squadrons came in their place with Turbinlite equipment, i.e. 20 Hurricanes and Havocs.

June 11: American 309 Pursuit Sqn arrived "looking rather travel-stained and tired."

June 15: "D.R.O.s contained a reminder regarding the local gardening rules, whereby no-one may have 48 hours leave unless he or she can produce coupons showing that they have done four hours gardening."

The Turbinlite experiment

For a time during 1942 High Ercall was the base for a "secret" unit using an innovative new method of night interception which was one of the most extraordinary stories of the air war.

Douglas Havoc bombers of 1456 Flight arrived with Turbinlite equipment. This turned them into flying torches, with a powerful light in their nose. The idea was that they would get close to roaming enemy aircraft in the darkness by initially using radar, and then would illuminate them. At this point an accompanying Hurricane fighter would shoot the enemy raider down. Because of all the equipment they carried the Havocs were not themselves armed.

The Turbinlite unit at High Ercall was shown off to the King and Queen. They were given a demonstration of Turbinlite interception, presumably in daylight. However, in action the concept was too complicated to work well. One of the main difficulties was co-ordinating the Havocs and the Hurricanes in the dark. When one was ready, the other never was. In any event, improved radar quickly made Turbinlite obsolete.

High Ercall's Turbinlite unit does not appear to have had any successes, but during the Blitz the base was a front line station and the Beaufighters of Max Aitken's 68 Squadron were kept busy and notched up a number of "kills" using more conventional methods.

The first was on the night of June 16/17, 1941, when a Beaufighter crewed by pilot Flight Lieutenant D.S. Pain, AFC, and Flying Officer Davies, the A.I. operator (i.e. radar operator), engaged and destroyed a Heinkel III, which came down at Timsbury, south west of Bath.

On October 12 another 68 Squadron crew, Pilot Officer Mansfeld and A.I. operator Sgt Janacek, a Czech, while on patrol from RAF Valley contacted five Ju88s and claimed two destroyed and one damaged.

On October 22, Pilot Officer W. D. Winward, and A.I. operator Sergeant C.K. Wood, made contact with a Ju88 which was shot down into the sea. One Ju88 damaged was claimed by Warrant Officer Welch and A.I. operator Pilot Officer Bennett in Crewe area on October 25. "Black smoke was seen to come from the port centre section of the e/a which disappeared in a steep dive to port"

The single "kill" in 1942 was on April 25, when Flying Officer Wyrrill shot down a Ju88 one or two miles N.E. of Builth Wells. 68 Squadron's Beaufighters had moved on by this time (although they were replaced by Beaufighters of 255 Squadron), and this victory may have been by a single-engined fighter from High Ercall.

Nor was it all one way. On October 22, 1941, Beaufighter no R2099, crewed by F/O J. Kloboucnik and A.I. operator Sgt Klvacek, became an operational casualty while on operational patrol from RAF Valley. The pilot requested permission to land at High Ercall at 2249 and again at 2255 but this was refused as the runway was temporarily obstructed by aircraft which could not taxi.

At 2303 the pilot last contacted RAF Atcham, but High Ercall was unable to get him again. An enemy aircraft was reported in the vicinity at this time and bullet marks were found on the wreckage of the Beaufighter which crashed about a mile south west of High Ercall, at Poynton Green.

The King is introduced to a Turbinlite crew during his 1942 visit. The heavily censored Havoc is in the background.
(National Archives)

'Mr Harris is dead!'

"Run for your life!" cried **Jim Harris** when he saw a stricken Mosquito was about to land on his office at High Ercall.

The planes were that day doing "circuits and bumps" and while on the phone to a girl in headquarters he noticed a lot of blue tyre smoke up the main runway. Looking for the plane which produced it, he spotted a Mosquito at about 150ft, with wheels down, one engine stopped and the other just ticking over. Shouting a warning, he dropped the phone and dashed for the door, but then stood transfixed in the doorway.

"I could clearly see the two pilots when suddenly the nose went down. The aircraft crashed vertically into the perimeter track, bounced into the air, slid onto the grass in front of me, burst into flames, and both engines went either side of me. Both pilots were killed, and it was apparent they had deliberately pushed the control column forward to give us a chance.

"The girl on the other end of the phone, who could also see the airfield and the fire, started screaming: 'Mr Harris is dead!' Fortunately this was not the case," said Mr Harris.

Mr Harris was one of the first to arrive at High Ercall, around June or July 1940 – months before the official opening. He saw the first planes to land at High Ercall airfield in 1940, and the last to leave 17 years later.

"The first planes that came in were three Harvards. The second one that landed forgot to put his wheels down. That was a bright start, wasn't it?" he said, estimating the date as July or August 1940.

Mr Harris helped recover the plane with a crane. "Amazingly enough, when the airfield closed in February 1957 the last plane out was also a Harvard, which was rather peculiar, I thought."

Mr Harris used to live at Broadway, Ketley, but moved in later life to Cricklade. He was at first a chargehand airframe fitter, and became Foreman of Trades in charge of a site.

He was one of the hundreds of civilians who worked at the base repairing, servicing, modifying and testing planes.

He recalls that an operational training unit was at High Ercall training pilots to fly Mosquitos in February 1944. Because of a shortage of pilots the previous step of training on twin-engined Oxfords or Ansons had been skipped.

"We had a lot of crashes and hairy dos."

The chief instructor was, he said, later a Group Captain Irvin Smith, who took part in the famous Amiens raid in which Mosquitos bombed a prison to free French resistance fighters inside. Another distinguished flyer was Max Aitken, who was in charge of a Beaufighter nightfighter squadron.

He witnessed the 1941 bombing raid. "We had a duty crew for receiving any aircraft that came in, and on that particular

A poor quality shot showing two Beaufighter crews of 68 Squadron, commanded by Max Aitken, at High Ercall. *(via Alec Brew)*

1942

June 16: "Airmen complaining about their food of late. General complaint today regarding both quality and quantity."
State of the station at the end of June 1942: Airmen, 1,286; airmen attached, 222; WAAF, 255; Army attached, 23; USA personnel, 309; RAF officers, 88. Total, 2,183.

July 1: 48 SLG opened (at Teddesley Park).

July 16: The station was honoured by a visit from their majesties the King and Queen...a demonstration of Turbinlite interception was given.

July 29: Fatal accident to P/O R.W. McDunnough (Canadian), Typhoon a/c of 257 Sqn. McDunnough was buried at High Ercall churchyard. "It was the first occasion it has been found necessary to use the picturesque churchyard in the village."

July 31: 309 Sqn USAAF moved to Westhampnett.

August 21: No 27 Fighter Sqn (US) arrive with Lightning a/c.

September 1: Mr G.Le M. Mander, PPS to Sir Archibald Sinclair, Secretary of State for Air, visited... "Unfortunately a projected visit by Gen Eisenhower, G.O.C. American Forces in the European Theatre of War, did not materialise."

September 21: The first locally made Horsa glider was towed away to Brize Norton by a Whitley.

October 4: 13 "Aerocobras" (sic) ferried in from Burtonwood for No 92 Sqn USAAC who were arriving shortly (i.e. on the 8th).

October 12: "Meal card system introduced in airmen's dining hall. System commenced owing to the prevalence of habit of airmen taking two meals."

October 17: Station soccer XI defeated 9th Batt. RAOC Donnington 8 goals to 1 in the first round, Shropshire Junior Cup.

day I was on duty crew," he said. "It was a pretty murky day with low cloud and this thing came out of the clouds. He went across 2 Site, noticed 1 Site, and dropped two or three bombs there."

At times, Americans were at High Ercall and he said when the ship carrying their Airacobras, a fighter with a tricycle undercarriage, was sunk, they were given 40 Spitfires instead.

"After the end of about a week there was not one left serviceable. As it was a tail-wheel aircraft they had to do a tail-wheel landing, but they were forgetting and hitting the props on the ground.

"After the war there were absolutely thousands of aircraft at High Ercall. John Dales scrap people had a big smelting furnace out there. We used to call the fields the Fortress Fields because we started off by scrapping Flying Fortresses.

"They used to cut the aircraft up and drop the engines out, and then put the planes in this big smelting unit and run out the aluminium into blocks.

"Some aircraft had to be scrapped even though they were good aircraft, because they were Lease-Lend and we were not allowed to sell anything that was Lease-Lend.

"The numbers were up in the thousands. The airfield was lined with Spitfires, Halifaxes, and Oxfords. We used to drop the engines out of the Oxfords and set fire to them because they were wooden, and then rake up the metal. They sold several hundreds of these Oxfords for 1/6d each."

Mr Harris left High Ercall at the same time as the last plane moved out, in February 1957. "By then at High Ercall we were working on motors and jet engines."

Jim Harris, left, and Wally Mitchell (chargehand fitter airframe) dismantling an Oxford post-war. *(Jim Harris)*

A line of newly-planted poplar trees at High Ercall airfield kept getting "shot down" again by Spitfires, according to **Tom Coupland**, of Wellington.

"We had to run up the engines of the aircraft, and they kept getting blown down. We used to get told off about it," said Mr Coupland, who was a civilian airframe fitter at the base. "I haven't been there lately, but the gap in the trees was still there a few years ago."

Mr Coupland arrived at High Ercall in 1940. "The main runway was only just being made then. There were no RAF there at all, apart from senior ones, officers and above. Everybody else was civilian. There were thousands of civilians at High Ercall from the beginning until the end in 1956."

Mr Coupland was employed by the Air Ministry. "Where I live now, in Woollam Road, these houses were originally built in 1939 and were called Air Ministry houses.

"There were a couple of air raids. Lone German aircraft came over and shot the 'drome up a couple of times. They just hit the hangar doors. We were under cover."

Eddie Wellings, of Crosby, Liverpool, said: "I arrived at High Ercall in May 1941 and was put into the unit responsible for communicating with aircraft at the airfield. When 68 Sqn, commanded by the then Squadron Leader Max Aitken, wasn't actually intercepting enemy aircraft, intensive training was going

Lineup of Spitfires on 29 MU in 1948. The control tower is in the centre of the two hangars in the distance. The photo was taken from J Shed, HQ Site. *(Jim Harris)*

on getting current and new aircrews up to full operational standard with the new Ground Control Interceptor equipment and VHF Radio Direction Finding equipment.

"What I recall most vividly was aircraft practically taking off the aerials of the tender if they were 'homed' – guided

Mosquito outside J Shed, 29 MU, in 1948. "We didn't have any towing gear for this, the only Mosquito we had left, so I had to taxi it everywhere," said Jim Harris, who loaned this picture.

Oxford and a Halifax serial number RG786 at 29 MU in 1948. Work is being done on the aileron of the bomber. *(Jim Harris)*

in – properly. With the radio tenders strategically placed at the end of the runway, a good homing certainly brought good vibrations."

Mr Wellings was posted to the Far East in August 1941.

A wartime colleague of Mr Wellings, **Mr W.E. Humphreys** of Hereford, recalled that they were both posted to High Ercall in the spring of 1941.

"We finished our radio course at No 1 Signals School, Cranwell, and were paraded to be told where we were posted and given railway warrants etc. When my name was called and RAF High Ercall I said to Eddie 'Where the heck is High Ercall?'. When they reached the 'Ws' he found that he was posted to the same station. He said that High Ercall was only about 10 miles from Shrewsbury and as his home was at Bayston Hill he was very lucky.

"As the Beaufighters were usually on night patrol we had to go on watch on the radio tender from 4pm to 8am originally, but as new radio operators arrived from Cranwell we started at 11pm and continued until 8am. After that shift we went to bed for a couple of hours in the morning and then had the rest of the day to ourselves.

"I asked my parents to send my cycle up by rail from Hereford and Eddie and I used to cycle to his home where his mother treated me as one of the family. We went into Shrewsbury to the cinema and then cycled back to High Ercall in time to go on duty at 11pm.

"There was no NAAFI in the early days but there was a small Salvation Army tent where we could relax when off duty, otherwise we just stayed in our billets when we could not get into Wellington or Shrewsbury.

Spitfire undergoing work outside J Shed, HQ Site, 29 MU, on January 30, 1948 (this date is written on the propeller). From left, Stan Morton, Wally Mitchell, Eric Edmondson, a Rolls-Royce contract rep, Jim Harris, and two others. Mr Harris says: "Certain Spitfire engines were removed and partly dismantled to change some seals. These seals had to be replaced and a jointing compound called Wellseal put on all joints and seals." *(Jim Harris)*

"I remember Max Aitken at High Ercall, but cannot recall hearing of him flying under the Iron Bridge. I know that on a quiet night he would fly down to an airfield in southern England and go on a sweep in a Spitfire.

"We had quite a character on Signals section. He was a Londoner and brought his car back when on one weekend pass. The station was scattered over a wide area with huts in corners of various fields and the cookhouse was about half a mile from our radio tender, so we had to walk quite a distance for meals.

"If this chap was on the same shift as us we would ride down to the cookhouse

Two views showing RAF High Ercall in the post-war days in which it was the graveyard for hundreds of aircraft. The photo, left, is dated March 11, 1948. The picture right is said to show over 700 aircraft.

with him and the 'erks' walking the other way would throw up a salute thinking he was one of the senior officers!

"In the autumn Eddie was posted to the Far East and about six weeks later I was posted to the Middle East where we each spent about four years of our RAF service, but that is another story."

Mr R.G. Heeks, of Pinvin, Pershore, arrived on April 25, 1941, when the base was still being built.

"As a Signals Radio Telephone Operator I, with others, should have been controlling the air traffic from the control tower, but that was still to be built, so we made use of a mobile radio van set in a field the other side of the road from the runway.

"Another thing that was not available was showering or bathing facilities, so each week we were transported by lorry to Shawbury and the luxury of hot water for a bath or shower, but we were limited to time that we could spend there.

"High Ercall was a dispersed camp, so if you were lucky you had a bicycle. I was lucky. Signals duties were very varied – aircraft control, telephone operating, maintaining the Glim lamps that were put down the side of the runway for night flying by making sure the batteries were fully charged – the flarepath had not been installed. At the end of the runway there was a Chance Light or floodlight to illuminate the runway during night flying, but it was only switched on when an aircraft was coming in to land.

"I left on September 13, 1941."

George Carter of Hadley, who worked at 29 MU at High Ercall from 1944 to 1957, recalled: "Soon after the war, Peter Rowell the test pilot would execute a falling leaf manoeuvre in a Tiger Moth to say Hello to his wife who lodged in Longdon-upon-Tern.

"One evening as we were walking down the road from No 3 site to a bus waiting on the Osbaston lane, he flew a Spitfire over Walton village and down the 3 Site road so low I thought the propeller would strike the tarmac. The Spitfire just cleared the roof of the waiting bus as we picked ourselves up out of the grass at the side of the road.

"On occasions the Lancaster squadron which was based at RAF Shawbury used High Ercall because of adverse weather at their home base.

"There is a well-known tale of the bus parked near Taylor's tea shop which got its top cut off by a Mosquito which then crashed in the field below Walton. They turned it back onto its wheels and drove it to the MT section without a top, like something at Blackpool Tramway.

"One one occasion a Venom (a post-war jet fighter) set off down the 108 degree runway, but midway the engine failed. The machine ran on, then over the grass area and over the road which leads to Moortown. The test pilot told us that he debated whether to retract the undercarriage but decided not to do so and escaped without serious injury when he came to rest in farmland."

1942

October 28: RAF Symphony Orchestra broadcast from the gymnasium on the BBC overseas service.

November 1: Broadcast from station of "Sunday Half Hour" in the Forces programme of the BBC, and also Forces Middle East.

November 13: Fatal accident involving Sgt D.T. Gale, 247 Sqn. Funeral at High Ercall churchyard.

December 6: "Station fire party received an outside call to High Ercall Village Hall – completely gutted."

December 11: Fatal accident to Sgt H.E. Baldry, 247 Sqn, Hurricane JS343 nr Moreton-in-the-Marsh.

December 12:: 92 Sqn USAAC left.

1943

February 24: Canadian Sgt Q.M. Shippee, 247 Sqn, crashed and was killed at Madeley, Shropshire.

May 5: Six Lancasters of 97 Sqn, Bourn, and four of 156 Sqn Warboys, and two Wellingtons, landed on return from ops (because of bad weather it seems).

May 7: Formation of 60 OTU (Mosquitos).

May 31: Accident involving Mosquito III HJ881 (W/O V.A. Clouder instructor, F/L G.W. Mason RCAF pupil) and Spitfire Va X4930 (Pilot Sgt McPherson) from Rednal in which all three killed. The Mosquito collided with one of a formation of four Spitfires on a familiarisation flight. The tail of the Mosquito was cut off and it crashed at Berwick, near Shrewsbury. Mason buried at High Ercall Church.

July 21: F/O Wilcox killed when Mosquito AJ892 piloted by him flew into the ground at Catherton Farm, Cleobury Mortimer. Cause unknown.

July 24: Fatal accident involving Mosquito at Pentrenant, Church Stoke. They were of 301 Ferry Training Unit, Lyneham, posted to High Ercall.

July 28: W/O Hodges and F/O Hemmings killed when Mosquito HJ634 of which they were pilot and observer respectively collided with Spitfire near Atcham while on camera gun exercise. Pilot of Spitfire, Major Asselin, also killed. (The Atcham operational records book gives a July 29 date for this crash)

August 13: Fatal accident to F/O P.W. Stokes DFC and a civilian passenger in Mosquito DD630. Crashed on aerodrome.

September 7: Fatal accident near Market Drayton – Mosquito DD685 (two Canadian crew killed).

September 16: Fatal accident near Shawbury, Mosquito DD678 pilot F/O P.R. Wilmot RAAF. He had been engaged in local formation flying with another aircraft after which he made a few steep turns, resulting finally in a vertical dive. Also September 16, a battle-scarred B17 Flying Fortress 239828 of 384th BG Grafton Underwood made a successful forced landing at 1800. It was returning from operations against the enemy over Nantes and three of the crew of 10 were suffering from wounds. Its radio was u/s making its home base unlocateable.

September 29: "Mr B.O. Mulligan, Air Ministry Horticultural Adviser, visited the station and expressed satisfaction with our efforts. Very disappointed that the station were not entering root crops for the Air Force Horticultural Show. In view of the fact that the airfield was constructed on what was reputed to be the finest land in Great Britain for root growing, we claim very little merit for what are undoubtedly some excellent results with carrots and turnips."

October 14: Mosquito HJ617 (pilot Sgt S.S. Reah, navigator Sgt E. Jenner) crashed at Elliston Farm, Coalville, Leicestershire, while on cross country flight. Both killed.

November 15: Mosquito DS701 (?) (pilot F/O Horn (Hare??), navigator F/O Abelson (?) crashed during night flying near Broadstone. Both killed.

December 12: An accident occurred on the perimeter track. 1st Officer Merce (??), a lady ATA pilot in a Fairchild aircraft ran into a civilian stoker, James Eccleston, causing him serious injury. Taken to Royal Salop Infirmary.

December 28: Three Mosquitos from High Ercall crash in separate incidents. All crews killed. Details as follows: a. Mosquito HJ826 (F/Lt Scholes pilot and F/Sgt Fox navigator) crashed and the occupants killed while attempting to land on one engine at Chedworth. b. Mosquito HX861 (Capt Rogers USAAC pilot and F/O Marcus navigator) crashed at Chedworth and crew were killed. c. Mosquito DZ751 Flt Lt Franklin pilot and W/O Twomey navigator crashed while on night cross country at Hoylake, Cheshire, and killed.

1944

January 20: Mosquito DD795 (Flt Sg Mitchell, pilot and F/Sgt Aylott, navigator) failed to return from a night cross country flight. No trace found. Posted as missing.

January 26: The station cinema was filled to capacity at 1830 hours when Major Kerner USAAC gave a most interesting talk on the United States of America.

March 14: Mosquito DZ718 F/O Galvin pilot and Sgt Bramwell navigator crashed in Northern Ireland on practice night intruder flight. They were killed.

April 6: Mosquito HX865 crashed on approach. Crew killed.

April: "There is no doubt that April in many ways set a new high standard for 60 OTU to maintain. On the technical side, the 30th April saw a record strength of 50 Mosquitos on the unit. Also flying times for the month constituted a record, the hours being 1,762 (day and night) for Mosquito, and 1,996 on all types – representing a 50 per cent increase on the March total... The activities of several ex pupils of the OTU deserve recording. W/C Mitchell DFC (ex 605 Sqn), now O/C training wing carried out a brilliant 'intruder' to Metz on 5th April, destroying three unidentified enemy aircraft and damaging three on the ground."

May 1: At 1803 hours Sgt Etherington (18 course) in Mosquito VI HJ818 developed trouble in the port engine on take off. He did not become airborne and hit a civilian motor coach at end of runway. No casualties. Motor coach badly damaged.

May 6: 1040 hrs Mosquito HJ699 Pilot F/Sgt J.L.T. Hinchliffe (Staff Pilot). This aircraft took off on an air test with as passenger Sgt P.G. O. Reynolds (from training wing orderly room). Engine trouble was experienced on the circuit and the pilot indicated that he would make a single engine landing. He crashed 200 yards from the runway. Pilot killed and passenger died of his injuries.

May 6: Mosquito crashed in grounds of 16th US General Hospital, Penley Hall, killing pilot.

May 31: "The unit (29 MU) holding has now exceeded 700 aircraft for maintenance and checking..."

June 14: 1059, F/Lt Wickham A.T. DFC (pilot instructor) and F/Lt Evans (pilot pupil) crashed on airfield in Mosquito JH863. Both killed.

July: 29 MU A/c dispersed at 14 SLG Overley and No 1 SLG Slade Farm.

September 10: 1415 in Dee Marshes range, Mosquito VI HJ816 crashed on air to ground gunnery exercises and pilot F/O Templer and navigator F/O Attwood both killed.

A 1942 view of the airfield. The information on the back of this print reads: "RAF Shawbury, June 29, 1942, RAF Official, High Ercall" and "11 PAFU, 4.6.42, 61/065395, 10.40, 6.5, 10,000, 1 1/8 333 yards approx." This photo is one of a number from Mrs Aileen Chimonides, of Annscroft, and belonged to her late mother, who used to work at RAF High Ercall right from its early days. Her name was at that time Miss Mary Egerton and she was a civilian teleprinter operator at the base, living locally, at Cotwall. While at RAF High Ercall she met Oliver Blake of the Fleet Air Arm. They married after the war.

1944

September 15: Battle of Britain parade. Together with units from the RN and Home Guard a 100 per cent muster parade held at 0900 on runway 350 with G/Cpt Tomalin DFC AFC taking the salute. The band of RAOC Donnington was also present.

September 25: 0055 F/L Johnson and P/O Else, navigator, crashed in North West Wales, hit a mountain in Mosquito HX862 on navigational training trip. Both killed.

September 29: 1550 F/O Roberts killed in a/c accident Mosquito near Peplow.

November 22: 1304 hours. F/O Liblikmaa (Polish) and Sgt Hara (Polish navigator) crashed at West Bromwich in Mosquito HJ650 and killed.

November 25: F/O R.W. Evans and P/O D.V. James, navigator, missing from night flight. It is believed that they were lost in the sea near Bridport.

December 12: F/O George and F/O Draheim in fatal crash in a Mosquito IV near Wittering.

1945

January 13: Avro Anson NK890 of 60 OTU crashed at 0055 near Lyneal. Killed were the pilot, navigation instructor, and four navigators under instruction.

February 4: At 0414 hours a Lancaster PB708 piloted by F/Sgt J.J. Mosley landed a High Ercall after being attacked over its base at Wigsley by a presumed Ju88. None of crew hurt but rear gunner had bailed out over its own base. Inner starboard engine had been shot out of action.

March 1: 2115 F/L Barker and navigator F/O Wilde took off on practice night operational patrol. At 2301 a Mayday call was heard but was very weak. Mosquito crashed near Andover. Believed to have struck an Auster in mid air as an Auster crashed five miles away at the same time. Barker injured, Wilde killed. The same crew flew into a high tension cable on Anglesey only a few days ago, but brought the aircraft safely back to base.

March 13: 60 OTU moved to Finmere and Hampstead Norris.

December: 29 MU holding 1,527 aircraft.

A furtive look through the hedges and trees to capture a glimpse of some wartime bombers. *(Aileen Chimonides)*

A four engined "heavy" under wraps. *(Aileen Chimonides)*

Dog team, 29 MU, 1943. Far left with Aircraftsman H Kennedy is "Jackie, VC" - which implies that Jackie got the Dickin Medal – the dogs' Victoria Cross. However this is unconfirmed. *(Aileen Chimonides)*

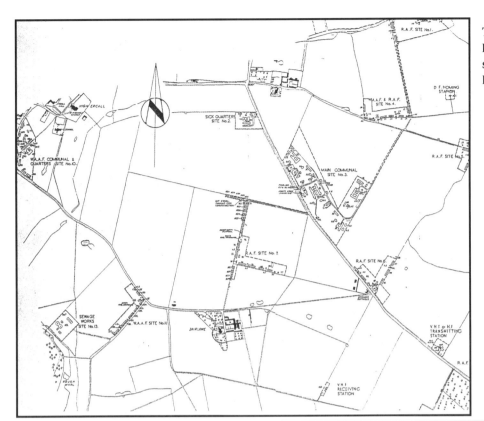

This secret map showing just part of the RAF High Ercall site gives some idea of the sprawling nature of wartime air bases. High Ercall village is on the far left.

High Ercall cricket team in August 1944. The names on the back of this photo are difficult to read, but seem to be: F/O Wolfe, F/O Wright, F/O Ford, F/O Minney, W/C Knowles, F/L Christie, F/O Weaver, F/O Gosbic, F/O Pearce, W. Yates, and finally what looks like RAF J Lewiliers. *(Aileen Chimonides)*

The young lad in the centre of the back row is Reginald Humphreys, part of the maintenance team – he was an electrician's mate and fitter's mate at High Ercall during the latter part of the war. He says next to him, back right, is Frank Higginson, who lived at Harlescott, and used to ride a bike to the airfield daily. He was the hot water fitter. "The sergeant in the air force uniform on the right of the picture, I think his name is Frank Bevan. I believe he married a girl from the Waters Upton or Cold Hatton area." Mrs Sue Clarke of Shifnal said: "My mother, Miss Lilian Hughes, is on the front row, second from left, holding somebody's hand. The women on the photograph used to clean the planes. I remember she said it used always to be a cold job in the winter." *(Picture via Allan Frost)*

Among the many accident victims from RAF High Ercall was Flight Sergeant Quentin MacPhail Shippee, who was flying with 247 Squadron and died when his Hawker Typhoon spun off a turn at 300ft and crashed in a field near Windmill Farm, Aqueduct.

The crash site is these days obliterated by the Brookside housing estate in Telford. According to local research, and also the Commonwealth War Graves Commission, he died on March 19, 1943. However, RAF High Ercall's own records give the date of the fatal crash as rather earlier than that – February 24 of that year. Perhaps the later date was when death was officially presumed.

The local Britannia Aqueduct Historical Society has quite recently researched the crash and, with the help of the Quebec Family History Society, was able in 2004 to get in touch with Mac Shippee's niece – he was known to his family and friends as Mac. His family supplied this picture of him.

Mac, whose father was American, went to university in the United States, and after a year at university joined the Canadian Air Force. He was 22 when he died, and is buried at St Cuthbert's Church, Donington, near Cosford.

High Ercall today

Although the runways are long gone, High Ercall has benefited from the continual use, until quite recently, of its main airfield buildings, which are consequently in good condition.

They were for years known locally as MOTEC. This was a Multi Occupational Training and Education Centre for the Road Transport Industry Training Board. Afterwards they became a training centre called Centrex, but they now await another use.

Hangars continue to be used for warehousing and a clutch of the dispersed buildings remain, in a derelict state, by the B5063.

The Cotwall to Crudgington road gives a good panoramic view of the old airfield site.

A September 2000 view down the old main runway.

The imposing control tower of RNAS Hinstock photographed in July 1996. Since this picture was taken it has been transformed.

Hinstock

Search as hard as you like in and around the village of Hinstock, but you will be lucky to find the airfield of that name. Royal Naval Air Station Hinstock is about as remote and isolated as you can get, tucked away along the country lanes of north Shropshire.

The Royal Navy called it HMS Godwit. This "warship which flew" is today one of Shropshire's best preserved wartime airfields, with many of the old buildings surviving, including the rare Admiralty-designed three-storey control tower, which is said to be one of only two of its type in the whole of Britain. A minor road runs along part of the old perimeter track along which planes would once taxi before taking off.

The site was requisitioned by the RAF in November 1939. Originally known as Sayerfields, it was then called Ollerton and was used by training aircraft at Tern Hill and later for storing aircraft. But in 1942 the Royal Navy was searching for somewhere to set up an instrument flying school. The airfield was developed, renamed RNAS Hinstock and, in the Navy way of doing things,

was commissioned as HMS Godwit in June 1943.

The main resident unit was 758 Squadron, the Naval Advanced Instrument Flying School, flying mainly Airspeed Oxfords. Tiger Moth biplanes were also a common sight at Hinstock and among other types seen there were Barracudas, Fireflies, Avengers and Harvards.

One of the main skills pilots learned was how to use a special radio beam to help them fly "blind". The beam was transmitted from the airfield and if planes flew along it the crew would hear a steady note. But if they were to one side they would hear either dots or dashes, depending on which side. Further tones helped pilots judge when they were approaching the runway. It was the start of blind-flying landing systems seen at all major airports today.

At the school's peak, 52 qualified instrument-flying pilots were being turned out a week. According to a 1946 newspaper report, there was only one fatality, and that on a day of perfect visibility.

Hinstock had a grass runway reinforced by metal tracking and its close proximity to Peplow (Childs Ercall) airfield only a mile or so to the south must have made things interesting for pilots in the circuit. In fact Hinstock and Peplow were to become virtually twin navy bases. In February 1946 they still had about 2,000 naval personnel and almost 400 Wrens between them.

In July 1946 the Fleet Air Arm's first gliders were used at Hinstock for advanced flying training, and Squadron Leader E.J. Furlong set up a new altitude record of 4,500ft for two-seater sailplanes. In November of that year a Royal Navy Lancaster, piloted by a Hinstock flying instructor and manned by pupils attached to the station's advanced flying training school, left a southern airfield on what was to have been the longest non-stop flight ever undertaken by the Royal Navy, a 1,200 mile hop to Malta. In the event the Lancaster landed in Sardinia.

Hinstock, this little bit of the Fleet Air Arm in Shropshire, was finally abandoned around February 1947 and a few months later was being used as a Ministry of Labour camp for displaced persons from eastern Europe. The site was sold in 1963.

'Like a country club'

In the spring of 1944 **Reg Howard** completed his advanced flying training in Scotland and was thirsting for action. His posting was to HMS Godwit. He soon discovered this was not, as he hoped, some new aircraft carrier, but a navy airfield in the heart of the Shropshire countryside. Sub Lt Howard was to see out the rest of the war as an instructor.

"I was met at Hodnet station and whisked away to the officers mess at Hinstock Hall. The squadron was in its formative days and when I arrived there were more senior than junior officers," said Mr Howard, of Eaton Constantine

Initially they operated from a grass field at Bratton, near Wellington, (see the Bratton chapter for his specific memories about that airfield) but as the squadron grew and began to take pupils it moved to Hinstock airfield which had a metal strip runway with a steep slope at one end.

"The navy had taken over Hinstock Hall as the officers mess. You lived like gentlemen. You didn't wear uniform unless you were on duty. The station was RNVR from top to bottom – there was no straight lace to be seen. There was discipline all right, but it was relaxed discipline.

"We were flying Tiger Moths and Oxfords. Initially I was being taught to be an instructor for a few weeks. And then eventually when they took on courses there were people coming in on a course for advanced instrument flying. I believe the idea was that naval pilots who had trained as most did with the RAF or the Americans in Pensacola had not much idea of instrument flying. In Pensacola they never saw a cloud.

"At Hinstock they had standard beam approach. It was a beam centred at the end of the runway which sent out a beam either side. When you flew in the centre of the beam you got a steady note, but if you were to one side you would get dots, and the other side you would get dashes. You could therefore keep a straight course.

"When the weather was bad they had a beacon, I think it was called a Y beacon, which sent out beams in all directions in sectors."

On one occasion while he was flying in bad weather it failed and he became lost, crash landing his Oxford without injuries near Holmfirth.

"Instrument flying is a tricky thing. You get a sort of vertigo in cloud. I think it caused a lot of crashes. It's a very strong feeling that your instruments are wrong.

Hinstock (Ollerton)

HMS Godwit
N5250 W00230
Runway:
04/22 c 4100 ft
Grass reinforced by tracking
Hangars:
P Pentad B Blister
M Mainhill
H Blister/S Shed (N/k)

c 1945

To Hodnet

To Ollerton

To Hinstock

To Childs Ercall

Map: Ian Pride

"On one occasion the CO Johnny Pugh took off in a Tiger Moth and as he did so hit a picket, a big concrete

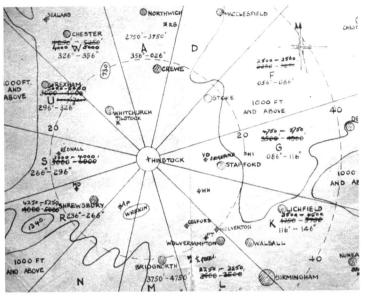

Reg Howard's instrument flying map with Hinstock at the centre.

lump with a ring on top for tethering aircraft. He knocked the wheel off but didn't know. When he came to land all he got was a Very light to warn him off. In the end they dashed out with a spare wheel and shook it at him to make him understand why. He made a very good landing actually," said Mr Howard, pictured left in the grounds of Hinstock Hall in about 1944.

"On another occasion the weather was pretty rotten down below and I was stooging around with a pupil. A colleague formated with me and indicated by hand signs that he had lost all his radio controls. I got through to the ground and 10 minutes later the chief flying instructor came up in a third plane and held up a blackboard to him which said 'Follow Me'. The three of us descended through the cloud and the one that was lame landed first."

Early in 1945 the RAF left nearby Peplow and the navy moved in. At last it enjoyed the luxury of three runways and being able to take-off and land

into wind. "Flying had finished by February or March 1946. Hinstock Hall has a big horseshoe-shaped drive. It's still there. Unfortunately they have taken the top storey off the hall itself. The Wrens were in Steps Farm."

George Preece, of Victoria Road, Bridgnorth, was an air mechanic in the Fleet Air Arm stationed at HMS Godwit from June 1944. "When I first went there we were billeted in bell tents next to the airfield. I suppose there was no room in the camp," he said. "One thing I remember was that the guard room on the airfield was a reclaimed cottage."

He also lived at Bridgnorth at that time. "It was quite handy while I was stationed there as I used to cycle home"

After a few months they were transferred to an ex-American army transit camp at Stoke-on-Tern and were taken to the airfield every day by bus.

He served at Hinstock until spring 1945 when navy pilot training was switched to Peplow when the RAF moved out.

Mr Preece remembers that they referred to the small airfield at Hinstock as Childs Ercall airfield. Confusingly, as we have seen, Childs Ercall airfield was also the original name of the much larger base nearby

E Flight of 758 Squadron at RNAS Hinstock in 1944 or 1945. Reg Howard is middle row, second from right. *(Reg Howard)*

which was later officially named Peplow airfield.

Richard Neal, of Benthall, Broseley, said: "I was sent to the Naval Advanced Instrument Flying School at Hinstock while waiting for an operational carrier-borne fighter squadron in the summer of 1943.

"'Boring' I thought. But bored I was most certainly not, trapped in the closed cockpit of a Tiger Moth a few days later gyrating violently to earth with only the altimeter, the airspeed indicator and the turn and bank needle to help me get out of the spin. It was a vital skill and mastering it gave one great confidence. Comfortable twin-engined Oxfords were used to teach us blind take-offs, flights and landings. We used the Lorenz Beam Approach, which brought us into the airfield at Hinstock on a bearing of about 217 degrees.

"Morse dots and dashes indicated left and right of beam respectively. A continuous note meant you were lined up with the 'runway' which you approached over an outer marker and then an inner marker beacon at a precise rate of descent until touchdown. We became able to take-off and land quite 'blind' until the last few hundred feet. Magic in those days.

"Having taught me to be accurate and safe, Hinstock then made me an instructor – which was not safe. One pilot tried to fly me through the control tower. I resisted his attempt but unfortunately transmitted my comments. Another pilot froze onto the controls of my Miles Master in a spin directly over Glastonbury tower. A passenger hung his parachute over the throttle lever in his

The cartoon rescued by Freda Davies from the officers mess.

Year		Aircraft		Pilot, or 1st Pilot	2nd Pilot, Pupil or Passenger	Duty (Including Results and Remarks)
Month	Date	Type	No.			Totals Brought Forward
—	—	—	—		—	—
				Dummy cockpit drill.		
Jan.	11.	Master. 1.		Sgt. Gannaway.	Self.	Cockpit familiarisation.
"	14.	Master. 1.		Sgt. Gannaway.	Self.	Cockpit drill.
"	18.	Master. 2.		Sgt. Gannaway.	Self.	Cockpit drill.
Feb.	3.	Hurricane.		Sgt. Gannaway.	Self.	Cockpit familiarisation.
August	1.	Oxford	DF.462	Lt. McVey.	Self.	Hinstock to Chetwynd. Chetwynd to Hinstock.
	1.	Master. 1.	T.8666.	F/Lt. Barwick.	Self.	L.F.P.
	1.	Oxford	DF.461	Lt. Scott.	Self.	3.A.
	3.	Oxford	HM.621.	Self.	Mid. Brewer.	I.F.
	4.	Oxford	HM.621.	Self.	Mid. Brewer.	I.F.
	4.	Oxford	H.M.621.	Self.	Mid. Brewer.	I.F.
	5.	Oxford	607.	Self.	Mid. Brewer.	I.F.
	5.	Oxford	607.	Self.	Mid. Lees Jones.	I.F.
	6.	Oxford.	462.	Self.	Mid. Brewer.	I.F. Spins
	7.	Tiger.	7610.	Self.		
	8.	Oxford	461.	Lt. Pridham.	Self.	Hinstock to

hang on until they drowned, by the way)," said Mr Neal, who went on to fly operationally with 1839 Squadron on HMS Indomitable in the Far East.

Mr Neal, part of whose logbook entries for his days at Hinstock are shown inset, added: "I'd like to thank the grizzly professionals of Hinstock (even the cockpit chain smoker) and the unsung ground crews. But thank God I was not asked to perform Lorenz beam approaches and landings on a carrier! It was dangerous enough fully sighted in a flat calm."

Frank Fuller, of Market Drayton, said: "At the end of World War Two, Sea Cadets from Wellington often visited the base and sometimes some of us had a flight. I remem-

cockpit on take-off. Most pilots would invert the aircraft and dive if I pushed the stick gently forward in cloud to produce negative G.

"Japanese ground guns, Zeros, Oscars and Tojos were more predictable and Hinstock's training saved me from ditching and sharks on three occasions (we were instructed to dodge the sharks, grab their fins and

A group of Wrens outside their billets at RNAS Hinstock, perhaps around 1943. There were billets around Hinstock Hall.

Peplow. Then I was moved to Hinstock Hall.

"I remember Ann Shelton (the famous singer of the era) coming to Childs Ercall for a concert. She held a concert there. I don't know if it was in one of the hangars or a building.

"Hinstock Hall was a beautiful place. It's where they used to dine. We had billets around the hall. I don't think anyone slept there as far as I know. We had our own dining place.

"There used to be a Butters bus which ran from Childs Ercall to Wellington, and we used to go to the Majestic. You had to be in by 9pm, and heaven help you if you were late, although I think on a couple of nights you were allowed out to 11pm."

ber flying from there in an Avro Anson in 1945."

When news came through of the Victory in Europe in 1945, for the first, and as far as **Freda Davies** knows, the last time, the Wrens stationed at RNAS Hinstock were invited to "splice the mainbrace" and join the men in a tot of naval rum.

Freda (seen in wartime, previous page), of Lockley Wood, Market Drayton, lined up with the other girls with her cocoa mug.

"It was so strong and I wasn't a big drinker anyway, so I took one sip and gave it away."

Afterwards she wrote "HMS Neversink" over the lintel of her cabin, where it stayed for many years until the huts were demolished. Freda, who joined the Wrens in December 1944 at the age of 17, served in the Air Engineers Office of HMS Godwit, initially serving at Peplow and moving to Hinstock in January 1945.

In the evening of VE Day she went with other girls into Hinstock to celebrate.

"Everyone was out. There were three pubs in the village and people just moved around them. I knew some of the villagers and we just had a great time."

After the war she was transferred to Plymouth and on to HMS Pembroke, before being demobbed in 1947. One memento she kept from the Hinstock days is a cartoon, rescued from the officers mess, which refers to 758 Squadron's farewell on being transferred to RNAS Culdrose, Cornwall.

One HMS Godwit veteran, who preferred not to be named, said: "I was stationed at Hinstock in 1942 or 1943. I went there into the Wrens. I was only 17 and a half and came from Trefonen, near Oswestry.

"I was billeted at Steps Farm, which is where our digs were. You could almost touch the aeroplanes at RAF

It's time for tea – or would it have been cocoa?

Airspeed Oxfords, like this one at Hinstock, were a familiar sight in Shropshire's wartime skies.

Above and below, communications aircraft at Hinstock in about 1944.

Instructor and pupil after a flight in a Tiger Moth. Reg Howard thinks he may be the instructor on the left.

Officers of 758 Squadron, RNAS Hinstock, probably in 1944. Seated, centre, is commanding officer Captain Johnny Pugh.
(This picture, and all others on these facing pages, loaned by Reg Howard)

Wartime Hinstock Hall, which was the officers mess. Notice the aircraft overhead. The hall is today substantially altered and reduced.

Rooms with a view

HMS Godwit is unique among Shropshire's old wartime airfields in that its historic and rare three-storey control tower of Admiralty design has been rescued from dereliction and sensitively restored into a luxury country home.

And, rather naturally, it enjoys stunning panoramic views over the airfield site and surrounding countryside.

While most disused airfield buildings in Shropshire are under constant threat of being swept away without a thought, and many old control towers have fallen victim to the bulldozers, it has been a remarkable and imaginative transformation.

The airfield and control tower had attracted interest in the past. In the 1990s The Bomber Airfield Society earmarked it as a possible site for a living museum in which the society would take over an airfield and turn the clock back to 1943.

The Hinstock site fell through mainly because traffic access is so bad on the country lanes.

The future of the decaying tower, which is not protected by being listed as being of architectural or historic interest, seemed uncertain until in April 2003 Becky and Stephen Lea were given planning permission to turn the building into a bed and breakfast, and also a home for the Leas.

The far-sighted councillors gave permission despite being urged by council officers to refuse the plan, which would surely have spelt doom for the building.

By giving it a use, the tasteful conversion has helped secure the future of this most unusual building which retains its historic wartime name – HMS Godwit – and, together with the associated equestrian centre, went on the market in June 2005 with a price tag of £1.95 million.

The control tower was on sale separately in January 2008 as a six-bedroomed home, with an asking price of £725,000.

Speaking then, Pat Kirk, Fine and Country branch manager, said: "The property is unique. It would certainly make a family home because of the huge size of it.

"It would perhaps appeal to someone from the city who is looking to move to the area and wants something a bit different, but it is the complete opposite to a chocolate box cottage in the country; some people absolutely love it and others don't, because it is very different," she said.

The four floors of the property all have balconies (the sales particulars said), and the third floor has a spiral staircase leading to the watchtower, and a penthouse style studio, equipped with its own kitchen and roof terrace.

It is set in more than 300 acres of land, and has an all weather menage and 12 paddocks nearby, although these were not being included in the £725,000 price tag.

The accommodation comprises entrance hall, utility room, dining room, sitting room, master bedroom suite, second bedroom suite and then all four other en-suite bedrooms, along with the penthouse studio and roof terrace.

Compare this modern view with the picture of the derelict building on page 67 and you can appreciate sensitivity of the conversion.
Above: one of the rooms.

The view from the control tower

Airfield buildings survive in the surrounding countryside

Hinstock today

The airfield site is so tucked away down country lanes that an Ordnance Survey map is more or less a must. It is reached by Ollerton Lane, north of the village of Ollerton, which is itself west of Childs Ercall.

There are surviving hangars on the eastern side of the airfield while the old control tower which, as we have seen, has been converted into a house, still dominates the scene. A minor road follows the old perimeter track for about a mile giving a good view across the flying field, and some airfield buildings can still be found in the surrounding countryside.

Hinstock Hall, once the officers mess, is a mile or two away, but a pale shadow of its wartime appearance after 1950s demolition.

There is new planting across the middle of the airfield which will, when more fully grown, break up the expanse, making it more difficult in the future to imagine it as a flying field.

Hodnet

The clunk of bat against ball at Hodnet's cricket pitch is a far cry from the days when the site had a more warlike purpose. Under spreading trees aircraft would be stored under camouflage netting. What is now the players' pavilion was an airfield building used by guards protecting their valuable charges.

And then when the planes needed to take-off, traffic on the Shrewsbury road was stopped and the aircraft were taken through a gap in the hedge across the road to the airstrip itself, south of the A53.

It seems almost incredible now, but this Shropshire village had its own airfield. Not, it must be said, a very big one. RAF Hodnet had a minor role, a bit part in the mighty drama of World War Two. It was a satellite landing ground, storing and dispersing aircraft from bases like RAF Shawbury and RAF Tern Hill. Not only did this take some of the pressure off the crowded and busy main bases, but at RAF Hodnet planes could be hidden under trees and camouflage netting, making them less vulnerable to air attack.

RAF Hodnet opened in June 1941 and, in addition to its storage and dispersal function, there was some circuit

Staff of RAF Hodnet in September 1941 in front of a Lockheed Hudson bomber, probably in the grounds of Hodnet Hall. Back, from left: Aircraftsman Hill, AC Moncrieff, Leading Aircraftsman Moon, AC Hodnerson, AC Corp, AC Manning, AC Edwards, AC Dewe, AC Hammond, LAC Cuss, AC Iles, AC Kemish, AC Robinson, AC Styles, LAC Andrews, AC Chambers. Centre row: AC Rhodes, AC Doyle, LAC Dowd, AC Springett, AC Hannah, AC Blevnev, LAC Newcombe, LAC John, AC Tedder, AC Tomlin, AC Tankard, AC Waltham, AC Evans. Front: AC Ward, LAC Smith, Corporal Clare, Cpl Bottomley, Flt Sgt Jennings, Flying Officer G.J. Pearn (Officer Commanding), Sgt Henderson, Cpl Williams, Cpl Arthur Braithwaite (from Hodnet, who had this picture hanging on his wall for years), another Cpl Williams, and AC Flux.

flying by Miles Master trainers from Tern Hill. The old upstairs dance hall at the Bear in Hodnet was used as early billeting, but the main accommodation seems to have been at Holyrood House across the road.

Among aircraft spoken of which were at Hodnet were small training types and also Spitfires, together with twin-engined planes like Wellingtons, Hudsons, Mosquitos, Ansons and Oxfords. Planes were dispersed between the A53 and Hodnet Hall – including the area which is now the cricket pitch – and in fields between the A442 Wellington road and the railway line, now disused.

They were taken across the road through gaps in the hedges which are still visible. The landing area itself was west of the A442, bounded by Green Lane to the south and the A53 to the north.

Hodnet's part in the history of the RAF finally came to an end in February 1945. Around this time some aircraft like Mosquitos were broken up at the southern part of the site.

Although it was a makeshift base, evidence still survives. Apart from the cricket pavilion, which was a combination mess room and kitchen, the old flight hut and mess room still stands, a derelict bungalow-like structure alongside the A442. The guard room which stood on the notorious Hodnet bends has been demolished. The modern Hodnet bypass cuts across the northern part of the airfield.

Small, undoubtedly. Insignificant, arguably. But RAF Hodnet is not yet forgotten.

Under camouflage

Yorkshireman **Arthur Braithwaite** was stationed at wartime RAF Hodnet – and it indirectly led to him marrying a Shropshire bride. He arrived in 1941 from RAF Tern Hill and was a corporal in charge of transport.

Arthur recalled that when the RAF arrived at Hodnet they initially slept in the upstairs dance hall at The Bear and paraded down to the airfield every morning.

Then they moved into messing huts at The Kennels, opposite The Grove, where there had been an army searchlight camp, and also took over Holyrood House. The cookhouse was downstairs.

"I was MT driver, which meant I had to look after the ambulance and the fire engine. And there was a van kept at Holyrood House. I slept at Holyrood House and my office was upstairs there.

"The aircraft used to be stationed under trees, camouflaged. They used to come in to be fitted with gun turrets, bomb racks and that. It was like a bit of a repair unit. There was only a small gang here, with riggers and fitters.

"We didn't have any crashes. They were all test pilots who brought in the aircraft. They used to light smoke bombs to tell the pilots which way the wind was blowing.

"When you go towards Wellington, the first bend you come to, there used to be an orderly room there where the officer and staff sergeant used to be. I don't know if it's still there – I think they took that one. The building where the guards used to sleep on the cricket pitch is still there."

Mr Braithwaite was posted to the Middle East just over a year before war's end and said at that stage the Hodnet base was on the point of closing. But after being demobbed he returned to work for a civilian pal at Marchamley Wood. It was then he met his wife-to-be Sylvia, from Wollerton.

Charlie France, of Hodnet said: "I was a lad during the war. The airfield huts were where the cricket field is now. We still use the huts for a pavilion and equipment shed. I can remember the hangars in that sort of field, between the cricket field and Hodnet Hall. They were steel structures with camouflage netting.

"The personnel, about 20 guys, were billeted at Holyrood House, which is opposite the groceries shop. They used to have their meals in The Bear, in the function room upstairs which used to be called the Bear's Parlour. I can remember there being ENSA concerts in The Bear and we used to be invited up. I can remember going as a lad and sitting at the back."

Jim Rhodes, who lives at Holyrood House (in 1998), was serving in the Army but said: "I remember the airmen marching up and down. I came home a couple of times on embarkation leave and I can remember seeing these chaps here. I had a coffee round here one morning.

"Corporal Parkinson was the corporal in charge of these chaps. His father was a parson. He married the butcher's daughter, Ada Morris, and he kept The Bear after he was demobbed."

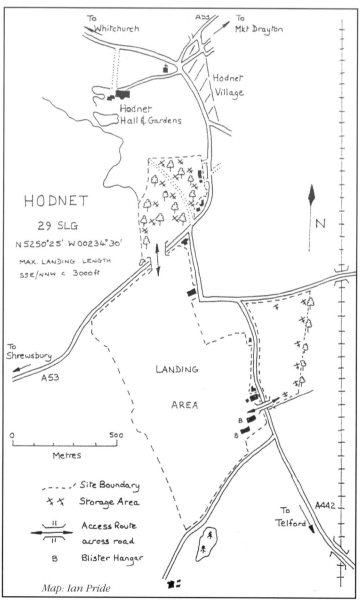

HODNET

29 SLG

N 52 50' 25' W 002 34' 30'

MAX. LANDING LENGTH
SSE/NNW c. 3000 ft

To Whitchurch

To Mkt Drayton

Hodnet Village

Hodnet Hall & Gardens

N

To Shrewsbury

A53

LANDING

AREA

B

B

To Telford

A442

0   500
Metres

- - - - Site Boundary
x x   Storage Area
         Access Route
         across road
B   Blister Hangar

Map: Ian Pride

Ron Cope, then a teenager living at Greenfields Farm on the southern edge of the airfield, remembers the hidden aircraft and said: "Sometimes there would be 30 or 40 planes. They used to come and go – it was more a storage base. Some days there would be a lot of planes landing, and then there would be nothing for perhaps a week or two.

"At the finish they had what the locals called the graveyard. Next to Green Lane at the bottom of the airstrip there were little fields that they broke planes up in. They destroyed no end of planes there at one time."

Albert Ward, of Walsall, was one of the first at Hodnet – he worked on the building of the airfield. "At the side of the runway they built some hangars and made them look like shops. They looked like shops from the outside. These 'shops', they put windows in the hangars, but there was not anything there – they were not shops as such.

"They brought the Spitfires in and took the wings off them and pushed them into the woods. If they wanted them, they assembled them and flew them out again. I was there when it started. It was when I left school. I was born in 1925. I left at 14. I worked in a poultry farm for 12 months. The wages were putrid. They were 10 shillings for 48 hours. Somebody said there was a job going at Hodnet making the tea for the men (i.e. the labourers). I went there and got £2 a week.

"It was only a straightforward runway, straight down and straight up. It did not go different ways. It was only rolled hard. We had big 10 ton rollers rolling the ground and then they put grass back on it. Quite a few planes came there, mostly Spitfires.

"I think the aeroplanes went into part of Hodnet Hall. They went across the Shrewsbury Road when they pushed them in. There was not flying up and down – they just brought them and parked them. When they wanted them, they flew them away. It was not used as an ordinary airfield. I lived at the time at Stoke Heath."

Hodnet today

Drive towards Hodnet along the A442 from the south. About a mile from the village, on the left of the road shortly before the roundabout of the modern Hodnet bypass, there is an empty, single storey building (see picture, right), which was the airfield watch office (control tower). It could easily be mistaken for a farm building – all part of the disguise of this "secret" base.

The landing area was in the fields on the left, and planes were also dispersed in fields on the right of the road, and in the grounds of Hodnet Hall, behind the wall as you drive up into the village. As you travel up into the village centre, Holyrood House, where personnel were billeted, is on the left near the top of the hill.

War diary

1940

December 2: "At Hodnet, Master N7597 crashed at Holme Farm, resulting in the deaths of F/O H.T. Buswell and LAC R.A. Chant." (These aircraft were from 5 FTS at Tern Hill and it is not clear if the accident was connected with the building of the airfield at Hodnet).

1941

June 12: Hodnet SLG commenced to function in the afternoon of this day. Seven Blenheim IV aircraft were flown in.

June 22: Numbers of aircraft at SLG Hodnet now seven Blenheim Mark IVs, five Defiants.

July 27: Eleven Hurricane aircraft arrive at 29 SLG (i.e. Hodnet airfield) from 48 MU, Hawarden, for dispersal.

August 18: All Hodnet SLG personnel moved from parent unit's billets at Market Drayton to Holyrood House and Assembly Hall, Hodnet.

August 31: Visit by Air Commodore Vincent who discussed the possibility of using the airfield by a squadron in the event on an invasion.

1942

January 1: Flying Officer G.J. Pearn, in command of SLG Hodnet since opening up, posted to parent unit.

February 10: Work commenced on Ministry of Aircraft Production hides.

March 31: Average strength of personnel at No 29 SLG during the period June 1941 to March 1942 was 45 to 50.

An airfield building is used as a cricket pavilion

An early meeting – around the mid to late 1930s – of some of the gliding pioneers on the Long Mynd with Charles Espin Hardwick, centre, with trilby. *(Keith Mansell)*

Midland Gliding Club

While all other airfields in this book came into their own in war, exactly the opposite happened at the gliding club on the Long Mynd, which shut down for the duration.

It is one of the oldest in the country and, at 1,400ft above sea level, is the highest. For over 70 years pilots have soared above the Mynd. But it almost all ended as soon as it began.

The Long Mynd attracted the interest of glider enthusiasts from the Birmingham area in August 1934, who were looking for somewhere reasonably local to practise what was then a new sport, which had been largely pioneered in Germany. What caught their eye was the west-facing ridge which stretches for miles along the Long Mynd. They knew that in westerly winds the ridge would deflect the air upwards – and that gliders in the upcurrent would be able to stay aloft.

In preparation for their visit, the farmer, Alfred Morris, of Snead Farm, Wentnor, cleared a strip 80 yards long by seven wide to enable the gliders to be launched. Among the team were Mr Charles Espin Hardwick, chairman of the British Gliding Association. The first flight was on August 11 by Fred Slingsby, a pioneer manufacturer of British gliders.

The glider was launched by bungee. In other words, it was catapulted off the side of the Long Mynd by a rubber rope. This method is still occasionally used today. The gliders on that historic day were aloft for about two hours.

When the gliders were there a second time, a crowd of around 700 turned up to watch, and got in the way of launches and landings so badly that gliding had to be suspended. However, the site had lived up to its promise. It was the start of the Midland Gliding Club, which initially had one sailplane, two gliders, and 40 members. A sailplane was a high performance glider.

But there was a problem. In March 1935, they found themselves in court. The Chancery Court heard an action by Max Wenner, who owned 5,000 acres on the Long Mynd, who claimed the gliding interfered with his grouse shooting. He won an injunction banning further gliding.

The gliding enthusiasts were not beaten. Within days they acquired the lease of a new site, further south, overlooking the village of Asterton. It proved an excellent choice and soon gliding records were being set. A hangar went up in 1936 and gradually the club complex began to take shape. As for Max Wenner, he met a sticky end in January 1937 when he either fell, jumped, or was pushed from an early airliner when returning from a visit to Germany.

In August 1938 Sub Lt A.N. Young, an officer in the Fleet Air Arm, broke the British amateur gliding record for a single seater, staying aloft 15hr 45 mins above the Mynd. But there was tragedy too. A few days later, on August 21, Major J.G. Stewart-Smith, of Kinver, was killed on his first flight. It was the first fatal gliding accident there.

On October 10, 1939, the club's activities were suspended for the duration of the war. What happened at the site during the 1939-45 period is a little unclear. An immediate post-war aerial photo shows strange markings across the flying field, which has been taken as evidence that trenches were dug to discourage enemy planes or gliders landing.

However, apart from the top of a hill being an unlikely choice for an airborne invasion, the usual way to deter such landings was to erect poles or scatter vehicles over the area. The markings may instead be traces of, say, hardstandings of some sort.

Over the years since the war the site has been developed and improved, and the flying fleet expanded. In 1954, the present clubhouse was added. Thanks to various land acquisitions, the club now owns all the flying field.

Glider pilots found new ways to harness the power of nature to stay aloft, and strides in design moved gliders away from the drag-laden, ground-loving types of the early days, to sleek machines of the skies. It is routine for pilots to fly long distances in a day and return to base. The record height gained by a glider flying from the Long Mynd is about 23,000ft.

Today the club continues to give ordinary people an introduction to gliding through trial lessons, gliding holidays and courses.

Amy Johnson at the Mynd

Top pilots have long been attracted to the Midland Gliding Club – and none have been more famous than Amy Johnson, the pioneering woman aviator.

Johnson, who was the first female solo pilot to fly from Britain to Australia, joined the club on the Long Mynd in October 1937. "The story was that she was not too much of an ace pilot," said MGC president Keith Mansell.

However, Johnson was clearly an enthusiast, as she appears to have been a member of several gliding clubs at once. She was still on the Long Mynd's books at the outbreak of war, when gliding was suspended. She died during a ferry flight in 1941, when she baled out of her aircraft over the Thames Estuary. Her body was never found.

Another colourful figure to have flown from the Long Mynd was Prince Bira, a Thai prince. Prince Birabongse Bhanutej Bhanubandh, to give him his full name, was a member from October 1945 to January 1951.

"He was more famous for his motor racing, before and after the war. He drove ERAs. He used to take his dog with him on cross country flights."

The prince did not have a trailer for his glider, and had a novel way of getting back to base if during one of his cross country flights weather conditions forced him to land.

"He would ring up a local removal firm and ask it to take him and his glider back to Shropshire," said Mr Mansell.

A pre-war visitor to the Long Mynd was Eric Lock, of Bayston Hill, who became an ace during the Battle of Britain. He would watch the gliders and is also thought to have met Amy Johnson.

Amy Johnson on the Long Mynd in about 1938. *(Keith Mansell)*

An image from Midland Gliding Club's 1937 Christmas card. *(Keith Mansell)*

1934

August 11: Fred Slingsby makes history when he is catapulted from the Long Mynd in his Falcon II glider, the first soaring flight from the hill.

September 22-23: Crowds watch second gliding meeting on the Long Mynd.

October 17: Midland Gliding Club formed at a meeting in the Mikado Restaurant in Martinau Street, Birmingham. Espin Hardwick elected first chairman.

1935

March 15: After a four-day legal case, Mr Justice Crossman effectively bans gliding from the initial Long Mynd site which he rules interferes with grouse shooting. However the MGC immediately finds a new site a short distance further south, overlooking the village of Asterton.

October 29: First unofficial flying meeting at the new site.

1936

April 4: Newly built hangar officially opened.

April 18-19: Formal inaugural flying meeting.

1937

October 24: Legendary aviator Amy Johnson signed up as a member and promptly made first solo flight in a Kite glider.

1938

August 18: Flying Officer A.N. Young, a visitor, achieves British duration record of 15 hours 47 minutes.

August 21: Club suffered first fatality when a Falcon III glider became ensnared by the launch rope during take-off and crashed.

1939

July: First camp of the new Air Defence Cadet Corps took place, training young cadets.

September 10: Last flying at the Long Mynd, permission having been obtained from the RAF.

October 10: Club formally closed for the duration of the war.

1946

July: Charles Wingfield makes British record long distance flight in a low performance glider, taking off from the Long Mynd and landing near Redhill, having been in the air for six hours and covering 147 miles.

1954

Present club house built.

1967-68, also 2001

Foot and mouth disease closes down flying operations.

The original caption for this picture was: "The First Tea – hostess Mrs C.E. Hardwick. Tea in the Club House at the opening of the Long Mynd Hangar, April 4, 1936. What Happy Faces." *(Keith Mansell)*

"Easter Camp, 1938." *(Keith Mansell)*

This photo from the immediate post war period shows strange markings on the airfield which may be associated with a wartime use. Unfortunately they are a mystery as nobody knows what they are. *(Keith Mansell)*

Glider pilots play a constant game of snakes and ladders in the skies. They seek out the rising air and avoid descending currents.

In the earliest days of gliding you simply took off from a high point and then glided to the ground. It was the Germans who found that if the wind was in the right direction and struck a ridge with suitable contours the air would be deflected upwards, and that gliders could position themselves within this air to stay aloft or climb.

It is this "ridge lift" which explains the hilltop position of the Midland Gliding Club near a five-mile west-facing ridge. When the wind is from the west, and sufficiently strong, gliders can track up and down the lift from this ridge. The down side, literally, is that in the lee of the hill there is a strong downward current, which pilots avoid at all costs.

A second way of soaring is to use thermals. These are rising currents of warm air on sunny days which eventually condense to form clouds. Gliders circle to stay within these narrow columns of rising air, and cumulus clouds often mark where they are.

Lastly there is "wave" which can take gliders to great heights. When wind strikes mountains, it creates a wave pattern in the air in the lee of the mountains, in the same way water hitting a boulder in a stream creates waves downstream. Gliders aim to position themselves in the rising part of these waves in the air and can be taken to much greater heights than the mountains which created the waves in the first place.

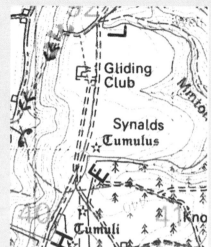

Gliders on the Long Mynd can on some days benefit from ridge, thermal, and wave lift. On others the air may be stable and there is no lift at all. In these circumstances the gliders simply return to earth at a rate which depends on the performance of the glider, known as the glide angle. A typical glide angle for a modern glider would be 1:34, meaning for every 34 feet it travels it will sink 1ft. However, high performance gliders have much "flatter" glide angles of around 1:50.

Midland Gliding Club today

To get there, simply follow the signs from Church Stretton and make the hair-raising journey up The Burway. The gliding club is at the south end of the Long Mynd in what must be one of the most spectacular and beautiful settings of any airfield in Britain.

There is a path which skirts the gliding field and, at the southern end, crosses it. Gliders can, and do, land on any part of the flying area and it is advisable to keep a close lookout at all times. The cables used to launch the gliders are a further potential hazard.

A better vantage point is from the higher ground just to the north, where many spectators like to park up for a picnic and watch the proceedings.

The club offers trial lessons for anyone wanting to try gliding and there are courses available for anyone wanting to take up the sport. There are no special requirements and generally if you are medically fit to drive a car, you will be able to fly a glider.

The crowded club hangar.

An Avro 504K at Monkmoor in 1927. *(H.R. Savage)*

Monkmoor

Monkmoor is the only one of Shropshire's airfields in which the flying field has totally disappeared, buried under the northward expansion of Shrewsbury. And, as one of Britain's oldest airfields, its heyday is now virtually beyond living memory. There are probably only a handful of people around who can remember flying taking place there.

But there are some reminders of its former use – huge hangars which were once part of the airfield are now used for business and commercial purposes. They are part of Britain's aviation heritage, as they are among the oldest hangars in the country, and rare survivors from the days of biplanes, rotary engines, and seat-of-the-pants flying.

The airfield at Monkmoor was created during World War One. The area was already in use by the military, with fields to the south of Monkmoor Road being used for cavalry training. And it was along Monkmoor Road, on the south side, that the large "Belfast" hangars were built. However, according to Shropshire aviation historian Ian Pride, a retired RAF officer, the actual flying field was north of the road. This meant the aircraft had to cross the road to get to the flying field, and there was a special gate built across

Monkmoor Road for this purpose.

Actually, there is some disagreement among aviation historians over whether there was also flying from the field south of the road – i.e. on the hangars side.

According to Flt Lt Pride's researches, it was in November 1915 that an airman called Green carried out test flights in a BE2 aircraft to judge whether Monkmoor would make a satisfactory aerodrome, and building started in April 1916. In 1917 a Vickers Vimy crashed there, having mistaken it for another airfield. It was opened in 1918 as home for the Observers School of Reconnaissance and Aerial Photography, and there are some early aerial pictures of Shrewsbury as a result of this use.

Unfortunately official records relating to Monkmoor are sparse, but the military doesn't appear to have been there long, and the military wind-down after World War One was very rapid. In March 1922 various hangars and buildings were sold and in December that year the aerodrome was sold to Mr J. Barber Lomax for £2,250.

However, there was civilian flying from the airfield in the 1920s and 1930s, including "joyriding" flights. Among visitors were Winifred Spooner, a famous lady pilot of the day, who had for the first years of her life lived at Woodfield, Port Hill, Shrewsbury. She and her brother Captain Frank Spooner landed at Monkmoor in September 1927. She made several subsequent flights into Monkmoor to visit friends.

During World War Two Monkmoor was the site of a salvage team which would travel to aircraft crashes across the country. Flt Lt Pride said: "It was not used as an airfield in the Second World War, but as 34 MU (Maintenance Unit). They used to call it one of the 'smash and grab' places. If there were any aircraft crashes they went to collect the bits to see if they could reuse them.

"During the V1 campaign in the south east of England Spitfires, Mustangs and Tempests used to go on 'Diver' patrols (to intercept and destroy the incoming flying bombs). The aircraft would intercept V1s and tip them over with their wings, and were consequently suffering a lot of damage. One of the jobs at Monkmoor was to mend wingtips. They used to travel from 34 MU to the south east."

He added that when two of the hangars were dismantled roof trusses from them were, he believes, used in the covered car park area at the back of the Lion Hotel in Wyle Cop, Shrewsbury, and at the Shropshire Dairy at Frankwell. At the end of the war the military use of Monkmoor ended again and the site was taken over for industrial and commercial purposes.

Shrewsbury historian David Trumper says: "There is still an area at the bottom of Monkmoor Lane where apparently grass won't grow because it was where they dumped engines and oil and so on which leaked into the ground and soaked it."

The only former Shropshire airfield to be obliterated by development, Monkmoor will never see fixed-wing flying again.

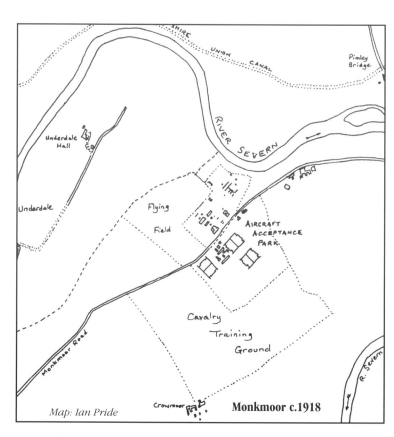

Map: Ian Pride   **Monkmoor c.1918**

'An enormously expensive airfield'

If **The Rev Wilfred Thompson**, who spent six weeks at Monkmoor at the end of World War One as an 18-year-old flying cadet, is right, then the airfield's sole achievement was to train him and 11 others at enormous expense.

He told of his experiences in a magazine article in 1984 – almost all first-hand memories of the airfield now are in written form.

"In November 1918 I was commissioned Observer Officer after having received, as an RAF Flight Cadet, specialised training in reconnaissance and aerial photography at Monkmoor, Shrewsbury, which was officially designated OSRAP, RAF (Observers School of Reconnaissance and Aerial Photography)," he wrote.

"We were to fly to France on November 13 but came the Armistice and the flight was cancelled.

"Monkmoor was a minute, pocket-handkerchief, airfield. It was constructed because Field Marshal Haig, Commander-in-Chief of the British forces on the Western Front, demanded his own Army Squadron to reconnoitre the entire Western Front to a depth of 30 miles behind enemy lines – a fairly risky occupation for the people assigned to the squadron. Monkmoor was to train the observers for that squadron and for none other. Twelve of us, selected on the results of examinations and practical work while flying, were to be the observers for the squadron.

"Our training must have been enormously costly. In the summer of 1918 a new airfield was laid out with large Belfast-trussed hangars, containing several DH4As (later DH9As) and a couple of fighters in case of enemy attack. All equipment and spare parts for these, and fuel, can't have been cheap. Then the staff was appointed – about six administrative officers including the CO, about eight officers' instructors and a Quartermaster-Sergeant, with their Warrant Officers and NCOs, a WRAF cook, several other WRAFs, batmen and their sergeant.

This was a postcard which appears to have been given as a souvenir to members of the public who went up on "joyride" flights. It is signed by the pilot. *(June Angell)*

"At the end of September we 12 pupils arrived for a six-week course. On November 13 we left on posting leave and by November 30 Monkmoor airfield had closed. Its construction and entire existence was to give one six-week course to 12 young men.

"What eventually happened to the former Monkmoor airfield? In May 1919 I was demobilised and in August of that year my father and I left London on bicycles, our travels including Shrewsbury. There we went up Monkmoor Road to find out what had happened to the airfield. The hangars and the tarmac apron had been sold to a poultryman, hen houses filled each hangar and the birds were scattered about the apron, pecking their food.

"The apron was fenced off from the airfield, which had been sold for a housing estate. Roads had been laid down and houses were being built, some were completed and a few were occupied. That was the end of Monkmoor airfield.

"A further distressing note. Delivery of the first DH9A was at dusk the day before I went on post-leave. I had asked my favourite instructor if he would take me up next morning and I would take some photographs. But next morning it was blowing a gale with torrential rain. Flying was out of the question and I left Monkmoor disappointed.

"After my leave, at home in London, I went to my posting, which was Marske Fighter Station in north east Yorkshire. My 11 Monkmoor colleagues arrived and brought sad news. The day after I left had been fine and Flt Lt Preece had taken up the DH9A with two sandbags for ballast. At 200ft the aircraft had stalled and crashed, killing the pilot. I deeply mourned my friend but was given furiously to think that I would have been his passenger."

Captain E.E. Fresson, who was to pioneer Britain's first airmail service in the 1930s, told of his Monkmoor memories in his 1967 book *Air Road to the Isles*.

"In 1928 I joined Berkshire Aviation tours, operated by Mr F.J.V. Holmes. He ran a joyriding circus with headquarters at Shrewsbury in Shropshire," he wrote.

"I remember seeing an advertisement in the aviation magazine Flight. It ran something like: 'Wanted, a pilot for the season, with experience of Le Rhone and Clerget motors.'

"As I had that experience from my war training and had given joyrides at Skegness at the end of the war with an Avro 504K with a Clerget motor, I applied for the job and got it.

"I motored up to Monkmoore (sic) airfield just outside Shrewsbury, and signed on. I was then shown around, and as we came to the gates which allowed the planes to be moved across the road to the flying field from the hangars, I was introduced to my prospective engineer, Bert Farminer. The poor chap was down in a deep hole digging for the erection of new gate pillars. I thought at the time that it was a peculiar job for a licensed air engineer to be at, but I soon got to know that in that organisation, or

Inside a hangar at Monkmoor, perhaps early 1920s. One of the trio (not known which) is Jack Baker, a mechanic. The aircraft is apparently a Vickers Vimy bomber being converted to passenger use. *(via David Trumper)*

in any joyriding organisation for that matter, one had to be a jack of all trades.

"I spent that summer joyriding in Shropshire, Lancashire, and then up in Scotland at Dumfries, and then Renfrew."

A letter in the Shrewsbury Chronicle in 1981 brought forth some letters in reply reminiscing about the site.

Sam Medlicott, of Handsworth, Birmingham, said: "Although I have not lived in Shrewsbury for 54 years, I do remember the aerodrome being built by McAlpine and Parkinson of Blackpool.

"I would be about 10 years old, doing a paper round for Mr Richard Mansell, of Wyle Cop, and on Saturday mornings after I had completed the round I used to go and meet my father who worked on the aerodrome. It was quite an experience, being wartime and seeing the prisoners of war, who also worked on the 'drome, being paraded ready to march off to the compound in Abbey Foregate by a small party of the KSLI regiment.

"I can remember Mr Jack Ince, a fruiterer from the corner of Roushill, Mardol end, taking over a hangar and turning it into a badminton court."

And one **A. Blackwall**, of Kenwood Gardens, Shrewsbury, took it upon himself to find out more about the level crossing gate by means of which Monkmoor Road could be closed for aircraft to cross the road from the hangars.

The editor of Motor Sport magazine, William Boddy, had previously visited, looking unsuccessfully for traces of the airfield and the gate.

"This gate put Monkmoor Airfield on a par with Croydon Aerodrome, which had a similar arrangement in the 1920s," said Mr Blackwall.

"Unfortunately Mr Boddy made his search in the open space beyond the sewage works, imagining this to have been the airfield. It was however apparently the cavalry training ground last used by the Shropshire Yeomanry in the days of horses."

Mr Blackwall found out that Mr Ron James, a curator of Clive House Museum, could remember living in Monkmoor Road towards the end of World War One and could recall drays bringing crated aircraft parts from the station for assembly in the hangars, after which they would cross the road and fly to their units.

One of his most fruitful sources of information was at the "Old Bush" in Abbey Foregate, where Richard Rowley, a World War One Royal Horse Artillery driver, could well remember the airfield.

"After leaving the army he had worked at a timber yard and had had the task of constructing a very large gate, sufficient to close Monkmoor Road. He could also remember

a discussion with Mr Walter Vaughan, by then the owner of the airfield, as to whether or not to set the massive gatepost in concrete.

"Other regulars at the Bush could remember that Mr Vaughan's son-in-law intended to develop the hangars for indoor tennis and skating. He did, however, in the late

According to the book "Wings Across the Border", this is a Super Drone motorised glider at Monkmoor in 1936. It stalled and crashed there in February 1937. *(Dorothy Chidlow)*

1920s, let some accommodation to Mr Holmes who, doubtless taking advantage of the gate, ran an air service to Manchester and certain other destinations. He was joined by another pilot who gave joyrides, possibly Captain Fresson.

"The gate was presumably removed when the airfield was built over and it is impossible now to establish its location from evidence on the site. The hangars, which were extensively restored by the RAF in World War Two and used as workshops again, occupy a considerable length of Monkmoor Road, opposite the Isolation hospital and from there towards Telford Way."

S. Cooper, of School Lane, Shrewsbury, said in a letter: "For the short period the station operated it was an ill-fated concern with a number of accidents. I saw many of the wrecked planes, some with their propellers buried in the ground."

He said the aerodrome had three twin hangars – i.e. six hangars – and after the Great War the first two hangars were bought by Mr Walter Vaughan, a retired Shrewsbury hatter.

"His son-in-law, a well-known banana king, Jack Ince, flew a plane off a field opposite."

Opposite Morris's Bakery, near the Welsh Bridge, one of the reconstructed hangars still stood, he wrote – although his letter implies it was a hangar from Shawbury.

"It was acquired by Messrs Lewis and Frogatt to serve as a garage. Today it is owned by a milk company."

Monkmoor mishaps

Monkmoor Aerodrome appears to have brought several crashes to Shrewsbury's doorstep, but surely none were more tragic than that in February 1919. Two flyers were killed when their DH9A aircraft nosedived into the ground in a field adjoining the aerodrome.

Mr Francis Price Edwards, licensee of the old Hero of Moultan pub in Wyle Cop, happened to be in the vicinity and dashed to the scene and tried to pull one of the victims clear, but just as he grabbed hold of him the petrol tank exploded. The victims were 22-year-old Lt Charles Evered Preece, of Hanley Castle, near Upton-on-Severn, and First Class Air Mechanic Harry Welch, of Ladywood, Birmingham.

A less tragic, but more dramatic accident which took place in the days of the Royal Flying Corps (i.e. before April 1918), seems to have grabbed the attention of much of the town as it unfolded, although a contemporary newspaper report does not make clear whether this aircraft was flying from Monkmoor – it could, for instance, have been flying from Shawbury instead.

Lt Edmund Montgomery, a 21-year-old Australian, was flying a "big biplane" when, over Coton Manor, he appeared to get into trouble. "He continued his flight, rapidly descending, then turned upside down, flew in that position over the Castle, the railway station, and across the river on to the Abbey Foregate side," said the newspaper report.

"Still in difficulty and realising that he must make a forced descent, the young officer righted his machine and came down with a swift slanting dive into the Abbey Foregate goods yard. He never for a moment appears to have lost his head; for in the final drop he made a plucky effort to reach a wide open space in the yard.

"Unluckily for him a part of the under portion of the machine caught by some six inches a railway truck and the impact threw the truck off the rails, smashed the engines

This giant Wellesley bomber landed on playing fields behind Monkmoor School on September 16, 1937. *(Bryan Corser)*

of the biplane, and threw the airman on to some loaded timber waggons." Montgomery suffered a broken leg and fractured skull.

"The descent was witnessed by people all over the town, and within a few minutes of the fall a large crowd collected. Some of those who got across to the goods yard secured parts from the biplane as souvenirs," added the newspaper.

There is a story that a Vickers Vimy bomber crashed at Monkmoor in 1917, having mistaken it for another airfield,

During World War Two an innocent Shropshire farmer found himself arrested for "spying" at the old airfield. George Bolderston was, rather bizarrely, mistaken for a Nazi agent. His daughter, Mrs Joyce Ashley, from Shrewsbury, told how he went to feed his bull in a field next to the airfield and was arrested as a "spy" at bayonet-point by the RAF.

"We lived at Crowmere Farm. It was all fields then and he used to walk across to the field next to the RAF base to feed the bull and water him. He had to draw the water for him.

"All of a sudden these RAF men came across to the field and put bayonets in his back. He was arrested for spying. They marched him off with a bayonet in his back. They interrogated him and let him go. We had the letter of apology from the Ministry for years. It was always a joke afterwards," she said.

Mrs Ashley, who was born in 1937, said the incident must have been in about 1942 as they moved from Crowmere Farm in about 1943.

She has no memory of there ever being any flying at the airfield at that time. "We left because the council was taking over all the land for housing." Crowmere Farm no longer existed, she added.

and talk too of crashes involving an Avro 504, a Bristol Fighter, and a DH2.

On September 16, 1937, a giant Vickers Wellesley bomber became lost, and circled around Monkmoor looking for somewhere to land. Perhaps it is a clue that Monkmoor Aerodrome was seeing little flying by then that the pilot decided not to put down at what the Shrewsbury Chronicle's report described as the "old aerodrome", and instead landed on playing fields behind Monkmoor School.

The newspaper, which moved heaven and earth to get a report and picture in its paper the next day, reported: "It seemed obvious that he was in some trouble, and more than once he attempted to come down by the old Monkmoor Aerodrome, where, however, certain difficulties faced him in the form of live electric cables which traverse the open space in front of the old 'drome, also the fact that children were playing in the fields close by.

"In an effort to avoid these, he finally chose to land in the school sports field, successfully negotiated some obstacles, struck a post, and, swerving, finally crashed into the iron railings at the top of Crowmere Road, where the undercarriage of his plane was severely damaged."

It said the pilot, Pilot Officer Riepenhausen, was on his way to Sealand, Cheshire, from Finningley, near Doncaster, on a triangular course and had lost his bearings.

"It is further understood that he had some trouble with his machine, and had also been puzzled by the appearance of the old hangars at Monkmoor."

He managed to get out of the aircraft unhurt, but dazed, and a crowd soon gathered.

There is a sad sequel. Flight Lieutenant James Eric Riepenhausen, of Birkenhead, died on October 11, 1940, aged 28, while flying a Whitley bomber of 10 OTU based at Abingdon. It crashed near Akeman Street landing ground killing the crew of six. The cause was thought to have been a large area of material stripping from the mainplane. He is buried at Flaybrick Hill Cemetery, Birkenhead.

Below: An oblique aerial view of Monkmoor around 1935 showing the airfield, top. Notice how the airfield straddled Monkmoor Road.
(Picture courtesy of Shrewsbury Museum Service)

Monkmoor today

The site of the old airfield can be reached by going down Monkmoor Road, Shrewsbury. Towards the end of the road the giant World War One hangars, which are still in business and commercial use, become obvious.

The flying field has completely disappeared. Some bits of the old airfield turn up, however, in unexpected places. The garage of the Lion Hotel, on Wyle Cop, has distinctive roof trusses which are said to have come from an old hangar at Monkmoor.

Above and left, the historic hangars at Monkmoor are still in use.

"19 Course, 61 OTU, Rednal and Montford Bridge, Aug 25-Nov 25 1942." **Rear row:** G. Cross, F. Merritt (USA), Buchanan (NZ), D. Wilkes (USA), D. Crowley, W. Cruickshank, W. Bailey, A. Bowker, L. Davies, L. Woods (Aus), G. Dobson, J. Boyle.
Third Row: J. Twomey, Johnson, J. Cole (USA), D. Cooke, R. Foster, T. Stonehouse (Can), R. Aubrey (NZ), L. Dalziel, G. Evans, Denholme (NZ), E. Karatau (?) (NZ), Collins, Russell (NZ), Johnson (NZ).
Second row: P/O R. Martin, P/O C. Fearn, W/O J. Lilburn, M. Murray (NZ), P. Cashen (Can), R. Dennamy, Russell, D. Dean, T. Holten (Aus), P. Newman (NZ), D. Darley, H.W.R. Hepplewhite, Barker (NZ), P/O Kirkwood.
Seated: P/O Heslyn DFM and Bar (NZ), P/O Thomas, Fl/Lt Smythe DFM, Fl/Lt (?) Dudeney, Fl/Lt Buchanan DFC (Rhod), W/Cmd Cheatle, Gr/Cpt Pearson- Rogers, Sq/Ld Thorne DFC, DFM and Bar, S/Ldr Rogers, Fl/Lt Ramsey, P/O Southwood, P/O R. Boys, P/O Miller. *(Sheila Hepplewhite)*

Montford Bridge

Montford Bridge airfield was Shropshire's wartime finishing school for Spitfire pilots. It was here that the rookie fighter pilots would hone their skills before joining combat squadrons. Throughout its life as a training base, RAF Montford Bridge was "twinned" with RAF Rednal, near Oswestry, which was the parent base. They both opened in April 1942, and were home for the rest of the European war to 61 Operational Training Unit.

From January 1945 Mustang III fighters began to be used by 61 OTU along with the Spits. The early part of the pilots' training was done at Rednal, and then they went to Montford Bridge for the final stages of their course, which included night flying.

In common with all training airfields there were plenty of accidents, including fatal crashes. In one unusual incident (which locals swear is true) a Dakota with a load of bananas clipped a hill and damaged a wing on a flight from South Wales and was diverted to Montford Bridge. It was guarded for two days and then when the bananas started to go off they were given to the locals. Some children had never seen a banana before.

On the departure of 61 OTU, the airfield was used by 34 Maintenance Unit, repairing and breaking up planes and gliders. A wide variety of types, up to and including four-engined bombers, were seen at Montford at this time.

There was also a small German prisoner of war camp. In fact the unit's barber and tailor were both German prisoners. Later surplus ammunition was stored on hardstandings at the airfield for disposal.

There were three runways, the longest of which was over 4,400ft long. At least two still exist today, although shrubs and vegetation have broken through the tarmacked surface. Also still standing, albeit derelict, is the control tower, and a few other wartime buildings. The wartime

Naafi became Grafton County Primary School in 1948, a link with the airfield which was cherished by the school.

A remarkable survivor is the multi-chambered underground battle headquarters, reachable down a metal rung ladder, although flooded to a depth of about five feet.

Apart from model aircraft, there is no flying at Montford Bridge airfield any more, although a few years ago it was used by a parachute centre and also by occasional crop spraying planes, and was called Forton airfield.

It is a shadow of itself in its heyday, but still recognisably a wartime aerodrome – and a dwindling number of disused airfields can say that.

School of aces

Pilots of all nationalities trained at Montford Bridge and one of them was one of the war's most famous aces, the Frenchman Pierre Clostermann, who finished the conflict with 11 air victories.

Clostermann spent five weeks at RAF Rednal in 1942 before spending the last three weeks of his training at Montford Bridge. He paints a bleak picture of the satellite airfield in his autobiography *The Big Show*.

"Without interruption, as soon as the weather cleared somewhat, we flew," he writes.

"Formation exercises in threes, fours, twelves, emergency take-offs, dogfight practice, air firing, course on tactics, on aircraft recognition, on elocution for speaking over the RT, etc.

"The cold was appalling. We lived in Nissen huts which had no insulating walls and keeping warm was a real problem. I used to go with John Scott, the baby of our team, who shared a room with me, and 'borrow' coal from a dump by the railway.

"John was very particular about his appearance, and it was a comic sight to see him, precariously balanced on barbed wire, passing greasy blocks of anthracite held distastefully between the thumb and forefinger of a carefully gloved hand.

"Then followed the homeric business of lighting the diminutive stove which had the task of warming our hut. Pints of petrol – filched from the bowser – were necessary to excite the faltering enthusiasm of the damp coal and wet wood.

"One fine evening, I remember, the stove, saturated with petrol vapour, blew up, and Jacques, John and I were transformed into Zulu warriors of the darkest hue.

"New Year's Eve came and went, very quiet and slightly sad in that remote corner. Then came the day of posting. Commailles, Menuge and I were to leave for Turnhouse in Scotland to join 341 Squadron, Free French Fighter Squadron 'Alsace', then in process of formation. Jacques, John and Aubertin were leaving for 602 Squadron in Perranporth.

"The die was cast. The real war was beginning. At last!"

An extremely rare picture of a Spitfire at Montford Bridge. In fact, this is the only such photo (so far) to come to light. *(via Robert Linney)*

A Yesterday's World romance

Raymond Baxter, who was to become one of the most familiar faces on television as presenter of Tomorrow's World, was an instructor on Spitfires at RAF Montford Bridge. And it was while there in the spring of 1944 that he met, at a party at the American-held Atcham airfield, the young American woman who was to become his wife.

The evening started inauspiciously for him. Dressed in his best RAF uniform, an ice cream sailed in the direction of him and his RAF colleagues as they joined the party.

Things got better. By the bar was a beautiful American girl in a green dress. He made a beeline for her and asked her to dance. She was Lieutenant Sylvia Kathryn Johnson of the US Army Nursing Corps.

When he left Montford Bridge – he says his time in Shropshire was six of the happiest months of his life – he returned to combat flying. On his favourite Spitfire, close to the cockpit, was painted his fiancee's name, "Sylvia K".

Baxter had been posted to Montford Bridge in February 1944 as an instructor having completed one and a half operational tours in Spitfires.

Baxter says: "There was an American OTU quite near (this was Atcham airfield). There was a good deal of feeling between the RAF and the United States Air Force at that time. It was not all brotherly love. Our pupils started getting involved in unofficial dogfights with their pupils in Thunderbolts.

Raymond Baxter back on "ops" after his Montford Bridge stay, with "Sylvia K" written on his Spitfire. *(Raymond Baxter)*

"Their colonel rang us up and said effectively: 'See here you guys, we better get our heads together before somebody gets his butt accidentally shot off. We are having a party in the mess on Friday. Why not come over?' We went over. There were swing doors at the entrance to the mess hall, as the Americans called it. There was a raging party going on inside. We threw open the swing doors and there we stood, four of us, in our best blue.

"I said 'duck' and an ice cream went whizzing over our heads and hit the doors behind us. Then the colonel came out of this melee and said: 'Say, did someone throw an ice cream at you?' The senior of our party, who was an Old Etonian, reacted with some sang froid, saying: 'No, no, no colonel, I'm sure it just slipped out of his hand.'

"I saw this beautiful, beautiful girl standing at the bar in a lovely green evening dress. I asked her to dance. We danced. I said: 'Either you are an English girl who has spent too much time with Americans, or you are an American girl pretending to be English.' She said: 'I'm from Boston'.

"So I had to marry her. That's what I said, and that's what I did. We fell in love. We decided we wouldn't get married until people stopped shooting at us. She was an American Army nurse with the 64th Field General Hospital stationed at that time at Oulton Park.

"On the favourite Spitfire which I flew later with 602 Squadron, I put 'Sylvia K', my then fiancee's name and first initial."

Their romance was played out in the countryside of Shropshire and Mid Wales, with trips in Baxter's MG.

Baxter left Montford Bridge on June 4, 1944. In later years, the couple returned occasionally to relive their memories. "It was all very nostalgic when we drove to Shropshire to the places we remembered. It was lovely."

'I was scared stiff'

Jack Hotchkiss remembers well his one and only flight from Montford Bridge airfield. "I went up in an Airspeed Oxford and we flew over both Birkenhead and Liverpool. I was scared stiff," said Mr Hotchkiss, of Broomfields Tenement, Montford Bridge.

"The pilot was a 19-year-old Canadian. He got in and threw his parachute in the back. I said I hadn't got mine

A wartime sports meeting at Montford Bridge. The woman is Peggy Tuffley, who was one of the winners. The officer with the moustache is Group Captain D. Finlay. *(Peggy Tuffley)*

on, and he said: 'Chuck it in the back – don't bother with it.'"

Mr Hotchkiss was given the flight because he was in the local Home Guard.

Grafton-born Mr Hotchkiss, who worked at Mytton Flour Mills from 1929 to 1966, recalls how there was airfield accommodation – huts – in various places in Grafton. "The WAAFs lived in huts just opposite the airfield the other side of the road at Grafton.

"On two occasions I was coming out of Shrewsbury on my push bike – I had been having a drink – and two WAAFs at different times stepped out and asked if they could have a ride, and I said 'where do you want to go to?' and they said 'Grafton airfield'. They got on the bar of my bike and I took them home. They had to be in at 12 o'clock I suppose and must have missed their bus home. In the officers mess they had concerts and dances. I have been there, but have never been to a dance. I was not a dancing man.

"They had one or two nasty crashes. One bloke was up over Ford. They had searchlights at Nib Heath about half a mile away and the searchlight got on him and must have blinded him. He came over the main A5 and hit a beech tree, then hit the crest of a building, crossed a road, and there was a big hawthorn hedge and he crashed into that. He would have been about 100 yards off the runway. Sergeant Spry was his name. I think he was in a Spitfire. He was killed outright.

"One dived into a bank at Grafton, not far away from the airfield. The propeller and the nose were down in the ground. I don't know whether he was killed.

"After the war the airfield packed in. Then they brought a lot of gliders here to be dismantled. Then the army had a certain amount to do with it and stored ammunition in the huts. When that was all cleared off, they sold it back to the three farmers which it belonged to."

Mr Hotchkiss recalls that the airmen would drink in Montford Bridge, Baschurch or at the Railway Tavern at Old Woods. "They have changed it now to the Romping Cat. The one at Montford Bridge was the Wingfield Arms, which is now called the Old Swan, and at Baschurch they used three pubs – the New Inn, The Duncan, and The Boreatton Arms."

George Tudor was born at a house on the corner of the airfield, only about 100 yards from the end of the main

A snowy wartime scene. *(Ian Pride)*

A 1948 aerial view. *(Ian Pride)*

War diary

1942

April 2: "Runways at Montford Bridge being retarmacked and will not be ready for another week. Move of unit (i.e. 61 OTU) postponed from April 8 to April 15."

April 15: Main move of 61 OTU.

June 20: AOC 81 Gp, A/Commodore F.J. Vincent DFC, attended pupils' passing out flypast.

1943

January 3: Accident involving F/Sgt Clostermann in Spitfire P7832 – burst tyre on landing, parked at edge of runway, run into by another plane (It is not clear whether this happened at Montford Bridge or at the parent station RAF Rednal).

February 17: Spitfire made wheels up landing.

April 8: Spitfires P8429 and 7921 collided in mid air, resulting in death of the pilot of the former machine, Sgt Moody.

May 28: Wheels up landing at Montford Bridge. Spitfire, pilot Sgt Norris.

June 8: Fire at the base caused injuries to 953955 A.C.2 Wakeman.

July 1: Investigation by W/C Stammers into fatal crash of P/O E.A. Evans.

December 28: Course 37 proceeded to Montford Bridge earlier in their training than usual, but this had been delayed owing to the bad weather earlier in the month and the time of training had to be extended.

1944

January 25: No 37 Course left.

April 30: AOC No 9 Gp visited to pass out No 41 Course.

May 6: Spitfire R6602, Pilot F/O Mare George Rivet, RCAF, and Spitfire X4821, Pilot W/O Joseph Irenee Wilbrod Nadeau, RCAF, collided at 12,000ft while engaged in battle formation. F/O Rivet baled out successfully but W/O Nadeau went down with his a/c and was killed. On the same day five Piper Cub a/c of the 83rd Artillery Div of the US Army arrived.

May 18: Interception training of formation of Liberators by Montford Bridge a/c under operations control.

December 16: Taxying accident involving two Spitfires. One written off.

runway. Spitfires were parked on hardstandings nearby and when the nearest was turned round the wing would come over the garden hedge.

During the building of the airfield the bulldozers and heavy equipment would be parked near the house overnight. His mother would boil hot water for the workmen so they could have a cuppa, which they would put in their billy cans, and his father Emery Tudor was given several flights at the airfield.

"One plane hit Dobson's ash tree and came down in the end of the wood here. I can vividly remember that.

The control tower at Montford Bridge in July 2001.

That was later on in the war. He came down the far end of the wood here on the airfield.

"The only bomb dropped here was dropped at Fitz. As far as I know it was a Jerry. They used to come up the Severn to Liverpool. It landed to the right of the church and broke one window in the church. There was a big crater for years. We used to go and play in the hole.

"At the end of the war, it must have been six or 12 months after the war, all round the villages were all the munitions from Nesscliffe, all up Yockleton, Westbury, all that. There were so many ammunition huts, all scattered around... this airfield was absolutely covered in ammunition. The Nissen huts were moved off all the farms and re-erected. This was absolutely a mass of sheds. The main runway, perimeters, anything with a hardstanding, was ammunition. The flying had ceased.

"My uncle was the architect for the airfield. He was William Thornhill. He used to come over from Sandbach

Flying control van at wartime Montford Bridge. *(Ian Pride)*

and stay with us for two or three days. We used to go through the gaps in the wire and onto the airfield and play."

Ninety per cent of the planes were Spitfires, he said. "The odd Wellington flew out of here and only very rarely, I think at the end of the war, when they were taking the Home Guard and people like that up."

A locally produced commemorative booklet for the airfield's 50th anniversary in 1992 also brought forward memories. Celebrations to mark the birthday included a Spitfire flypast.

Among memories of the airfield were those of **Mrs Ruby Everall**.

She said: "I was living at Broomfield Farm at the time and they took 11 acres of land off the farm. We got used to it at the farm. It did not upset the animals or chickens when they had to come so low to land.

"My son John was born in 1943 and I used to put him out in the pram and he would sleep through it all.

"We had a fright one night. What turned out to be one of our own airmen dropped a canister of incendiary bombs in the field by the garden and they spread all round the house, just escaping the stack yard, which was

a blessing.

"One fell on the house in a gutter over the bathroom. We did not notice it at first, but when Frank my husband got a ladder and went up to see what had happened he lifted a tile and the rafters were red hot, so we had to carry water up and then it started coming through the ceiling in the bathroom. A nice mess. Anyway, we managed to put it out.

"It was very frightening. Of course, it was a mistake. They should have dropped on some waste land a mile or so away."

And **Rex Cartwright** told how one of the visiting aircraft was a B24 Liberator.

"This parked on a hardstanding near the Mytton turn and had an engine changed. This aircraft was supposedly carrying General Slim – that was the story at the time."

One unnamed local recalled: "Aircraft were parked on concrete pads along the roadside leading off the perimeter track. Maintenance was carried out in the open and small blister hangars.

"Take-off and landings were quite spectacular with the roar of the Merlins on take-off and the spluttering and misses of landings. The smell of the aircraft was another very noticeable attribute – the 100 octane fuel, the smell of the dope (paint, which smelt of peardrops – amyl acetate).

"The first B17 to crash in the UK in the Berwyn Mountains saw a visiting B17 on Forton Heath for the first time. Also visiting was a C47 Dakota. This may have brought a crash crew.

"One of the last aircraft I remember landing was a Typhoon which came in over the Forton Heath road and made a typical Typhoon landing, a series of great leaps and touchdowns – a most ungainly performance."

After initial training in Canada, **Ray Racy**, of Bristol, was stationed at, in turn, Tern Hill, where he flew Miles Masters; Chetwynd, where he flew Hurricanes; and then in Spitfires at Rednal and Montford Bridge.

They were "blissful experiences for me, and I cannot recall times when I have been so in tune with my environment. Even at Tern Hill, it took on an almost mystical quality and that, I think, became particularly intense at Montford Bridge."

Mr Racy was at Montford Bridge in October and November 1944. He was with 61 OTU and had gone there from RAF Rednal for final training before joining an operational unit.

"We were flying mainly Mk V Spitfires," said Mr Racy.

"At Rednal I had teamed up with two or three Polish pilots, with whom I used to venture into Shrewsbury at nights. They were very animated, lived for the day, and were a lot of fun. They had also come to Montford Bridge.

"One of them I came to like and respect enormously. His name I will never forget – Dek Mayevski. He was my image of a Polish aristocrat – tall, elegant and with aquiline features. We used to play snooker together occasionally when we were killing time, as often happened on the unit. He spoke excellent English, and we talked about all kinds of things. I remember one evening he said to me with passionate emphasis: 'I want to *live.*'

"Almost immediately after moving to Montford Bridge I was sent on a night flying cross-country exercise. As I recall, it was a triangular route from Montford Bridge to Hawarden in Cheshire, returning via Newcastle-under-Lyme and Shrewsbury to base. The whole trip was to be mapped out only by beacons at the appointed turning points.

"I was given the beacon signs, mapped out my course and took off. I quite enjoyed night flying; the air conditions were so smooth without the frequent daytime thermals. It was a bit like riding in a first class railway carriage. I made the initial turning point at Hawarden without any difficulty and flew SSE towards Newcastle. As I passed by, it started to rain, but I could just make out the blacked-out town beyond my port wingtip. I wondered what the people in that dismal-looking town might be thinking of me flying nearly overhead.

"Finally, and with some relief after a somewhat apprehensive trip, I landed safely. Curiously, I often found that I made a better landing at night than I did in the daytime. Perhaps it was due to the smoothness of the air and the absence of wind. Anyway, I reported in and went to bed, satisfied that all had gone reasonably well.

"Next day I heard that Dek Mayevski had been killed. He had been on a similar night cross country. Apparently he had flown into a hillside somewhere in south Shropshire. And this was the man who had so much wanted to live, and had so much to live for. I was devastated. I had lost a friend, and as so often happened in wartime, one whose life had so much promise and who had ended it in tragic futility."

Mr Racy was posted to 154 Squadron at Biggin Hill, flying Mk VII Spitfires with extended wingtips and pressurised cockpits for high altitude. He was taken a prisoner in the last weeks of the war after force landing in Holland.

Virtually the last out of Montford

Bridge was **J. Elwyn Roberts**, of Oswestry, who was at Montford Bridge for about seven months during 1944 and 1945.

"I was an RAF postal clerk and I found myself in the RAF Post Office at Rednal. After about three weeks the adjutant told me that the postal clerk at Montford Bridge was being posted to near his home town and that I was to go there to replace him.

"I lived out of camp at Rednal and the adjutant told me I could live out from Montford as well and that it would be a cushy job as it had no counter service.

"I distributed mail in the morning and collected mail to take to the sorting office in Shrewsbury in the afternoons. I used to be back at the airfield by about 3pm and as there was nothing else to do the CO there, who was a Squadron Leader, would tell me to go home.

"In the months of March to May 1945 there was a great deal of activity. Bulldozers moved in and were digging large holes around the perimeter of the airfield. We tried to find out why, but everything was hush-hush. Then about two weeks later lorries started coming in loaded and going to the holes that had been dug.

"And what do you think they were doing? We got talking to the drivers. They were dumping equipment, which consisted of car and lorry batteries, radio equipment, radar goods, typewriters and office equipment and a host of

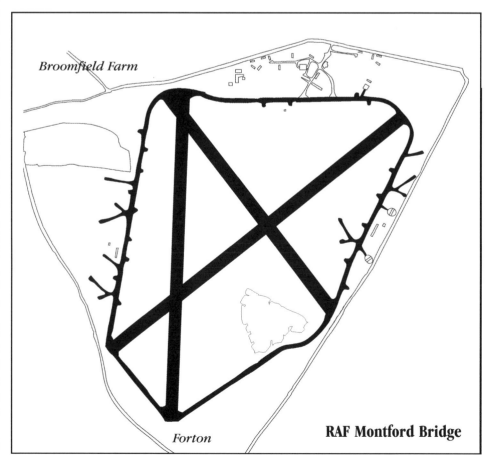

Broomfield Farm

Forton

RAF Montford Bridge

98

other goods, the majority of which were all brand new. When the holes were about half full, the soil was filled in to the holes and rolled hard by the bulldozers. What a waste.

"Just after that time the CO told us they were closing Montford as it was of no further use and that we would all be transferred to Rednal. A few weeks later the CO called a big meeting in one of the hangars and told us that Rednal was being closed and Group were moving to Keevil.

"In late May all personnel had gone including the two postal clerks and RAF Police and guardroom, and the only

two left was myself and a mechanic from the other part of the camp.

"We were told to lock up all buildings and make everything secure and then to padlock the airfield gates and follow the others to Keevil.

"The other chap was also from Oswestry and lived out as well.

"So they told us we could come down after the last weekend in my own small Austin Seven, bringing all keys with us. And I was given a batch of petrol coupons for my own use, and that was the end of Rednal and Montford."

1945

April 3: Spitfire Vb AD513 swung on landing and u/c collapsed.

May 9: Taxying accident, Spitfire Vb.

May 12: Flying accident involving Spitfire Vb. Cat E.

June 20: Montford Bridge placed on care and maintenance basis.

June 21: 61 OTU commanded by Group Captain Miller and composed of 131 officers, 189 NCOs, 1,011 airmen and Mustang a/c moved from Rednal and its satellite station, Montford Bridge, to RAF station Keevil. The personnel of 61 OTU stationed at Montford Bridge consisted of S/L Burra-Robinson, chief flying instructor; 30 other officers, 35 NCOs and 200 airmen. Also on June 21, visit of Wing Commander G.F. Dell, Commanding No 2 MU RAF Altrincham to RAF Stn Montford Bridge to report on the suitability of the station for the storage of explosives.

July 1: W/C Taylor, O.C. 34 MU and technical officers visited Montford Bridge to determine its suitability for occupation by that unit.

August 8: Airfield handed over to Maintenance Command.

1946

January 2: Strength of 34 MU as at January 31, 1946: RAF officers 21, W/Os and SNCOs 72, ORs 412. WAAF officers 2, Senior NCOs nil, ORs 66.

March: a/c repaired, 3 Mustangs, 1 Proctor, 1 Stirling, 1 Tempest.

May 31: Unit strength included 38 German POWs.

April: "The forty German POWs have been employed on domestic and suitable technical work on the station. Their living site has been surrounded by a wire fence. A canteen has been opened under the management of the camp leader. A copy of the Geneva Convention is available to the prisoners."

July: "German prisoners of war were employed on suitable work on the unit, including the jobs of unit barber and tailor".

September: a/c completed included Mosquito, Lincoln and a Wellington.

1947.

July 14: Main party of 34 MU moved to Sleap.

August 27: "Marching out", Montford Bridge. C&M party took over.

Hep's last resting place

Harry "Hep" Hepplewhite flew Spitfires from RAF Montford Bridge in late 1942 and on one occasion was vectored to intercept German Ju88 bombers while on convoy patrol.

The date, according to his logbook, was October 12 and the enemy planes were seen "on the deck" 25 miles from Liverpool. His patrol gave chase but was unable to intercept.

Hep had trained in America and on his return to England was transferred to 61 OTU. He went to Montford Bridge in October and trained in Spitfires there until mid-November, with convoy patrols thrown in for good measure. Later in the war he served in 136 "Woodpecker" Squadron, flying Spitfires at various

locations in the Far East.

His widow Sheila, of Bayston Hill, said: "When he died we had his ashes scattered over Montford Bridge airfield." The couple came to Shropshire in 1984 and her husband showed her round his old wartime haunts, including the Wingfield Arms (now the Old Swan), which was used as the "local" by pilots at Montford Bridge.

Montford Bridge today

In the village of Montford Bridge, take the minor road to Forton Heath and Mytton. The airfield quickly becomes apparent after about a mile. Many wartime buildings still stand.

In the nearby village of Grafton, what is variously described as the airmen's wartime dining hall or Naafi was used as Grafton Primary School (below), and the connection with the airfield was honoured on the school's badge, which features a Spitfire. The school closed in 2006 but it remains in use as the Grafton Centre of Condover College.

Only a few feet from Forton Heath Farm is the old wartime underground operations block. The complex is reached through a shaft down an iron rung ladder. "If there was an air raid, the officers would go in here," said farmer Mr Graham Hanmer.

Although the Hanmers didn't

move in until 1953, he believes that the farmhouse was used by the RAF during the war, when a farmer called Barnett had it.

His daughters must have been pretty, as old RAF boys making nostalgic returns to the station have fond memories of "those Barnett girls".

At least two of the runways – including the main runway – are still tarmacked, although in some places overgrown and interrupted by trees and shrubs which have grown through the surface.

The decaying control tower still stands looking out over the flying field. "I wouldn't knock it down unless it became dangerous. If the Government wanted to pay to do it up, I wouldn't mind. Some work now would maintain the brickwork," said Mr Hanmer.

A few years ago crop sprayers used the old airfield, but that died out. A parachute club also died out.

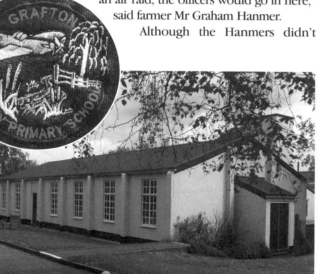

Maintenance crew at Peplow in its HMS Godwit days. This picture is from the collection of Mr G.H. Preece (second from right).

Peplow

Childs Ercall, Peplow, Eaton-upon-Tern – whatever name you choose to give it, this was a big bomber training base in the heart of north Shropshire. Aircrews trained up at the airfield before joining operational squadrons spearheading the Bomber Command offensive.

It started life as RAF Childs Ercall. But in August 1943 the official name was changed to RAF Peplow – although the airfield is not particularly close to Peplow – to avoid confusion with RAF High Ercall. Local people have in any event tended to call it Eaton-upon-Tern airfield.

With a main runway over a mile long, it was built to full Bomber Command standards. Although it was not a front line base, the training at Peplow was spiced up from time to time with "nickelling" raids, usually over France, in which the Wellington bombers would drop propaganda leaflets.

This had its hazards and RAF Peplow is possibly unique among Shropshire airfields in that it lost a plane in a mission over enemy-occupied territory. A Wellington from Peplow failed to return from a leaflet raid over Lille in 1944.

Today several of RAF Peplow's hangars survive, together with a handful of wartime buildings, and a minor road runs in part along the line of the perimeter track along which the Wellington bombers would taxi. The three concrete runways, rather unusually, intersected at one point. This arrangement was generally avoided because it meant one bomb or one crash could put all three runways out of action. They are now dug up.

In 1998 officers at North Shropshire District Council tried to insist that some of the old buildings were demolished as a condition for giving planning permission for a new store. Happily aviation enthusiasts lobbied the councillors and successfully persuaded them that the buildings were a valuable part of aviation heritage.

The airfield started life modestly as a relief landing ground for RAF Tern Hill in early 1941, being used by Master trainers, but in late 1942 development started to turn Childs Ercall into a bomber OTU (operational training unit).

It opened in much revamped form in August 1943 as 83 OTU and throughout its life the principal plane in use was the Wellington bomber, although there were other types like Hurricanes.

In October 1944 glider training started here with Horsa gliders and Albemarle tugs.

Although RAF Peplow was only a mile south of the naval airfield of RNAS Hinstock (known as HMS Godwit), there were no collisions in the circuit and indeed at the end of the war RAF Peplow itself became a naval base, and the two airfields were essentially operated as one unit as the Fleet Air Arm's main instrument flying school, called HMS Godwit.

It is said that one runway (it is not entirely clear at which airfield, but probably Peplow) was marked out as an aircraft carrier flight deck and the planes were guided in by a batsman. Among the aircraft operated were rare birds – Royal Navy Lancasters.

The airfield closed at the end of 1949.

Crewing up

Harry Sutton DFC was posted to 83 Operational Training Unit at RAF Peplow on September 17, 1943. "This was the first time in my training that I would be flying a fully operational aircraft, namely Wellington IIIs and Xs.

"It was a very concentrated course of day and night flying up to operational standards, and it was where I first met the rest of my crew, namely sergeants G. Caps (navigator), Peter McKeller (bomb aimer), Jonny Walker (wireless operator), and Roy Millington (rear gunner). My crew was increased by two more sergeants, Bob Smallwood (mid upper gunner) and Peter Penn (engineer) when posted to Heavy Conversion Units, flying Stirlings, Halifaxes and Lancasters.

"The course at Peplow consisted of two hours Ground School per day covering aircraft type, Hercules engines, dinghy drill, emergency exits, hydraulics, meteorology, navigation, astro navigation, bombing technique, high and low level etc.

"The local pub we used was the Seven Stars just down the road from camp, and also The Swan at Childs Ercall.

"There was friendly rivalry among most crews and I can remember one incident when one of my own crew, namely Sgt Jonny Walker, climbed on to the roof of the next Nissen hut and dropped a Very cartridge (smoke puff) down the chimney into the stove below. There was a very quick exodus, as you can imagine!

"While I was stationed at Peplow I was engaged to a girl telephonist at the Post Office Exchange in Lymm, Cheshire. She used to phone me quite often and she got to chat to the telephonist on the Childs Ercall switchboard – which was in an ordinary house – and when she knew that my fiancee wanted to come over and see me, she kindly invited her to stay in her house for a few days. I understand that the actual switchboard was quite minute!

"While she was over visiting me, we went to a dance at Hodnet in the local village hall, where we mingled with and chatted to some of the locals, who made us very welcome. I might add that we are still together after 56 years of marriage."

Mr Sutton, (extracts from his logbook, left), from Warrington, later flew 15 "ops" from RAF Elsham Wolds with 103 Squadron and then added a further 16 operational missions with 625 Squadron at RAF Kelstern.

"I am still an honorary member of the Lancashire Aero Club and although I still fly, do not hold a flying licence."

YEAR 1943		AIRCRAFT		PILOT, OR 1ST PILOT	2ND PILOT, PUPIL OR PASSENGER	DUTY (INCLUDING RESULTS AND REMARKS)
MONTH	DATE	Type	No.			
						Totals Brought Forward
NOV	6	WELLINGTON	MZ X III	SGT PRICE	SELF	CHECK CIRCUIT
NOV	6	WELLINGTON	MZX III	SELF	CREW	C&L'S O/S/A.
NOV	4	WELLINGTON	MZ Z III	F/O KING	SELF	CHECK CIRCUIT
NOV	4	WELLINGTON	GS T X	SELF	CREW	C&L'S O/S/A.
NOV	8	WELLINGTON	MZ Z III	W/O POWELL	SELF + CREW	DUAL X-C. BASE - RHYL - DOUGLAS - RHYL - MELTON MOWBRAY BASE. AIR FIRING 4 STICK BOMBING
NOV	9	WELLINGTON	GS Q X	SELF	CREW	SOLO X-C. BASE - MELTON MOWBRAY - DARLINGTON - SCARBOROUGH - GOOLE - SAFFRON WALDON - TRUNO - FARRINGDON - BASE. AIR FIRING 4 STICK BOMBING.
NOV	10	WELLINGTON	MZ C III	SELF	CREW	SOLO X-C. BASE - RHYL - MULL GALLOWAY - FISHGUARD - DOUGLAS - RHYL - BASE. AIR FIRING H.L.B
NOV	14	WELLINGTON	MZ S III	SELF	CREW	H.L.B. 8 BOMBS.
NOV	18	WELLINGTON	GS D X	SELF	CREW	H.L.B. 8 BOMBS.
NOV	22	WELLINGTON	GS L X	SELF	CREW	H.L.A. 8 BOMBS
NOV	25	WELLINGTON	GS H X	SELF	CREW	OPERATIONAL NICKEL TARGET. ST. QUENTIN.

Dennis Chetwood, of Llys Road, Oswestry, said: "I served at Peplow as an electrician Group II (L.A.C.) in the engine change hangar from 1943 to 1944.

"At that time Wellingtons were in service and I think we were in Bomber Group 93.

"Some time prior to the invasion we changed to Albemarle tricycle undercarriage twin-engined aircraft for glider towing. The gliders in service were Horsas and American Wacos. They were tubular framed, covered with fabric and with a plywood floor, much lighter than the Horsa and were almost airborne on run-up for take-off, unladen, of course.

"I was on recovery party on various occasions to crashed gliders. On arrival at the crash site, loads of children would arrive within minutes and in some cases were at the site before us. Where they came from was a mystery as there were no signs of habitation for miles.

"Of course we were a good source of extra food that we had with us, and chocolate.

"I remember one occasion we were host to a number of

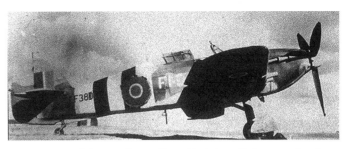

A Hurricane of the Bomber Defence Training Flight at Peplow in October 1944. *(via Alec Brew)*

Flying Fortresses. The pilot of one said to me: 'Where's this place, bud?' I told him and his reply was: 'Where the hell's that?'

"Another thing which may be of interest was the delivery of aircraft to Peplow by ladies of the Air Transport Auxiliary, who did a marvellous job. I recollect my surprise on entering an aircraft which had just parked on the apron outside the hangar when the pilot took off his helmet revealing a very pretty girl with long hair.

"After the invasion the unit was run down. I was in the care and maintenance (party) until being posted to RAF Penrhos in North Wales."

Bill Bates was the only one of his bomber crew, with whom he had "crewed up" at Childs Ercall airfield, who was to survive the war.

A tail gunner, he arrived there in the late summer of 1942 or 1943. He recalls that between 500 and 600 navigators, bomb aimers, pilots and gunners were called into a big hangar – engineers were crewed up at a later stage – and given six hours to form themselves into crews.

So he linked up with a navigator from Sheffield, a wireless operator from Croydon, and pilot Stan Beatham from Leeds.

Later on Mr Bates flew on operations in Wellingtons and Lancasters from RAF Kelstern in Lincolnshire. His colleagues died on a bombing raid in September 1944. He was not with them that fateful night because he had been grounded for three days with a minor ear problem.

"I reported to the gunnery leader and as he couldn't find another gunner, he had to go himself. He was on his second tour and was killed. I can always remember his girlfriend coming for his little car on the hardstanding a couple of weeks later. She was crying her eyes out. I felt terrible. By

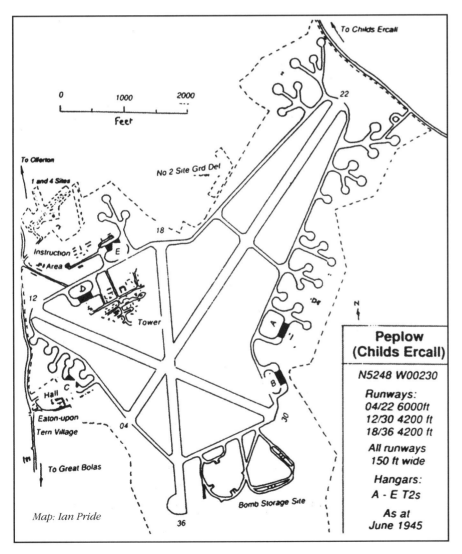

0   1000   2000
Feet

To Olerton

1 and 4 Sites

No 2 Site Grd Def

To Childs Ercall

22

18

Instruction
Area   E

12

Tower

D

A

N

B

04

30

Hall   C

Eaton-upon
Tern Village

To Great Bolas

Bomb Storage Site

36

Map: Ian Pride

**Peplow
(Childs Ercall)**

N5248 W00230

Runways:
04/22 6000ft
12/30 4200 ft
18/36 4200 ft

*All runways
150 ft wide*

Hangars:
A - E T2s

*As at
June 1945*

This aerial view, dated February 24, 1944, makes an interesting comparison with the map on the previous page.

rights I should have gone instead of him."

While at Childs Ercall Mr Bates was a sergeant and lived at Harp Lane, Dawley, which was handy because when he was not flying he could cycle home to spend the night.

His stay at Childs Ercall was for about three months, training on Wellington bombers, with cross country flights and the like.

"What amused us is that outside Peplow you would be walking down a lane and see some sailors. We said, what the hell are sailors doing in Shropshire? Of course, they were from Ollerton (nearby RNAS Hinstock) and they flew Wellingtons. It was funny to see sailors in Shropshire."

Servicemen wanting to get off camp could, he remembers, get a Butters Bus to Market Drayton or Wellington.

Mr Bates died aged 82 in June 2005 and his ashes were scattered over RAF Cosford, where he worked in the museum as a guide for 20 years.

Further memories of wartime servicemen who served at Peplow were gathered in a special millennium project led by Mrs Ruth Newby of Eaton-upon-Tern. The aim was to produce a leaflet or booklet.

Among the contributors was a **Mr Hawkins**, of Welford on Avon, who was at Peplow from June to October 1944.

"It was on our last night cross country flight when we

War diary

1943

July 15: Official opening date.

August 1: Various delays in the arrival of key personnel and in completion of certain buildings meant it was not until this date that the station transferred from an "opening-up" basis to that of an OTU, the resident unit being 83 OTU. "The station has been redesigned for use as a three-quarters OTU, having been built and used previously in four different categories. Three permanent runways – 2,000 yards, 1,400, 1,400 with full night flying facilities."

August 17: No 1 course, having completed ground training at other stations, returned to this station and commenced flying training.

August 20: Name of station changed to RAF Peplow, owing to confusion between RAF Station Childs Ercall and RAF Station High Ercall. Aircraft on the base were Wellingtons and Martinets.

September 9: First fatal flying accident, three killed, two injured.

October 17: First "Nickel" operational exercise (i.e. propaganda leafleting). Eleven aircraft took off and all returned safely.

October 30: Visit by A.O.C., Air Commodore A.P. Ritchie AFC, who inspected airmen's dining halls, the station having been advised that it had received first place in Group Dining Hall competition.

November 3-4: Three Wellingtons were engaged on a Nickel exercise and returned to base (there were regular such exercises during the month).

November 30: During the month there were four minor accidents, three involving Wellington aircraft, and one an Oxford.

December 13-14: Five successful leaflet sorties.

December 22-23: Two successful leaflet sorties. One Wellington X made a successful flapless landing, after damage to the aircraft from heavy flak.

Peplow aircrew in 1944 or 1945 outside the Sutherland Arms, Tibberton. Third from left is Flt Lt R. Hooper and third from right is W/O Wally Young. *(via Ruth Newby)*

crashed in Wales, and only myself and the rear gunner survived. The village in which we crashed was Cenarth, near Newcastle Emlyn. After many years the local historian contacted me, and with the co-operation of military and civilian organisations, a commemorative service was held in the village church on September 4, 1994," he said.

And **Mrs Rita Lovett** (nee Robinson), of Shoreham, an MT driver from 1943-45, said: "I was one of the first WAAFs to be posted to Peplow in the spring of 1943. We lived in Nissen huts, about 24 in each. The heating was a coke burning stove in the middle of the hut.

"For some time I went out with one of the (instructor) pilots. One of his pupils was the actor Michael Rennie, who was well known then and after the war for playing heroic parts, but not too keen on flying, and he later asked to be taken off flying, saying it was too dangerous.

"Desmond Donnelley, who later became an MP, was also at Peplow. My pilot friend, Ian McPherson, became a professional footballer after the war and played for Arsenal."

The northern part of the old main runway. The hardened surface has been dug up, leaving a grass strip.

Reeves returns

In May 2004 George Reeves returned for the first time to the air base at which he served 60 years previously and found, to his surprise and delight, the building in which he served was still standing.

His wartime workplace is now part of a haulage yard, but he was able to go to the site and identify the telephone exchange in the operations block.

Standing on the remnants of the runway, with the only sound the buzz of model aircraft, he said: "Back then it was all bustle and aircraft. To see all this derelict, it's much better than wartime. People were getting killed then."

Mr Reeves, born on November 14, 1914 and from Teddington, Middlesex, came to RAF Peplow on May 7, 1943, as a corporal taking the role of telephone exchange supervisor. He left in October 1944.

"I was here for 15 months and I was very happy here. The signals officer was Squadron Leader East, and he was a gem. In the telephone exchange we had four WAAFs, two LACs, one other corporal, and I was the supervisor.

"Before D-Day all private calls, both from sergeants and officers, were logged and charged to the two messes. After D-Day, all that stopped. We had mostly Wellingtons, which were known as Wimpeys after a cartoon character. We did have one or two big stuff come in now and again.

"We had cycle races around the perimeter. I came third. There were dances at Peplow for which I did the posters, as I had previously worked on newspapers as a linotype operator. I went to one dance and somebody from the Army pinched my bike, so I pinched somebody else's.

"My billet was a Nissen hut. There were about 20 people in it. When it was night flying they used to go down to the cookhouse nearby and bring four or five slices of bread and we used to toast it over the stove in the centre of the billet. During the winter the smell of toast was irresistible.

"One night, coming from the cookhouse, there was a police blockade on the road and I was 'unfortunate' not to have a rear light on my bicycle, as of course were many others. I was fined 10 shillings which was a lot of money in those days, and this was on a road which ran through the camp!

"When I left Peplow my medical consisted of a salute to the M.O., a 'Good Luck' from him, and 'about turn.' I was posted to Burma."

1944

January 13: Four Wellington aircraft took part in an ASR search for missing crews of USAAF aircraft. This was the first time this unit participated in such an operation.

February: Aircraft strength: Wellingtons 38, Martinets 4.

April: Nickelling operations conducted on various towns and cities in occupied France, including Chartres, Orleans, and Tours.

May 19-20: Six aircraft detailed for a Nickel op on Lille. One failed to return. Crashes for May: Wellington X, LP568 starboard engine failure, Cat E; Wellington X, HE830, engine failure, Cat B; Wellington X MF590, engine failure, Cat B; Wellington III, BK463, Missing, Cat E; Wellington X, LN550, port tyre burst, Cat AC; Wellington III, BK462, ran off perimeter, Cat AC. Personnel strength: RAF officers 248; W.O.s and S.N.C.O.s 558, OTRs 949, (WAAF officers 7, SNCOs 7, OTRs 332.)

June: During "Salute the Soldier" week at Peplow, for which the station had a target of £2,500, the total raised was £5,750. During the month the perimeter track was resurfaced and work progressed at Cherrington Moor bombing range near Newport, this being constructed by unit labour under a "self help" scheme. The anticipated date of completion for use was estimated as mid-July.

June 5: Cycle tour of Haughmond Abbey.

June 6: Award of the Air Force Cross to Flt Lt (A/S/Ld) R.L.L. McCullough DFC announced in London Gazette. This award for devotion to flying duties (non-operational) particularly while on the strength of Peplow's OTU.

June 13: Theatre visit to Birmingham to see "Watch on the Rhine".

June 22: Visit to Uriconium Roman city.

July: There were seven flying accidents during the month, two of which were fatal, one Wellington crashing in the sea (during a night cross country) and the other being a Hurricane which was in a mid-air collision with another Hurricane from Hawarden (seven dead for the month).

July 20: First use of Cherrington Moor bombing range this night. Also during the month a party visited the Fairey Aviation Works, Manchester. Afterwards visited the Opera House to see John Gielgud, Peggy Ashcroft and Leslie Banks in "Hamlet".

August: 83 OTU strength – total officers including WAAF 313; senior NCOs including WAAFs 518; other ranks 1,107.

August 7-8: Twenty five Halifaxes from 6 Group diverted to Peplow after bombing troop and gun concentrations in the Caen area.

August 24: Wellington JA453 crashed at night south of Aberporth after signalling that one engine was u/s.

August 26: Wellington HF517 and MF590 (or 589) collided at night on Bullseye exercise near Halton.(one survivor baled out). Total with August 24 accident was 15 dead this month.

September 21: Judged best representative in 93 Group for Air Ministry Dining Hall competition.

October 12: Wellington C crashed in ploughed field near Tern Hill. Crew killed. Six dead.

October 28: Albemarle and Horsa glider airborne for Brize Norton. First glider take-off from this airfield. Aircraft on strength at end of October 1944: Wellingtons 41, Hurricanes 5, Martinets 1, Masters 2, Oxfords 1.

October 28: Station ceased to be a Bomber Command OTU of 93 Group and was taken over by No 23 Group for Number 23 Heavy Glider Conversion Unit.

October 29: 20 glider instructors reported and were allotted to A.B. Night Flights. Eleven Tug Pilots reported and were allocated to Tug Flight under Flt Lt Robertson.

November 10: Night flying carried on till 0400 hours, then stopped by very bad visibility. Total tows day 32, night 22. "Six Horsa and six Albemarle by day and two Horsa and two Albemarle by night now being used as these numbers seem most efficient for operation and runways only."

November 11: Wellington aircraft from 14 OTU Market Harborough in a mid-air collision with a Seafire near Lilleshall. All occupants of the Wellington killed and their bodies brought to Peplow.

November 30: Aircraft strength: Albemarle 68, glider 48. Personnel. Officers RAF 128, WAAF 7, senior NCOs 306, WAAF 8, ORs 1,301, WAAF 312.

December 11: Special mass landing exercise and ground fighting. Tow of 12 aircraft each. F/O Tyson and 2nd Pilot, Sgt Kemp, crashed in Horsa on landing. Both badly injured. Horsa written off. Total tows six.

Peplow today

Aim for Eaton-upon-Tern and then take the minor road signposted to Childs Ercall. This road skirts the old airfield, using in part the perimeter track.

Several hangars remain, as do some derelict station buildings, but the control tower has long gone. Flying still takes place thanks to the activities of remote control aircraft enthusiasts.

The rare bombing teacher at Peplow has been given a "hat" to help protect the historic building from the elements.

It is owned, along with various other airfields buildings, by Dave Williams.

"It's a very rare building – a twin bombing teacher simulator. There are only one or two left in the country – most of them in the history books are singles. They could teach two groups at a time, one at each end," he said.

"I want to make sure it doesn't fall into any more decay."

With no grants available, he financed the work himself. And his thanks? – Being reported to the council for doing it without planning permission (since granted retrospectively).

The building is seen above right in its summer 2008 state, although the work is incomplete, as Dave wants to glaze it.

"Then it will be both weatherproof and waterproof. I just want to keep it in the best condition I can."

One of the huge hangars, still in good condition

Rednal

RAF Rednal meant one thing – Spitfires. It was here that pilots were familiarised with the legendary fighter and operational flying techniques before joining a front line squadron.

The base opened in April 1942 when 61 Operational Training Unit moved in from Heston, Middlesex.

It had three runways, one of 1,600 yards and two of 1,100 yards, and at peak strength around 1,600 servicemen and women were stationed here.

Accommodation was dispersed in surrounding woods and fields for a considerable distance, and bicycles were standard issue.

With the base being in the middle of nowhere a special arrangement was made for the trains on the railway line which runs near the aerodrome to stop.

Many famous pilots were at Rednal at one time or another, including Pierre Clostermann, Ray Heslyn, "Screwball" Beurling who was an instructor, and pre-war

Circuits and bumps by a student pilot in 1942. *(Picture courtesy the Imperial War Museum, negative no. CH6455)*

hurdles champion Don Finlay, who was a commanding officer.

In July and August 1944 Rednal was busy accepting wounded flown straight from Normandy in Dakotas to be treated at special military hospitals in Shropshire.

In the last few months of the war 61 OTU began to re-equip with Mustang fighters and in June 1945 the unit moved to Keevil in Wiltshire.

Rednal was finally sold in 1962.

Over 60 years on from its heyday, aviation is not dead at Rednal. It has been the home of The Classic and Vintage Aeroplane Company which flies vintage planes at air shows.

And the airfield was used for a test flight of a scaled down version of the Global Challenger balloon in which Richard Branson and Oswestry's Per Lindstrand hoped to circumnavigate the world, although in the event did not succeed.

Rednal remembered

Eddie Mazur from Shrewsbury is one of a rare breed. He was in the Polish air force but after the defeat of his home country escaped to Riga where he was interned by Latvians and taken to a camp near Moscow as a prisoner – Russia and Germany were at the time allies.

Salvation came when Germany invaded Russia in 1941 and the Polish pilots were allowed to come to Britain. Eddie joined 61 OTU at Rednal at the end of 1943.

"I remember I was a Flight Sergeant then. We were billeted on the north side of the airfield in the woods there and we had bicycles," said Eddie, pictured above during his time as a sergeant pilot at Rednal in 1943.

"My Spitfire V was a very nice aeroplane. I flew many Spitfires but that's the one I liked best."

He was at Rednal for about two months. "I had a lot of friends. I have survived, and they have gone." He recalls that while practising high level bombing one of his dummy bombs missed the target by so much that it killed a cow on a farm west of the airfield.

Ben Jesson, of Cornwall Drive, Bayston Hill, arrived in 1942. "We had all started on Spitfire Is but went on to Spitfire IIs where the pitch control lever worked in the opposite way. As a result one pilot tried to take-off with the propeller in coarse pitch, which is like trying to move off in a car in top gear. He didn't really get off the ground and crashed into the railway line and was killed."

Mr Jesson, who was at Rednal for six to eight weeks and went on to fly operationally in the Balkans and Italy, said of the Spitfire: "It really was a marvellous aeroplane to fly."

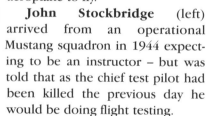

John Stockbridge (left) arrived from an operational Mustang squadron in 1944 expecting to be an instructor – but was told that as the chief test pilot had been killed the previous day he would be doing flight testing.

"I had been flying over Germany at zero feet and getting shot at, so this was a pleasure. I also met my wife, Marjorie Cotgreave, while at Rednal – she was at the post office and grocers shop in Queens Head," said Mr Stockbridge.

Reg Todd MBE of Primrose Drive, Shrewsbury, said: "We had a chap on the staff there, David Southwood, who was the radio instructor. He was ex-BBC and one of the Children's Hour uncles." Mr Todd, who flew at Rednal from May to August 1943, added: "We used to ride into Ellesmere and do the pubs to death. On one occasion another chap, a Dutchman, and myself rode to Shrewsbury stopping at all the alehouses on the way, finishing off at the Post Office Inn in Shrewsbury. We took the train back."

Mrs Doris Harper, nee Clarke, said: "During parts of 1944-45 I had the pleasure of serving there as a WAAF wireless operator, working in the signals section of the station.

"At times I helped out at the 'Homer'. To get to this isolated part of the station we had to cycle round part of the German prisoner of war camp. I remember they used to hurl abuse at us through the wire fence.

"The Homer was a building away from the main airfield where we helped to get the planes back to base if they were lost or on the wrong track.

"In our spare time we formed a dramatic society of which I was a member. In April our production of 'A Murder Has Been Arranged' toured many of the RAF camps in Shropshire.

"Rednal was a very happy camp. Our commanding officer at the time was Group Captain Don Finlay (ex-hurdler) and second in command Wing Commander Gray (New Zealander – ex Battle of Britain pilot).

"I was one of the WAAFs to represent Rednal on the VE Day parade march through Oswestry."

Margaret Thorogood served at Rednal as a WAAF from 1942 to 1945 in the control tower as a controller's clerk, logging flights, calling crash crews if anything went wrong, and often operating the Tannoy.

"It was a very happy place. We were a half Polish station and it was quite hard to pronounce their names," she said.

The tower was in radio contact with pilots, and this could sometimes be heartrending.

Mrs Thorogood, who was at the time Margaret Hay – landing her with the nickname "Maggie Straw" – said: "The awful part was hearing so many last words. It was awful when you knew somebody was crashing. You saw it happening. For about a year afterwards I had very bad nightmares over what I had seen."

Mrs Thorogood made a nostalgic return to Rednal to find the control tower, once the showpiece of the station, a derelict wreck.

"It's tragic," she said.

Battle of Britain pilot **Paddy Barthropp** was pleased when his OTU moved from Heston to Rednal in May 1942, as he was brought up in Shropshire.

In his autobiography he says: "Only one snag. We were the first to land there and the contractors had built the control tower facing a local farm and not the aerodrome. Not ideal for an OTU."

After a couple of days, he and his pal Cassidy were detailed for dual formation flying and beatup to demonstrate to a new intake "how it should be done."

"I didn't realise it at the time, but he was still suffering from an overdose of benzedrine from the previous night and following our display we came down for a perfect formation landing. The only snag was that Cassidy had forgotten to put his undercarriage down and was slithering along the runway behind me amidst a shower of sparks and bits of propeller.

"That night we went out on a binge and on our return from Oswestry I took a wrong turn and drove my car into a lake."

His commanding officer, "Lovely" Parker, had had enough of him and he was sent packing back to an operational squadron. Barthropp was later shot down and taken prisoner. He died in 2008.

Mr E. A. Roberts, of Oswestry, said: "In 1941 I was posted to Rednal to works flight and at the time there was no flying training taking place because there was no building. The staff consisted of a 60-year-old Warrant Officer, one corporal tipper driver with 7 yard lorry (sic) plus five airmen including myself, plus eight tents and a few cooking utensils.

"From the time I arrived at the site by the canal it rained straight for three days and nights. I shall never forget it. Boots were quickly turned green with mildew and life was just one long misery. But I digress!

"We quickly set to and erected the sergeants mess and thankfully stowed the tents away. That was only the start."

War diary

1942
April 15: Main move of 61 OTU to Rednal.

1943
July 18: Sgt J.A. Sharkey (Australian) was flying Spitfire when "Whilst acting as target a/c during cine gun exercise pilot noticed bullets entering the cockpit. He discontinued the action and returned to base, and made splendid landing. Unaccountable mistake by Sgt Rinde (Norwegian) who had been briefed before the exercise and whilst engaged in cine gun exercise pressed the firing button instead of the cine button causing damage to Sgt Sharkey's machine."

August 25: Airwomen Turner and Robertson killed by train while walking on railway line near base. Two others, named Finch and Poll, injured.

August 26: During dinghy drill on The Mere, Ellesmere, Flight Sergeant Early drowned.

October 13: "Today the vanguard of the film unit, Independent Producers, who are to make a film of the book 'Signed with their Honour' arrived on the stn. The film unit will eventually have here a Wellington aircraft and nine Gladiators and they are expected to be here for two or three months."

November 4: Gladiator II F/Lt H.D.L. Flower crashed while force landing due to fog.

November 24: Gladiators, F/Lt Kleimeyer and Lt Bache in mid air collision.

1944
March 15: F/Sgt J.R. Newman flying Spitfire R7022 was killed while night flying at 2035 hours, crashed in a field adjacent to the communal site (airfield not stated, but will have been either Rednal or Montford Bridge).

June 29: "General Lee (U.S. Army) landed at Rednal at 0820 hours in a Dakota, taking off again for Hawarden at 0940 hours. His visit was nothing to do with Rednal."

July 3: "The evacuation of the American wounded from Normandy to Rednal started today. They are being flown here direct from the beachhead in Dakota aircraft."

August 5: Nine Dakotas landed from France with 24 wounded in each (there were regular such arrivals of aircraft with Normandy casualties during this period at Rednal).

September 16: Baltimore a/c took off and crashed about half a mile from the airfield. Caught fire. Two killed – Wing Commander Wilkerson and Major Cross (who had arrived the day before to observe the training programme at the OTU).

December 19: Mustang III arrives at Rednal.

A Spit comes to grief with an undercarriage collapse at Rednal.
(via Alec Brew)

The first of a series of official pictures dating from 1942 following a young pilot – Pilot Officer G.C.H. Walsh, of Wallington, Surrey (left) – through his training at 61 OTU. "The pupil arrives at dispersal point for his first day's flying." *(Picture courtesy the Imperial War Museum, CH6446.)*

"She's off the deck." *(Picture courtesy the Imperial War Museum, CH6452)*

"There she is – and treat her gently." The instructor introduces the pupil to his first Spitfire. *(Picture courtesy IWM, CH6448)*

The Rednal cast of A Murder Has Been Arranged in spring 1944. *(Doris Ha...*

pitfire by the control tower,
ate unknown.
via Michael Davies)

d how small he feels, tucked
n behind the Spitfire's long
ine cowling!"
*cture courtesy the Imperial
r Museum, CH6450)*

"It's not all work, though, and now and then there is time for a little relaxation."
(Picture courtesy the Imperial War Museum, CH6462)

Instructor and student pilot after his first solo.
(Picture courtesy IWM, CH6454)

Wilkie's last flight

The life and times of a distinguished bomber pilot were remembered in a ceremony on the hillside near RAF Rednal where he lost his life.

The tribute to Wing Commander David Wilkerson was 60 years on, to the minute, from that fateful day in September 1944 when "Wilkie" was killed aboard a Baltimore aircraft that crashed at Tedsmore Hill, near West Felton.

The tribute was organised by Hugh Cawdron, for whom the 27-year-old RAF pilot, who held the DSO and DFC and had survived 47 operational missions, was a childhood hero.

Wilkerson commanded 578 Squadron at RAF Burn in Yorkshire, and then became a senior instructor at the Empire Flying School at Hullavington, Wiltshire, which involved him visiting various training establishments, and it was while returning from Rednal that the aircraft in which he was a passenger crashed in the early afternoon of September 16, 1944.

Representing the modern-day RAF at the ceremony was Squadron Leader Martin Locke of RAF Shawbury, who is an ex-Vulcan bomber pilot, and was also representing the Shropshire Aircrew Association of which he is president.

Wilkie was a cubmaster, which is how Mr Cawdron originally got to know him in the Epping Forest area, so the Scouts were represented by Colin Gittoes, District Commissioner of Shropshire Borders.

The ceremony was held at a wooden cross erected on the crash site a few years ago by Mr Cawdron.

Among the 20 or so other people who attended were some local residents who could recall the crash and its aftermath.

Mr Cawdron said that since the age of eight, David Wilkerson had been his hero and friend.

"Tragically, the pilot had failed to notice that overnight rudder locks had not been removed from the aircraft," he said.

The plane came down and broke in two. Wilkie and a South African officer died, while three others in a part of the plane which careered down the hillside survived.

"One terrible morning, which haunts me still, David's mother called at my home with a brown paper parcel containing David's scout uniform.

"She could hardly bear to tell us that David had been killed. She asked that when I became big enough, would I wear the uniform. I did."

He pulled out the one remaining piece of the uniform he still had. "It's the sheath knife that we as kids admired so much."

Prayers were led by Weston Felton vicar the Rev Brian Hayes and during the closing verse of "Oh God, Our Help In Ages Past" a Griffin helicopter from RAF Shawbury crewed by Captain Phil Rudd and civilian instructor Tam Hazan flew past overhead in tribute.

Sixty years on, Wilkie had been remembered.

1945

January 3: 61 OTU started using Mustang IIIs in training fighter pilots, as well as Spitfires.

February 17: "It was reported that a number of German POWs had escaped from the Oswestry POW camp. Immediately on receipt of notification a rigid patrolling system was put into force around and in the camp."

February 18: "In the morning an airman found a German POW sitting in the cockpit of a Mustang a/c. He gave himself up without a fight and on being searched was found to have in his possession a half pound of black pepper in a tin and a knife handle sharpened to a razor's edge. The prisoner was returned to the POW camp. Later in the day it was reported that all the escaped prisoners had been recaptured."

March 7: "Soccer: Station XI 7, Montford Bridge 1. A very good win for Station side."

June 20: RAF Station Rednal and its satellite at Montford Bridge placed on care and maintenance basis w.e.f. 20.6.45.

June 21: 61 OTU commanded by Group Captain Miller and composed of 131 officers, 189 NCOs, 1,011 airmen and Mustang a/c moved from Rednal and its satellite station, Montford Bridge, to RAF station Keevil, the main party arriving at Keevil in two special trains.

An aerial view of the old airfield. This picture was taken in 1998.

One who didn't get away

One of the incidents at Rednal airfield still talked about is the day a German prisoner of war tried to escape in a Spitfire.

And Margery Rosser has more reason to remember it than anyone – she was the young WAAF who discovered the German fugitive in the cockpit.

Mrs Rosser, who lives near Hereford, said: "I popped out to the plane at about 6.30am. I know it was winter as the wings were very icy and I was slipping about.

"I climbed up to fill it with fuel, pushed the cockpit open, and there he was.

"I screamed and the whole squadron came rushing to me, the group captains and the officers and all the chaps I worked with. They all ran.

"The German was a very innocent looking chap. He was asleep, but soon opened his eyes when I screamed. It was a very blood-curdling scream. It was wartime and one didn't meet a German prisoner of war face to face very often, I can tell you."

Mrs Rosser, then Miss Margery Lamb from Liverpool, who had been conscripted into the WAAFs as a flight mechanic, said of the German: "He was gorgeous. He was

very tall and blond."

The Group Captain arrived and the German got out of the plane and clicked his heels. He could not speak English and those around him could speak no German, but the Group Captain invited him into the officers mess for cocoa before the Military Police arrived.

Margery, who was by now at the back of the crowd, said: "The German would not go until he had found me, which was rather disconcerting. I always remember that because I was trying to hide by this time.

"He insisted that I went in with him for this cocoa. I went in and felt very stupid and out of place. I was glad to drink my cocoa and say goodbye. He clicked his heels and bowed – he was bowing and clicking his heels to everybody."

Written accounts since say the German, who had escaped from a nearby prison camp, was armed with a sharpened knife handle, although Mrs Rosser has no knowledge of this.

"Of course he didn't produce anything like that to show me. I would have died of shock."

And although histories say the plane involved was a Mustang, Mrs Rosser says it was in fact a Spitfire.

A fatal collision

The fortunes of two young Rednal airmen became fatally entwined on August 22, 1943, in the wartime skies above Shropshire, when their planes collided during a mock dogfight. Jean Noizet died. Henri Goldsmit survived.

In 1977 the site where Noizet's Spitfire had plunged to earth at Hincks Plantation, Lilleshall, was investigated by Shropshire's Wartime Aircraft Recovery group. His remains were recovered for burial, over 30 years after his death. Some wreckage from his plane was put on display at the RAF Museum at Cosford. And when aviation historian Michael Davies saw it, it sparked his curiosity and he was overtaken by a burning desire to find out more.

"The display made no mention of his name, and just said the pilot had perished. I left the display but kept coming back. I had to find out who he was," said Mr Davies.

Soon he discovered the name, and that Noizet (above) was, like Goldsmit (right), a Belgian based at Rednal.

The culmination of his investigations into the life and death of Jean Noizet was a 96,000-word book, called The Limitless Horizon, which is as yet unpublished.

Undeterred, Mr Davies, of Shrewsbury, completed a companion book telling the other half of the story, that of the pilot who survived, managing to land his damaged Spitfire at Halfpenny Green airfield.

And he traced Goldsmit's widow and invited her to Shropshire, and she read the draft of his book – also unpublished so far – called A Lost Tomorrow.

For Henri, his narrow escape was only to give him little more than an extra year of life. He fought during the Normandy campaign and as more of Europe was liberated was able to land near Brussels and see his parents.

He was 28 when he was shot down and killed in November 1944.

Henri's widow Yvelline Hay and her daughter Michelle were invited by Mr Davies to Shropshire for a nostalgic visit in the autumn of 1998.

After reading Mr Davies' account, she said: "It was fascinating. Michael has done the most incredible research and what is most interesting is that I knew nothing about this part of his life.

"He was not allowed to talk about his training or what he was doing and when he came home for the odd weekend he didn't want to talk about it.

"I am so glad to have found out what he was doing. It isn't sad at all," she said.

"He finished his tour of operations, I think in October 1944," said Mr Davies. "But he was called back because they ran out of pilots – they were losing an awful lot of pilots. He said to a friend of Yvelline's 'In all probability, I've had it now'.

"Sure enough, he was killed when he was shot down over Holland by flak."

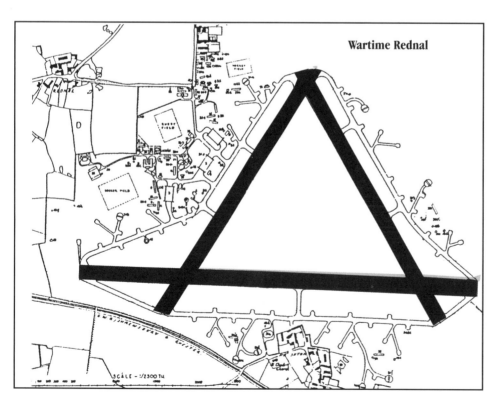

Wartime Rednal

Anatomy of a crash

He was American, keen as mustard, and desperate to fly. But his life's story was brought to a dramatic and tragic conclusion by an oak tree in a Shropshire field which still stands, a silent witness to the fatal last flight of Sergeant Mike Kassaneff of Chicago.

Sergeant Kassaneff, aged 28, was the pilot of a Miles Master III trainer from RAF Rednal which hit the tree at Sandy Hill, just north of Ellesmere, on September 13, 1942.

He was terribly injured and died later that day. His pupil, Kenneth Bowler, 21, from Harrow, was killed instantly. Ken was a "prospective aircrew candidate" making, it is believed, his first flight.

It was just one of many crashes which claimed the lives of young men flying from Rednal.

Surprisingly, even today there are eye witnesses who are able to shed new light on incidents such as these.

At the time the Kassaneff crash was officially blamed on "unauthorised low flying" (see accident report, right).

Witnesses recall the aircraft coming over Ellesmere Mere and then doing a climb, a half roll and a dive, from which it flattened out but never climbed above the tree. This may point to it being in a high speed stall in which pulling back on the stick has no effect.

Five years ago Sue Pawlak, who lives at Portage, Michigan, embarked on a quest to find out more about the crash which claimed the life of the husband of her Aunt Ginny (still alive at the time of writing).

John Michael Kassaneff was born in Chicago in 1914. He married Virginia Houdek in Hammond, Indiana, in April 1937.

The last view from the cockpit – the fatal tree looms

When war broke out in Europe he was determined to fly fighters.

"He was unable to in the USA because you had to have two years of college, but in Canada you only had to have a

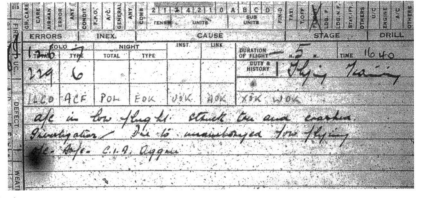

high school education. So Mike went to Toronto and enlisted in the RCAF on May 15, 1941," said Sue.

"Both Ginny and Mike's mother were not happy about him going. In fact, his mother was so upset, as he was an only child, that she passed away soon after.

"Ginny was notified of Mike's death but never knew details of what happened and where exactly he was buried. She joined the Women's Army Corps in hopes of getting to England to visit his grave. She figured it was the only way she would see his grave. Unfortunately, she never got there. She was sent to North Africa and then to Italy."

Widowed Ginny later remarried and had two girls and a son. Now 89, she lives alone.

"In talking with Aunt Ginny about Michael, she still gets tears in her eyes. He was her first love. She still has all the letters he wrote while in Canada and England. She still reads through them."

Mike Kassaneff was so keen to fly that he joined the RCAF (Picture: Sue Pawlak)

Ken Bowler may have been making his first flight. (Picture: Tom Bowler)

In the autumn of 1943 a film crew descended on Rednal to make a movie about the exploits of the RAF during the fall of Greece in 1941. "Signed With Their Honour" was based on a novel by Australian war correspondent James Aldridge.

According to a website on British wartime film production, it was a project by Denham studios who brought along nine (or 12 – sources differ) Gloster Gladiator biplane fighters and a Wellington bomber to act as a camera plane. Accidents soon left three Gladiators hors de combat.

Among the pilots of the Gladiators was Squadron Leader Reginald Jack Hyde, a New Zealander, who flew defensive sorties in the three famed Gladiators Faith, Hope, and Charity during the siege of Malta.

The director was Vernon Sewell and the producer was Paul Soskin. The film unit comprised lighting cameramen Osmond Borradaile and George Stretton, camera operator Grant McClean, camera assistant Jim Body and special effects expert Douglas Woolsey.

Also present were editors Clive Donner and Gerald Hambling.

Shot entirely in and around Rednal, filming took place over about three months. However, the website says production was abandoned – no reason is given.

What happened to the footage is an intriguing question. Maybe in some film vault there is, waiting to be discovered, a fascinating and unusual film record of RAF Rednal.

Another extraordinary chapter in Rednal's wartime life is also connected with film. In July 1943 a Spitfire pilot on cinegun exercises unaccountably pressed the wrong button and fired live ammunition at another Rednal Spitfire, hitting it and forcing it down.

Happily the pilot, apart from no doubt being much aggrieved, appears to have been unhurt.

Rednal's association with film continued after the war – it is said to have been used for filming some scenes of the 1950s film The Red Beret.

Rednal today

Come off the A5 road at Queens Head, near Oswestry, and follow the minor road to Rednal which runs alongside the canal. The road between Rednal hamlet and Haughton passes directly over the airfield site, following in part the line of two of the runways.

Many wartime buildings still stand, including perimeter defences and the control tower. Part of the site these days sees plenty of shooting – as a paintball adventure centre.

One runway continues to be used occasionally by light aircraft. Ask around and you will also come across a memorial to a pilot whose Spitfire crashed into farm buildings on the edge of the airfield.

All in all, Rednal is one of the more rewarding of Shropshire's disused airfields to visit.

Rednal's control tower is in a poor condition.

RAF Shawbury in 1939. *(Ian Pride)*

Shawbury

RAF Shawbury has a good chance of becoming one of the first airfields in the world to reach its 100th birthday. It has seen it all – from nimble biplanes to the sleek machines of the jet age.

It was from here that the first British aircraft to fly round the world took off as part of a pioneering series of long range flights.

While no fighters or bombers went to war from the airfield, the war came to Shawbury instead, with several unwelcome visits from Luftwaffe raiders.

Already one of Britain's oldest air bases, it is also one of its most important. For it is at Shawbury that all helicopter pilots for the Army, Royal Navy, and Royal Air Force receive their basic training.

Military air traffic control training is also done here. And scores of aircraft are stored in its specially dehumidified hangars.

RAF Shawbury has enjoyed two lives. The flat fields north west of the village were chosen as an airfield in the First World War and flying training started in 1917 in the days of the Royal Flying Corps – the RAF was not formed until April 1918.

Unlike today, the airfield hangars and buildings were grouped on the west side of the grass landing area. Soon the skies were massed with aircraft of many types, the Avro 504 being the favourite trainer.

One of the commanders was Major Arthur Tedder, later to be "Father of the Royal Air Force" Lord Tedder.

With war's end the station quickly closed and the fields returned to agriculture. But it was not the end of the RAF Shawbury story.

The 1930s was an era of expansion for the RAF. Eyes once more fell on the site, and the base was about to enjoy its second life. A major building programme began. Flying at RAF Shawbury "mark two" started in 1938.

With the coming of war, the base fulfilled some unglamorous but vital functions, like pilot training – mainly using the Airspeed Oxford – and aircraft storage. Accidents were frequent, with 38 in August 1941 alone. German raiders struck four times in 1940, without inflicting serious damage or casualties.

Concrete runways were laid in 1942 although the main runway was substantially lengthened southwards in the late 1950s so the base could act as a diversion airfield for V-bombers.

Two pilots who trained at Shawbury – Squadron Leaders R.A.B. Learoyd and J.D. Nettleton – later won VCs.

Aircraft were dispersed in fields for literally miles around. A hangar survives today as far away as Preston Brockhurst.

In 1944 the Central Navigation School arrived as the base became responsible for all navigator instructor training, and pilot training moved away. The year 1950 was another major landmark in Shawbury's history when air traffic control training arrived.

Flying training returned in 1976, but this time in the form of helicopters. Types such as the Whirlwind, Wessex and Gazelle became familiar sights. And for thousands of air cadets, Shawbury provided their first taste of flying, in Chipmunks.

RAF Shawbury has not only survived the "rationalisation" of the RAF, but has had a new lease of life with the formation on April 1, 1997, of the tri-service Defence Helicopter Flying School.

The Griffin and Squirrel helicopters are familiar sights in the skies round about, and various sites across Shropshire are used as practice landing areas. Apart from places like Tern Hill and Chetwynd, some local farmers have agreements with the base by which they allow the helicopters to set down and take-off on their land.

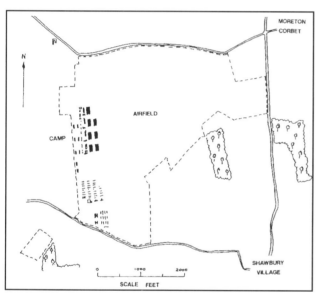

RAF Shawbury in 1918, when the airfield accommodation and hangars were on the west of the site. *(Map: Aldon Ferguson)*

When the sirens sounded

John Vaux, who was stationed at RAF Shawbury from 1940 to the end of 1941, recalls: "I joined up as a 'Ground Gunner' which soon became part of the RAF Regiment. On being issued with khaki battledress and a rifle I soon decided it was not for me, and remustered to aircrew, eventually ending up on Lancasters as a navigator.

"I have some odd memories of Shawbury, such as the day the sirens sounded and two Wellingtons flew over at 400 feet with German markings. Consternation!

"I was a radio operator on a thing called an Armadillo, a truck with a large concrete box which held a radio operator, a Lewis gunner and an odd bod to shoot his rifle and throw the six grenades provided, and a driver of course.

"There were four of these beasts to defend the station from airborne invasion.

"The famous golfer Henry Cotton was put in charge of catering. He did wonders.

"I can also remember an Oxford in a screaming spiral dive, its pupil presumably frozen at the controls. He made a hole 20 feet deep just north west of the hangars and was given a full military funeral with a three foot long coffin. A bit hard on the relatives.

"On another occasion a Boulton Paul Defiant nightfighter took off one morning and hit a Fairey Battle, decapitating the two occupants before crashing and blowing up.

"The station was attacked early in 1941 when a number of incendiary bombs were dropped all over the place but hit nothing so did not reveal we were there. Some fell quite close to six Blenheims and, of all things, an ancient Handley Page Heyford of Imperial Airways, one of their 24 seat airliners from about 1926. How it got to Shawbury, or why, I cannot imagine. It did not stay long but if it had survived what an exhibit for the RAF Museum at Hendon it would have been.

"One last thing. There was one Flight Sergeant Howell, S.P. He was an unholy terror to young officers and other ranks. He was in fact enormously good for discipline and morale, for if you were going on leave and got past his eagle eye at the Main Gate, then one really was well turned out and smart, a real boost for one's ego and morale. But if he stopped you...!"

From a very old and tatty sketch (probably illegal) done on the Wem side of Shawbury where one could often see quite a number of aircraft other than Oxfords, such as Blenheims, Beauforts, Whitleys (hideous) Wellingtons and once a Whirlwind. I think in this sketch we see a Beaufighter, a Whitley and what must be a Beaufort. A Fairey Battle flies low over the parked aircraft. Opportunities to sketch were rare.

One of a series of sketches John Vaux made while at Shawbury.

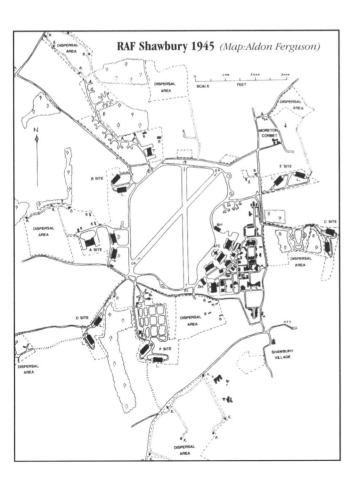

RAF Shawbury 1945 *(Map: Aldon Ferguson)*

War diary

1938
February 1: No. 27 Maintenance Unit formed to store, maintain and modify aircraft.

1939
January: Arrival of first aircraft, 12 Blenheims.
November 7: First wartime fatality when Acting Pilot Officer G.H.H. Coates crashes into The Wrekin in an Oxford.

1940
May: Aircraft establishment, 66 Oxfords, 23 Battles, and 40 Harts and Audaxes.
June 27: Lone enemy bomber attacked at 0055 during night flying, attracted by the flarepath. No buildings hit and no casualties. Blackout immediately improved.
July: Shawbury to Moreton Corbet road closed to improve security.
September 5: Three 10kg bombs dropped near the MU dispersal at Acton Lea. No casualties.
September 25: About eight explosive and 15 incendiary bombs dropped. No damage or casualties.
November 14: Beacon on B site strafed. No damage.

Art for RAF's sake

A talented artist was put to work at RAF Shawbury – painting camouflage on the aircraft. "They discovered that he was an artist in civilian life, so that's what he did in the air force," said Mrs Beatrice Hely-Hutchinson, of Ludlow, daughter of Stephen Harris, who was called up into the RAF in 1939.

"I think he was given free rein. I don't think there was a set pattern. He was at Shawbury, but not for all of his service. I think he was demobbed in 1947.

"It was rather hard to get information out of him, but he did say about the camouflage.

"He said how extremely boring it was at Shawbury. He hated it. There were a thousand men billeted there. He was an educated man and he disliked the jazz and all the culture of the day.

"He was rather a loner who kept himself to himself. The legend was that there were 900 copies of 'Blighty' delivered to the camp and one copy of The Times.

"He did not really fit in to camp life. The Wing Commander let him have a shed on the airfield to draw in. The only things that survive are drawings of his air force friend Cyril."

Stephen Harris died in 1980 but some of his paintings can be viewed on the Bridgeman Art Library website.

In 1998 an Australian woman visiting Britain presented RAF Shawbury with a collection of rare photographs of the aerodrome. Mrs Jane Johnson called at the base to hand over an album of photographs taken by her late grandfather, Harry C. Harvey of 5th Squadron, Australian Flying Corps.

Mr Harvey, who gives his rank in the album as 1st Air Mechanic, served at Shawbury towards the end of World War One. His photos must have been taken in 1917-18.

Mrs Johnson, from Osborne Park in West Australia, who was on holiday in Britain, had had the album in the bottom drawer of a chest in a spare room for years. Almost all the WWI pictures on these pages are from his album (all following images courtesy of RAF Shawbury).

"First crash at Shawbury aerodrome. An Avro across a road."

"A heavy fall of snow at the aerodrome. Three friends and myself."

"Portable hangars"

0/400 bomber in 1918

A Maurice Farman.

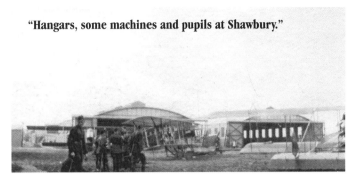

"Hangars, some machines and pupils at Shawbury."

"Sopwith Camel crashed at Shawbury."

"The dope room."

Bristol Scout

"Hoisting wind vane on top of hangar"

"Four Avros at Shawbury Aerodrome, also showing flying ground"

"German prisoners at work"

9 Training Depot Station in October 1918 (also facing page)

Priory School CCF (Air Section) field day in 1953. Michael Owen, who now lives in Grimsby, is centre. They were about to set off on a two-hour flight in the Avro Lincoln in the background. *(Michael Owen)*

The presentation of the Shrewsbury borough flag to the Central Navigation and Control School, Shawbury, on July 21, 1951 *(RAF Shawbury archives)*

Can you see it? "Trees" and "hedges" were painted on the airfield as camouflage early in the war *(Ian Pride)*

This B47 which landed low on fuel was a surprise visitor in 1955

Aries adventures

A series of record-breaking long-range flights has secured RAF Shawbury a place of distinction in aviation history. Known as the Aries Flights, after the first sign of the zodiac, they pushed forward the frontiers of knowledge in navigation.

The most famous was in October 1944 when a Lancaster, named Aries 1 and under the command of Wing Commander D.C. McKinley, took off from Shawbury on the first round-the-world trip by a British aircraft.

Flying via Prestwick, Reykjavik, Dorval, Washington, San Francisco, Honolulu and Samoa, Aries reached Auckland on November 1.

It visited bases in New Zealand, Australia and New Guinea before returning by Ceylon, Masira, Egypt and Malta but on reaching England had to be diverted to RAF Lyneham due to bad weather.

The flight had covered 42,000 miles over 53 days. The return trip broke the official Australia-to-UK record by over 50 hours, taking less than 72 hours.

Other flights followed, including a series of research flights over the North Pole, for which the plane was streamlined and sported polished bare metal.

In May 1945, operating from Iceland and Goose Bay, Aries became the first British aircraft to overfly both the geographic and magnetic North Poles. Aries continued to set many more records in long range flying but sadly was later scrapped.

In October 2004 the sole surviving member of the famous 1944 record-breaking flight made an emotional return, at the age of 87, for anniversary celebrations at Shawbury.

Herbert "Bunny" Dean, from London, was an electrician on board the Aries. Mike McKinley, whose father, the late Air Vice-Marshal David McKinley captained the 10-man Lancaster crew, was also at the event, at which Mr Dean presented the officers mess with a signed picture of Aries which was painted by artist Rob Evans.

Mr Dean said: "We took off around the world from Shawbury and were away for 53 days. It was no holiday and we went on a trip to do a job and, believe me, it was well done."

Aries I at Shawbury on October 21, 1944

1941

January: Arrival of detachment of No. 6 Anti Aircraft Co-operation Unit.

1942

April 1: No. 11 Flying Training School renamed 11 (Pilot) Advanced Training Unit.

May 2: First fatality of new (P)AFU when Sgt Pilot A.R. Whittington seen to dive his Oxford vertically into ground at Hadnall.

June 5: Two permanent runways opened.

June 15: Collision between two Masters kills Sgts Powloka and Pacahan. Both buried in Shawbury churchyard.

1943

January 16: No. 1534 Beam Approach Training Flight formed.

February: Establishment of 11 (P)AFU now 152 Oxfords and four Ansons.

1944

January 31: 11 (P)AFU moved out to Calveley to make way for the Central Navigation School.

February: CNS arrives with 42 Wellingtons and four Stirlings. Base became responsible for all navigator instructor training, and development of navigational equipment and techniques.

Modern Shawbury trains helicopter pilots for all three services.

Shawbury today

RAF Shawbury continues to dominate the village, just as it has done since the 1930s. It is an active airfield in full use, mostly by helicopters, but its runways can take fast jets and it does have visitors from time to time, such as aircraft refuelling on their way to air displays.

The helicopters based at Shawbury also use Tern Hill, Chetwynd, and Nesscliffe for practice, together with various other sites where public-spirited landowners permit them to land.

Prince William was one of the more high profile students at the base – he was at Shawbury for several weeks in the spring of 2008.

Anyone wanting to visit RAF Shawbury or its dispersed sites should of course not attempt to do so without receiving official permission! However it is possible to get an overview across the airfield from the busy A53 to the south.

Aircraft at Shawbury were dispersed over a wide area during the war. This surviving Robin hangar at Preston Brockhurst was disguised by having windows painted on, chimney stacks added, and a black and white half-timbered finish.

Sleap

In the summer of 1943 an extraordinary double tragedy hit Sleap airfield which, the story goes, has left the control tower haunted by the ghosts of two WAAF girls.

Within the space of only a few days the control tower was twice run into by bombers, leaving many dead and injured.

The second incident caused the most loss of life. Soon after midnight on September 7 a Whitley bomber hit the tower while taking off and burst into flames. Seven died – four in the plane – and, on the ground, Norman Peate and WAAFs Vera Hughes and Kitty Ffoulkes. The tail gunner was badly injured and two WAAF Met staff were badly burned. Corporal Peate is buried in St Martins churchyard.

It was a case of lightning striking twice. In the early hours of August 26 a Whitley had swung as it landed and hit the tower, killing the pilot and air bomber and seriously injuring the rest of the crew. Three on the ground were hurt, including one Wing Commander Robertson, but "about 15 personnel miraculously escaped injury" according to a contemporary report.

Today the repaired control tower still stands as the clubhouse of Shropshire Aero Club, symbolising the continuation of the flying tradition at Sleap, one of the few wartime Shropshire air bases which still sees regular flying.

Like most of the county's airfields Sleap – which is pronounced "Slape" – was a training base, although there were Whitley missions from here in 1943, dropping leaflets over enemy occupied France. Hidden in the countryside near Wem, it was reached by a new track which was dubbed the Burma Road.

One wartime event which is particularly remembered is when 31 American B17 bombers landed after diverting from their bases at Molesworth, Grafton Underwood and Great Ashfield in East Anglia after a bombing raid in

Whitleys at dispersal, Sleap, 1943. The WAAF by the trafficator (Standard van) is Vera Hughes who was killed soon after this photo was taken when a Whitley – probably one of those in this picture – crashed into the control tower. Rosemary Hayes (later Mrs Rosemary MacFadyen) is on the three ton Albion on flare path duty. *(Phil Ede)*

November 1944.

And there is a rumour that a Messerschmitt 110 is embedded deep in the rubbish tip near to the Tilley gate on the north side of the airfield. But claims that Guy Gibson was at Sleap are a mistake, no doubt caused by a confusion with a Wing Commander Gibson based at the parent airfield at Tilstock and who, unlike the famous Dam Busters leader, survived the war.

Sleap was a satellite to Whitchurch Heath airfield (which was later renamed RAF Tilstock). The advanced party in January 1943 stayed at Sleap House and the first recorded use is when a Henley force landed on January 10. Regular flying did not begin until the arrival of the Whitleys of 81 Operational Training Group in April. Its role was to train bomber aircrews, but in early 1944 Sleap's duties were extended to training crews for glider towing of airborne troops. Soon the lumbering Whitleys towing Horsa gliders were a familiar sight in the run-up to the great airborne operations like D-Day and Arnhem.

Gliders could be just as dangerous as powered aircraft. In November 1944 a Horsa trying to land hit a contractor's hut on the edge of the airfield, killing the pilot. By the end of the year Whitleys were being replaced by Wellingtons. Other types on the base included Ansons and Oxfords.

The station was used by RAF Shawbury for a while after the war, closing around 1949, but being revived as a satellite in 1958 and later used to train RAF air traffic controllers, with early jets such as Vampires being among the visitors.

In 1949 one of Sleap's hangars was turned into a film studio during the making of the movie *Gone To Earth*, which was filmed on location in Shropshire.

The RAF finally left in 1964, but Shawbury-based helicopter pilots still do some hover training and night training at Sleap.

Flying 'flying coffins'

Tim Yates, a wireless operator-air gunner, said: "The first time we landed at Sleap they had not finished it. We were the first aircraft to go there. There was a big mound of soil between two of the runways.

"It was a satellite airfield to Tilstock and we would have been in a Whitley. Whitleys were called flying coffins, although to be fair they were very safe – they just looked like a coffin."

Mr Yates had completed a tour of operational duty with 214 Squadron flying Wellingtons from Stradishall, Suffolk. His logbook records that he was posted to Sleap on March 9, 1943. His first flight was two days later and he remained there until December.

"I was doing cross country flights and a certain amount of ground instruction. We were training crews for Bomber Command. The officers mess had the best chef in the air force. She had worked at the Ritz before the war. She was brilliant.

"We had a very good wing commander, Wing Commander Carter. If we could not fly he was, like me, a keen poker player and we had good poker sessions with the C/O. The second in command was Squadron Leader Lockwood."

Mr Yates, who was chairman of Shrewsbury Town for over 20 years, was at the time a Flying Officer. "Sleap was very much a friendly, small station."

Herbert Griffiths' father Harry had two farms, Lower

WAAFs from Sleap relax with some furry friends. *(Phil Ede)*

Houlston and Houlston Manor, but had to yield many acres from Lower Houlston for the new aerodrome. Mr Griffiths, of Calverhall, worked as a youngster on the farms.

"We were getting aircraft literally passing over the buildings. They were so close you could almost touch them with a broom. There are trees there now which had the tops cut off because they were trying to take-off and had trouble gaining height.

"On one particular morning I was milking and one came particularly low, took the tops off two trees and crashed into the third. My brother and I ran to it. By the time we got to them the crew had got out and it was on fire. Their clothes were burnt and their skin was hanging from the hands, arms, and face."

Having an airfield on the doorstep had bonuses. "They would say 'come and have a ride with us' and I went up in Whitleys and Wellingtons. Being young, it was exciting. At that age you are sort of adventurous."

He also helped out by keeping down the numbers of hares and plovers, which were getting sucked into air intakes. And things worked the other way, with WAAFs and airmen helping pick mushrooms at the farm and WAAFs picking fruit in the Griffiths' orchard.

Sleap ground crew. *(Phil Ede)*

Some of the fitters, of both sexes. *(Phil Ede)*

Another benefit was that he would use a bowl to scoop up puddles of spilt fuel from plane refuelling, mix it with some paraffin – "it was high octane" – and use it in his Bull-nosed Morris.

On one occasion a large number of Flying Fortresses were heard circling in the fog. Low on fuel, they landed nose-to-tail.

A crew member told him: 'Buddy, we just followed the red light in front.'

"There was not a casualty. It was miraculous. They had orders that as soon as they landed they had to get off the runway, and of course they just sank, and there were these Flying Fortresses stuck in the mud," said Mr Griffiths.

He recalls one morning a German bomber fly-ing low past the farm, followed some minutes later by a Hurricane. The bomber jettisoned its string of bombs between Myddle and Baschurch. "I think some of the holes are still there now."

Post-war uses of the airfield included tyre and brake testing for Goodyear.

Flying Officer Harold Pimm (seen left) had completed 33 operational missions as a rear gunner when he arrived at Sleap in 1943 and was to spend over two years there. He began as an instructor and then helped develop a rear gun turret trainer.

On the day the B17s flew in he was duty officer.

"It was just what I needed as a sprog pilot officer. I finished up having to get beds made up on the sitting room floor of the officers mess." (A total of 560 Americans were accommodated at Sleap and Tilstock, where further bombers landed).

"We used to go to Wem which was the next village and the only place we could get to. They ran a local bus from the station on a Saturday evening as far as I can remember. There was either a cinema we could go to or eight or nine pubs."

Mr Pimm, from Henfield, Sussex, returned to Sleap twice in later life. The turret trainer, the only one of its type in the country, was still there on his last visit in 1996, although the basin-like structure onto which the images of attacking fighters were projected had partially collapsed.

Brian Davies has lived at New House Farm, Sleap, all his life. "I remember them building the aerodrome. They had so much land off our farm and there were three farms they took completely. The aerodrome used the same road we used and we had to have a pass to get in and out.

"I remember two aeroplane accidents. In one a plane was taking off and hit the control tower, and another one was coming in and hit the control tower. We heard this terrific explosion."

One day during World War Two **Bill Winnall** was working in the fields by the airfield when an unfamiliar aeroplane appeared in the sky.

"A Flying Fortress came over. This was quickly followed by three more, which were an unusual sight in that area" said Mr Winnall, whose parents at that time farmed Noneley Hall Farm adjoining the airfield.

"After that the area became full of Flying Fortresses

A turret trainer, the only one of its type, at Sleap in the 1990s. Sadly the 25ft diameter projection bowl visible here collapsed in 1997.

circling the aerodrome," he added.

Although the bombers operated from airfields in East Anglia, occasionally fog would make it impossible for them to land at their home bases after raids, and they would

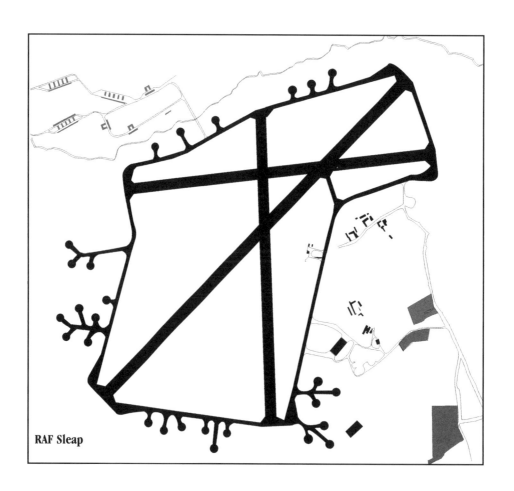

RAF Sleap

divert to bases where conditions were better, which could be some distance away. It was one of these occasions that Mr Winnall witnessed.

Norman Peate was one of the victims when a bomber hit the control tower. He is buried at St Martins. *(Phil Ede)*

"They started to land on the runway which pointed directly towards us working in the fields. Some of them had burst tyres, and they would hit the runway and then shoot off in different directions across the airfield.

"The red danger signals were being shot up from the control tower warning them not to come in, but it made no difference.

"In all, between 30 and 40 landed on the airfield. They had just returned from a bombing raid over Germany and their own base had become fogbound.

"Sleap was the first airfield they could find where they could land safely. We were told later that some had also landed at the airfield at Prees, which was known as Tilstock airfield."

Mr Winnall can remember the tragic incident in which a bomber crashed into the control tower.

Later, when there were no longer any guards at the base, he would cycle through the airfield, following the perimeter track, to visit a young lady in Preston Gubbals who would later become his wife.

"Going across the 'drome was a short cut of about five miles," he said.

Charles Emberton, of Shropshire Aero Club, said: "When Runway 28 was in use the Horsas' exercise often finished in the fields at the end of the runway, for if a Whitley was not gaining height quickly enough the glider was jettisoned without delay. A very hairy occupation for both pilots.

"If you examine the structure of our little tin hangar at the far end of the airfield you will be able to see the main wing spars from Horsa gliders of those bygone days.

"I lived below the 'late downwind leg' for runway 'Zero Six' and spent most of my school holidays sitting on a wooden stile by the Ellesmere road entrance to the airfield idolising the aircrew and fitters fussing round their charges. One momentous day I was invited over the barbed wire onto 'sacred' ground and up the ladder into the nose of a Whitley and allowed to 'work the joystick'. My feet never touched the cycle pedals all the way home!

"On another occasion, after having maintained an all-day vigil at Sleap, I was wending my weary way home when suddenly the circuit became alive with 37 B17 flying Fortresses which appeared out of the dusk from nowhere. I turned back just in time to see them all stream landing, each turning onto the grass at the end of his landing run and switching off. What a night!

"At the end of the war the airfield was closed and started to deteriorate, but a few years later it was reopened and was operated by RAF Shawbury as a GCA School using Chipmunks and Ansons, later to be replaced by Provosts and Vampires. This role ceased in the autumn of 1968 so that now we have it all to ourselves."

Mr Emberton and five others founded the Shropshire Flying Group in 1954-55.

War diary

1943

January 1: Advance party of 81 Operational Training Unit proceed to Sleap. Accommodated at Sleap House.

January 10: Henley L3280 force landed owing to fog.

April 8: First a/c arrives at Sleap at 1800 hrs.

May 3: Whitley on night cross country from Sleap crashed near Wem and caught fire. All crew killed.

June: Whitleys involved in nickel raids over occupied France, e.g. Amiens and Caen.

August 26: 0310hr. Whitley V LA937 crashed when landing into watch office – cause unknown. Pilot and air bomber (both RCAF) killed, others of crew seriously injured. Three ground staff seriously injured – ACW Viney and ACI Ferguson and Wing Commander Robertson. "The aircraft was a total wreck and considerable damage was caused to the watch office, about 15 personnel miraculously escaping injury. The building was temporarily repaired and in operation by 0900hrs." Wing Commander Robertson was the less seriously hurt of the three. He was the chief instructor (or became it) and later base C.O. He was repatriated to Canada later.

September 7: "Whitley N257 crashed into control tower while taking off at approx 0015 hours. Four members of crew of five killed – P/O R.W. Browne, pilot; Sgt W.D. Kershaw, air bomber; P/O E.L. Ware, navigator; Sgt E. Young, wireless operator/air gunner. Injured member admitted to RAF Hospital, Cosford, Sgt S. Williams, air gunner. Three members of ground staff also killed – Cpl N.W. Peate; ACW1 V. Hughes; ACW2 K.M. Ffoulkes. Two injured – ACW2 H. Hall (Met), admitted Cosford; LACW A.B. Jowett (Met)."

September: Station strength 591 plus 91 WAAFs.

September 24: A Fortress with 19 ferry pilots as passengers landed in poor visibility.

Long's quest

One of the wartime experiences which was particularly memorable for Richard Long was the day he crashed on the doorstep of a Shropshire country mansion – and was then invited in for a cup of tea .

But it always nagged away at him that he did not know where this happened and in recent years he launched a quest to pinpoint the site.

The upshot was, that with the help of readers of the *Shropshire Star* with long memories, he was able in 2002, at the age of 82, to return to the site of the drama – Loppington House, near Sleap airfield from which he had taken off.

Or at least, what was said to be the site of the drama. While some thought it was at Loppington House, one

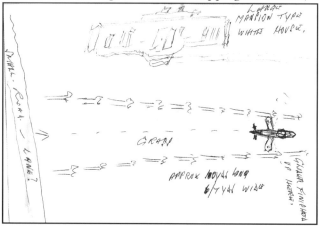

Richard Long's drawing of his crash helped to identify the location, although the avenue of trees has since disappeared.

gentleman, Bill Turner of Tilley, just south of Wem, recalled seeing a glider come down at Trench Hall, Tilley.

"It wasn't exactly a crash landing. He made a perfect landing except for ripping part of the wings. There was an avenue of trees by Trench Hall then," said Mr Turner.

Mr Long had come down in spectacular fashion in the middle of an avenue of trees, which ripped both wings off.

"Me and my co-pilot and one of the RAF chaps with us walked to the house and this gentleman there said: 'What the hell's happened out there?' There was an aircraft with no wings and no engines in front of his house. He was really surprised," Mr Long said.

While they waited to be picked up the man and his wife arranged tea and biscuits.

"It's something that's always bothered me. I have always wanted to go back. He did mention the name of his lovely house, but after all these years, names seem to vanish."

Mr Long, who took part in the D-Day and Arnhem operations, had taken off in a Horsa glider from Sleap airfield on December 29, 1944, and was at only about 500ft when the rope from the tow plane came adrift.

Staff Sergeant Long and his co-pilot looked around for somewhere to land – they were over a built-up area – and quickly chose a grass "runway" between two lines of trees in front of a large white mansion.

"I came over a road or lane at about 50ft with full flap, and directly I touched down both the wings started to disintegrate, leaving pieces of plywood all over the place."

Mr Long and his co-pilot, together with eight RAF aircrew passengers who were aboard because they had never been up in a glider before, escaped unscathed.

Mr Long, who served in B Squadron, the Glider Pilot Regiment, said: "The elderly chap looked like a military man. He had white hair, and a white-ish moustache, and spoke rather nicely, and his lady was about the same age."

Mr Long was afterwards called to see the commanding officer at Sleap and commended for his landing, but given a "right rollicking" for writing off a £5,000 glider.

Invited to make a nostalgic return, 60 years on, he was flown over Loppington House. He also went to RAF Shawbury to see a project to build a full-size Horsa glider replica in tribute to the wartime airborne forces. He then visited Sleap airfield itself.

1944

January 1: Tilstock and Sleap transferred from 93 Group Bomber Command to 38 Group – a new formation to train crews for towing gliders for airborne troops.

January 15: All gliders t/f to Sleap.

April 11: Wing Commander Gibson took a Stirling to Sleap and carried out two lifts with a Horsa glider.

April 29: 81 OTU carried out full scale airborne exercise. Nine Whitley tugs and glider combinations took off at 45 second intervals, carried out a short cross country and were mass landed at Sleap. All gliders achieved the aim of quick concentration on the ground. The exercise was the first attempted and was "generally very satisfactory".

May 18: W/O Double (navigator or bomb aimer – reports vary)

of RAF Sleap fell out of Whitley at 1,400ft at 1115hrs. Body found at approx 1415 hours after search led by Anson aircraft.

July 23: Boxing tournament held in No 1 hangar, Sleap. First use of the station's new boxing ring, built by Workshops.

November 16: Total of 62 B17 Flying Fortresses diverted from Molesworth, Grafton Underwood and Great Ashfield after a daylight raid on France. 31 were accommodated at Sleap. 560 a/crew accommodated at the two bases.

November 10: Horsa glider LH384, attempting to land, struck contractors' hut at edge of Sleap a/f and crashed. Pilot killed.

1945

April 30: Station strength, officers 101, other ranks 593.

The night of horror

Radio operator John Martin was sent from Tilstock to Sleap to replace an operator injured when a bomber crashed into the control tower – and narrowly escaped the same fate. When he arrived he saw a large hole in the control room wall, already bricked up, from where the port engine of a Whitley had come through.

"I had the comforting thought 'Well, lightning doesn't strike twice in the same place.' In less than two weeks I was to be proved terribly wrong," he recalled in the book *The Driving Force*.

His duty on the fateful night was from 1700 to 2300, but half an hour before he was due to go off watch a message came through to expect diverted bombers returning from operations. Control officer Flt Lt Mattingley asked him to have a late supper and return to be on standby. He suggested he got his head down in the small rest room to be available in case of a "flap".

Returning about 2345, he met Canadian control room officer, Flying Officer Brooks, who was now on duty for the night, and who confirmed he knew about the standby arrangements. He was chatting, said Mr Martin, to two pretty young WAAFs. He went to the rest room on the first floor and lay listening to the RT chatter coming over the loudspeaker in the main control room.

"I suppose it must have been soon after midnight when I heard the voice of the airfield controller, 'Freshfield U-Uncle taking off'. Then the roaring crescendo of two Merlin engines as a Whitley revved up for maximum power to get its heavy bulk off the ground. The sound seemed to be getting very near!

"Suddenly an urgent warning shout over the loudspeaker: 'Look out control, he's heading for you', followed immediately by a tremendous crunching explosion. The whole building shuddered and night was turned into day as a vast conflagration ensued."

Mr Martin rushed to the door but was unable to get out, so baled out of the window, and ran back to the crash area.

"A horrific scene met my eyes. The aircraft had ploughed into the ground floor of the watch office and burst into flames. It was obvious that the only possible survivor might be the rear gunner. Happily he was eventually extracted from the turret.

"I approached Flying Officer Brooks who was visibly distressed but it was not until I heard him say, in an agonised voice, 'Oh my God! Those two poor girls,' that I realised the WAAFs on MT duty had been in the room which had taken the full force of the collision."

Sleap today

Head north from Shrewsbury towards Wem. About three miles south of Wem there is a signposted turn to the airfield off the B5476. This takes you down the road to the airfield which was dubbed "the Burma Road".

Sleap is an active airfield and the control tower is home to Shropshire Aero Club, members of which are proud of the heritage of the site. Light aircraft are regularly seen in the skies and a gliding group also operates from here. There is also a small museum close to the control tower run by the Shropshire Wartime Aircraft Recovery Group displaying items recovered from wrecks, models, and other items of memorabilia. (Check for opening times).

With a bit of imagination, it is not hard to imagine what Sleap was like in wartime.

Seemingly peaceful Tern Hill has a dramatic and often tragic history.

Tern Hill

Shropshire's oldest air base has seen days of glory, extraordinary drama, and tragedy. It can point to the Battle of Britain and the Blitz among its battle honours.

During much of 1940 and 1941 its marauding Spitfires, Hurricanes, and nightfighting Blenheims hunted down Luftwaffe intruders, scoring a number of successes. Together with High Ercall, Tern Hill was Shropshire's "ace" air station.

But even during the period when Tern Hill was showing its teeth, its most enduring role was continuing – training. There was also a Maintenance Unit at the huge, sprawling complex which took up much of the surrounding countryside.

It meant it was a busy and often lethal base which took a steady toll of young lives. It seems likely that there were more fatal accidents at Tern Hill than at any other Shropshire airfield.

It was also on the receiving end of bombing, both in war and peace. A raid by a lone bomber in 1940 destroyed many aircraft and caused casualties. And a visit by the IRA in 1989 left an Army accommodation block blown apart, happily without casualties.

From its earliest days, the air station has been training pilots. And it does so still. Although RAF Tern Hill closed in December 1976, the airfield is still owned by the RAF, while the domestic site is the Army's Clive Barracks. The airfield is used on weekdays by helicopters from RAF Shawbury, and at weekends by gliders from the Air Training Corps.

Its links with aviation go back to August 22, 1906, when balloonist Percival Spencer took off from Shrewsbury Flower Show, with passengers Major Atcherley, who was Shropshire's chief constable, and Mr G. Ingle of Oakengates. Landing at Tern Hill, they received great hospitality from the locals.

The story goes that Major Atcherley afterwards told the authorities that it would be a good spot for an airfield. True or not, work on preparing the base began in September 1916 and squadrons arrived in December.

Training was on types ranging from Avro 504Ks to Sopwith Camels and Handley Page bombers.

RAF Tern Hill closed down in 1920. Two hangars were used as stabling and a third for indoor schooling of horses by Max Barthropp, while the airfield itself was used as a gallops.

But in the mid-1930s the RAF decided once more to use Tern Hill and on January 1, 1936, No 10 Flying Training School formed there, heralding the start of a major rebuilding and expansion.

Some sources claim that Dam Busters hero Guy Gibson trained at Tern Hill. More certain is the claim that another Victoria Cross winner, Wing Commander J.B. Nicholson, trained there.

Along with the training in biplanes such as the Audax and Hart, a maintenance and storage unit was formed in 1937, which maintained and repaired a wide variety of aeroplanes, from Spitfires to Lancaster bombers.

In early wartime the airfield was extraordinarily busy with a threefold function – home to fighters to combat German bombers; home to over 200 training planes, such as Miles Masters; and home to the major repair and maintenance unit.

To cap it all, during the height of the Blitz it served as No 9 Group Sector Headquarters, controlling fighters in a swathe of north west England and North Wales.

Tern Hill was a grass airfield and prone to flooding, which was not put right until two relatively short runways were built at the end of 1941.

With the Blitz over, the operational fighter squadrons faded from the scene and Tern Hill settled down into a training and repair role which continued after the war.

In the early 1960s helicopters arrived from the Central Flying School.

According to Shropshire aviation historian Ian Pride, when the Army took over in the late 1970s the name Borneo Barracks was chosen, before it was quickly renamed Clive Barracks. "Apparently the first Army CO did not wish to be known as the Wild Man of Borneo," he said.

Today part of the old RAF complex serves as Stoke Heath Young Offenders Institution (still known by older folk as "The Borstal"), and a hangar is the Maurice Chandler sports centre, while other buildings have various storage and business uses.

And 100 years after that balloon dropped in, they're still flying at Tern Hill.

Hurricanes of 306 "Torunski" Polish squadron at readiness at Tern Hill in November 1940. *(Picture courtesy of the Imperial War Museum, Image No. HU 4580; Collection No 6904-06)*

The day the bombs came

October 1940 brought Tern Hill's finest hour – and one of its darkest days. At 7.21am on the 16th a Junkers Ju88 swept low over the airfield and dropped its load of four high explosive and six incendiary bombs. It then came round again shooting everything up.

It happened so quickly that not a shot was fired back.

One of the hangars packed with planes was hit, causing an inferno in which 13 Avro Anson trainers were burned out, and 23 aircraft of various types, including two Blenheims, were damaged.

Nobody was killed but a civilian was seriously injured, and there were slight injuries to four others – one civilian, an airman, and two sappers.

"No panic whatever. Personnel took this attack in their stride and appeared to regard it as a natural occurrence," recorded an official afterwards. For many years the damaged hangar, now demolished, was left with its roof off and was dubbed the Sunshine Hangar.

The attack came within a week of Tern Hill's best day. On October 11 Spitfires of 611 Squadron claimed a "bag" of three raiders destroyed, one probable, and one damaged, at the cost of one Spit damaged by return fire, and one pilot seriously injured when he force landed near Kidderminster after getting lost in the dark.

Tern Hill was strategically placed to intercept German bombers on their way to raid the industrial north west or shipping in the Irish Sea, and during the momentous years of 1940 and 1941 a succession of fighter squadrons – Spitfires, Hurricanes, and a detachment of Blenheim night fighters – did battle from there.

Most of the time the patrols, many of which had the added hazard of being done at night, proved fruitless and frustrating.

The first success came when Pilot Officer R.A Rhodes in a Blenheim of 29 Squadron chased a Heinkel all the way across the country on August 18, 1940. Having shot off all

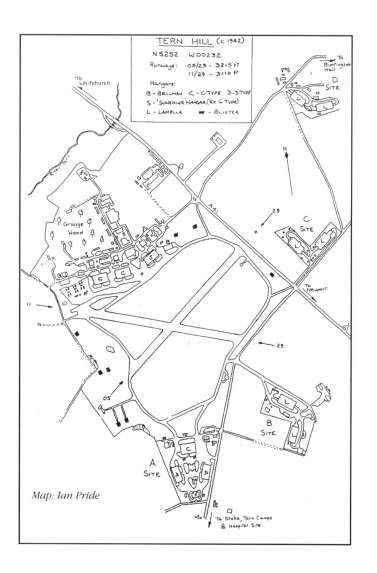

Map: Ian Pride

War diary

1916
September: Work on the preparation of the station begun.
December: Aerodrome occupied by 34 (R) Sqn commanded by Major E.L. Gower and 43 (R) Sqn. These squadrons remained at Tern Hill throughout 1917.

1917
About November: 30 Training Squadron (later called 6 Training Squadron) and 33 Training Squadron (later 8 Training Squadron) formed.

1918
From the middle of this year the only unit at Tern Hill was 13 Training Depot Squadron.
July 30: Major C.E. Brisley, C/O of 13 Training Depot Squadron, was killed in a crash at the aerodrome and buried at Market Drayton cemetery.

1919
March 9: Aerodrome narrowly escapes total destruction when two hangars burn down.

1920
As far as can be ascertained, the station was finally closed down this year.

the ammunition in the front guns, he manoeuvred along-side so his rear gunner could open up. The enemy landed in the sea near Cromer. Exactly a week later Rhodes was killed.

Some squadrons were simply out of luck.

Hurricanes from 605 Squadron arrived in April 1941 and stayed for two rather unhappy months without shooting down anything.

One night they were stood down to allow a couple of squadrons of Defiants to use Tern Hill to be nearer to an anticipated German raid on Birmingham. The Defiants promptly shot down a Heinkel.

1936

January 1: Formation of No 10 Flying Training School.

October 7: 2200 hours. A fire started near the northern edge of the block of officers quarters. It resulted in the complete destruction of all quarters, and the majority of officers and pupils lost their entire kit and belongings. Local fire brigades were unable to control the fire in any way in the stiffish breeze which was blowing. The mess itself was just saved. The loss of all the officers' quarters nearly resulted in the closing down of the school, but by taking over other accommodation, the unit was just enabled to carry on.

October 20: 2000hrs. Fire started in one of the officers' huts. Arson suspected.

1937

May 29: Total of 18,125 visitors on Empire Air Day.

June 1: 4 Aircraft Storage Unit (24 MU from about April 1939) formed. Ultimately planned to use nine hangars.

1940

June 5: Group Captain HRH the Duke of Kent visited, inspected Link trainer, training aircraft and pupils' lectures.

July 9. Seven Spitfires of A Flight only, 611 Squadron, arrived from RAF Digby, Lincolnshire. "The road convoy (1 Albion, 1 articulated, and a Humber Snipe brake) left at 1450, with another dozen airmen and the rest of the stores. All signposts have been removed during the last month and the drivers were ignorant of the route. They did not arrive until 2300."

July 22: A Spitfire landed on beach at Colwyn Bay after cooling system failure.

July 23: At 0130hrs an enemy raider dropped bombs half a mile away from the aerodrome. Nine landed in fields, one on the Tern Hill to Hodnet road, and one, which did not explode, in a stream. Damage was slight, temporarily blocking a road and blowing a few tiles off the railway station roof. "At the time the training school was night flying, at least three planes being in the air, and all the usual flares and lights were lit. In addition, it was a brightly moonlit night. No alarm was given until 0140 (i.e. ten minutes later)."

July 29: Two 29 Squadron Blenheims sent to Tern Hill every evening for patrol duties in Mersey area. Patrols controlled from RAF Digby.

August 18: Pilot Officer R.A. Rhodes in Blenheim L6741 with Sgt Gregory as air gunner patrolling Mersey area vectored onto a bandit and at 0228hrs, when about 15 miles south west of Chester, intercepted a Heinkel bomber. Shot down into the water after two hour chase about 10 miles west of Cromer Knoll.

September 10: From today four 29 Sqn Blenheims available at Tern Hill.

September 21: Blenheim L1507 hit floodlight on landing after being shot at by AA guns.

October 1: Operational part of 611 Sqn now wholly at Tern Hill.

October 11: At 1730 'A' Flt of six 611 Sqn aircraft took off to patrol Anglesey and attacked three bandits out of the sun. One raider crashed into water about 50 miles west of Holyhead, second crashed into hills about 10m south of Caernarvon, third crashed in flames near Capel Curig. The same day other Tern Hill Spitfires attacked two Dornier 17s near Prestatyn, one of which was seen diving towards the sea. "The total bag was three destroyed, one probable, and one damaged. Our losses were one damaged Spitfire (P7356) landed at Sealand, and one Spitfire (P7323) and pilot seriously injured, Sgt K.C. Pattison, who force landed at 1945 at Crooksey Green (sic), near Kidderminster. It is not believed that this crash was a result of enemy action, but was due to the pilot being lost in the darkness."

October 16: On a dull, rainy morning a Ju88 flew over aerodrome at 7.21 at 1,000ft and dropped four 250kg high explosive bombs and six incendiaries, and strafed the camp, causing a fire in 'C' hangar and serious injuries to one civilian employee. One other civilian and four service personnel were slightly hurt. Thirteen Ansons burnt out, two 29 Sqn Blenheims damaged, and about 20 training aircraft needed repairs. One hangar destroyed, another damaged.

November 7: 611 Sqn Spitfires return to Digby on relief by Hurricanes of 306 (Polish) Sqn from Church Fenton. A dispersal point for the squadron was provided in the south east corner of the aerodrome, where an old cottage, an army hut, and a Lamella hangar were made available.

November 8: First 306 Sqn patrol, over Liverpool and Manchester at 20,000ft.

November 13: Patrol, Coventry, He 111 or Ju88 attacked by three Hurricanes, one of which was damaged by return fire. Bandit escaped in cloud.

November 16: No 5 Service Flying Training School headquarters staff arrived and the station was taken over from No 10 SFTS.

November 26: Collision between S/Ldr D.R. Scott in a Hurricane and an Anson flown by two pupils. S/Ldr Scott in hospital. Also this day LAC P.G.W. Paul killed in a flying accident to Master N7427 at Gardenfields Farm, Cuddington and LAC W. Bethel was killed in a flying accident to Master T8397 at Uffington.

December 2: At Hodnet, Master N7597 crashed at Holme Farm, resulting in the deaths of F/O H.T. Buswell and LAC R.A. Chant.

December 12: At Nannerch, near Mold. Master T3326 crashed, resulting in the death of LAC E.R.J. Catworthy.

December 17: At Tern Hill, Master T7691 crashed resulting in the death of LAC H.H. Joseph and dangerous injuries to A/F/O W.N. Basson.

December 24: Practising dawn flying this morning, F/Lt H.W. Tennant crashed and was killed.

A treasure trove of planes

First hand memories of Tern Hill's World War One days are obviously impossible to find now, but retired RAF **Wing Commander Paddy Barthropp**, an ex-Battle of Britain pilot, can shed light on the inter-war years. He says his father Max used the WW1 buildings during this period.

"He had 120 horses in training. There were two huge hangars which were stables and a third for indoor schooling of horses when the weather was bad. It was the first one in the country.

"They had a lot of old aeroplanes from World War One in the hangars, both bits and pieces and some complete planes. As kids we used to play in them. There were SE5s and Sopwith Pups and Camels. If you got your hands on them now they would be worth a fortune. God knows what happened to them," said Mr Barthropp, of Lymington.

Jim Ward, of Stoke Heath: "I think it was on a Thursday morning that they bombed the airfield. My grandfather, William Webb, was in the next field to the aerodrome. They were topping swedes when they started machinegunning, and so he ran to a walnut tree. They never hit him.

"I was milking at the time. It was an asbestos roof on the cow shed and you could see the vibration go along the

"Avros at Tern Hill" in 1917 or 1918. *(Harry C. Harvey)*

asbestos. I ran outside and saw the plane in the distance.

"They had hit the hangar and the biggest part of the hangar was demolished. They called it the Sunshine Hangar afterwards.

"There were quite a lot of accidents. There were two planes that collided just over here where we are living now. One crashed at Stoke Grange, and the other at Helshaw Grange.

"The one was in bogland. They tried to retrieve it with

1941

January 12: Marshal of the RAF Viscount Trenchard visited the station and addressed various parades of officers and other ranks.

January 13: Thirteen Hurricane patrols in one night. In landing Sgt Pietrzak hit a Master which had crashed near the flarepath and damaged a wing of his machine.

February 13: P/O Bielkiewicz crashed and was killed, and Sgt Jasinski crashed and was slightly injured.

March 4: A film unit working on a record of Polish service in England arrived to take shots of No 306 (Polish) squadron.

April 1: Arrival of Hurricanes of 605 Sqn, which replaced 306 Sqn which left for Northolt. "The general opinion of our new home seems to be unfavourable. Our dispersal point and offices could be better and there is the usual feeling which attends a 'lodger' unit."

April 2 to April 23: Nine airmen of 5 FTS killed in flying accidents.

April 3: "The Controllers seem pleased with the prospect of talking to English pilots after the difficulties of understanding the Poles."

April 7: Sgt Kestler collided with a Spitfire flown by a Czech MU pilot, Sgt Martinec, near the base. Both killed.

April 10: "Two Defiant squadrons arrived to use our base to be nearer to Birmingham for an expected attack which materialised. The Defiants got one Heinkel, but lost two aircraft through R.T. failure, and crashed a number through bad weather landing." These Defiants were from 256 Sqn at Squires Gate and 96 Sqn at Cranage.

May 26: "Although we have not felt too comfortable on this station, we are sorry to be going now."

May 30: 605 Sqn left for Bagington.

July 11: Master N7567, piloted by LAC Butterfield, overshot on landing, and ran into and killed Leonard R. Johnson, an employee of Messrs British Runways, who was rolling the perimeter track.

August 6: Spitfires of 131 Fighter Squadron arrived from Catterick.

September 25: "Commandant Jullerot of the Free French Forces and an official of the BBC visited the Instructional Section on this date and interviewed pupils of the Free French Air Force. The object of this visit was in order to obtain material for a broadcast of the Free French Air (Force) training."

October: Half the aerodrome unserviceable because of runway construction.

1942

April 13: No 5 SFTS ceased to exist. 5 (Pilot) Advanced Flying Unit came into being.

1943

January 21: CFI of 5 PAFU Wing Commander A.W.M. Finny killed in a flying accident. Got into spin, pupil baled out.

August 29: AC. Johns, an airman of 24 MU, killed on an unauthorised flight – he took an aircraft without permission, did aerobatics over the aerodrome, and then dived into the ground.

1944

April 21: HRH Prince Bernhard of the Netherlands visited, stayed the night in the mess, and the following morning toured station and in afternoon visited Condover and RLG at Chetwynd.

horses to start with, I believe. They had no luck. They dug round to try and release it, and it went further in. Eventually they fenced round it and had a service and left it."

His brother **Albert Ward** worked on the Tern Hill complex as a civilian. "In Chapel Lane, Stoke Heath, there used to be a cafe. I believe it was called the Silver Slipper, and nicknamed the Gumboot Cafe.

"At Tern Hill, they used to bring Lancasters that had crashed and repaired them. Where the Borstal is now, they rebuilt the engines. They used to have a test bench up there, which ran 24 hours a day testing the engines before they put them into the aeroplanes.

"We lived at 8 Helshaw Cottage, Stoke Heath. When they were building the runways the Irish labour camp was right opposite our house.

"I don't know what date it was, but me and a friend who is dead now were on the A41, by the Borstal (now Stoke Heath Young Offenders Institution), and a German plane and an English plane were having a dogfight there. We were standing there like fools listening to them. You could hear the bullets hitting the fields. The German plane was shot down and the pilot was buried in the cemetery at Stoke-on-Tern. I think it had crashed somewhere between Tern Hill and Market Drayton."

This incident is conceivably that of October 22, 1941, when a Ju88 was shot down near Woore. Two of the crew baled out and were taken prisoners. Two were killed. They were buried with service honours at Stoke-on-Tern cemetery on October 23. The Tern Hill C/O was present.

Mr Ward added: "One dull morning a plane came over as I was going to work. I thought 'funny, he is low.'

"There was then an explosion. It had bombed the aero-

Tern Hill in April 1947. Just right of centre is the site of what is now Stoke Heath Young Offenders Institution. *(Albert Ward)*

Frank Chatham, who loaned this photo, which is blurred in the original, says it shows the first funeral at Tern Hill in WWI.

drome. He had gone down the three hangars, but only hit the one and then came round again and machinegunned the part he bombed. I believe there was one person killed by the bullets.

"There were plenty of crashes by the trainers. There was one crash at the back of my brother's farm. It tipped the corner of the thatched cottage and ran into the hedge. That was a Harvard, I think."

Frank Chatham, of Crickmerry, near Market Drayton, was a mechanic at Tern Hill Garage on the A41, and saw the RAF arrive in the mid-1930s. The garage was knocked down to make way for the camp entrance.

"The old wooden hangars were knocked down and rebuilt in bricks and mortar. The field was a rabbit warren, and they killed all the rabbits to make way for the landing ground."

Ken Goodwin, of Rosehill Road, Market Drayton: "We moved into this area in 1939, to Tyrley Castle Farm.

"It was extremely busy. Just as an example, all the airmen used to have a bike to cycle around the airfield to go to and from their place of work. They used to have weekend passes and all biked up to the farm opposite what is now Tern Hill roundabout, and would leave their bikes in the house yard over the weekend, and walk to the railway station at Tern Hill.

"It was nothing to see that yard full of 1,000 cycles in there. They would pick them up on their way back from weekend leave."

Empire Air Day, May 1936.

Above, a pupil at Tern Hill about to start his solo in 1942, and main picture, with his instructor. *(Pictures courtesy the Imperial War Museum, CH6474, CH6473).*

Below, the canteen and dining hall in about 1937. *(Ian Pride)*

Canteen and Dining Hall, R.A.F. Tern Hill, Market Drayton.

An Avro Anson in front of the tower as seen in a May 1938 newspaper

This photo probably dates from the late 1930s. On the right is Cyril Swain, known as Sid Swain, of Wem. He was shot down and took part in the Great Escape in 1944, but was one of those recaptured and shot.

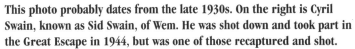

"Sports, Tern Hill aerodrome," in about 1918. *(Harry C.*

Below, the logbook of Howell Jones of Guilsfield during his time at Tern Hill in the second half of 1941.

Two memorable crashes

Rookie pilots, bravado, bad luck and crowded skies all contributed to a dreadful record of air crashes at Tern Hill in both world wars. Of all the many crashes, two stand out, for different reasons.

In 1978 air wreck enthusiasts investigating a buried plane at Helshaw Grange, close to the airfield, came across the remains of the pilot.

He was 19-year-old John Toplis Carr, from Eastbourne. His Miles Master trainer had been in a mid-air collision on April 10, 1941, in which the other pilot, LAC D.M.W. Hartley, also died.

The salvage team of the time, finding the wreck of Carr's aircraft sinking in dangerously boggy ground, abandoned recovery attempts.

There was a funeral service in situ, and the crash site was simply fenced off and left. After Leading Aircraftman Carr's body was recovered 37 years later, relatives were traced and he was given a military funeral.

Albert Ward, who worked as a civilian at the Tern Hill complex, can recall another crash, surrounded by rumour, which was especially remarkable and tragic.

The story was that a student pilot who recklessly flew under a railway bridge between Tern Hill and Crewe was court martialled, stripped of rank, and grounded.

Some time after this humiliation he stole a plane. "The plane he took was, I believe, a Harvard. He was doing all sorts of aerobatics with it. It was panic stations at the time. He then dived it out of the sky into the doorway of his own billet in Tern Camp. They reckon he committed suicide."

This incident must be that of August 29, 1943, in which Aircraftsman Second Class Johns died on an "unauthorised flight" in, not a Harvard, but a Master. Records show that Johns had been grounded for some reason and had not flown since March 19.

In the afternoon of August 29 he went up to a Master at "D'" dispersal point and, when a Flight Sergeant Ford got out of the front cockpit, he got in, saying he was going to taxi it across to the night flight dispersal.

It was realised something was amiss and attempts were made to stop him as he taxied, but he taxied to the end of the east-west runway and took off, and proceeded to shoot up the Maintenance Unit.

Johns then climbed to 1,500ft and started a slow roll to the left. When vertically banked on coming out of the roll, the nose dropped and the plane did a steep diving turn into the ground, setting fire to a 24 MU hut.

The Court of Inquiry described the crash as an accident and it led to a rule that grounded aircrew should be posted to non-flying units as soon as it became clear they were not suitable for further training.

Almost 50 years after RAF Tern Hill survived a destructive Luftwaffe attack, the base was bombed again – this time by IRA terrorists.

In 1989 two bombers sneaked into the base, by now the Army's Clive Barracks, and at the time of the attack housing the Parachute Regiment. They planted bombs by the packed accommodation blocks in the middle of the night.

Luckily they were spotted by guards. The barracks were evacuated before the bombs exploded with devastating effect (see picture, right). Instead of the huge death toll the IRA had hoped for, there were no serious injuries. But it had been a near thing.

A shocking aspect was that the bombers were able to escape, even though their getaway driver had abandoned them, and the quiet of the night had been riven by gunfire. It was also apparently Army policy at the time for sentries to carry unloaded rifles – in other words, carry them without their magazines attached. This policy was quickly changed.

In the excitement, nobody bothered to tell the police the base was under attack. The bombers have never been caught. Kevin O'Donnell, who was a student at nearby Harper Adams Agricultural College, was a prime suspect.

He was even nicknamed "Bomber" by fellow students. In an unrelated case, he subsequently appeared at the Old Bailey on gunrunning charges. The evidence against him was strong, but he was acquitted.

He was killed in a shootout with the SAS in Northern Ireland in 1992.

The pictures above and below are rather puzzling, as the original source says they were taken at Tern Hill – the plateau nature of the site seems to corroborate this – but they feature a Turbinlite Havoc. The Turbinlite unit was stationed at RAF High Ercall, not Tern Hill, so may have simply been visiting. The photo above is dated May 17, 1942, and below, May 12, 1942. *(via Andrew Thomas)*

Drawing on some happy memories

Hector Goldsack arrived at 24 MU, Tern Hill, in 1942. This is his story...

My first duties were to be in the newly appointed Airscrew, (Propeller) Repair Section in a recently built hangar on C Site.

This section was to be engaged in the servicing and repair of aeroplane propellers and their constant speed units. Many suffered damage either directly by enemy action with bullets or fragments passing through them, or indirectly by striking something or contact with the ground from an undercarriage failure. The repairs were very critical in their demands as any deviation from the tight criteria of accuracy and dynamic balance could easily destroy the aircraft and its crew.

During the commissioning of the facility the usual gremlins manifest themselves. On one such occasion a block and tackle carrying a load and running along an overhead runway secured high in the hangar roof provided a dramatic cure for constipation when it ran off the end of the trackway. The builders had apparently omitted to the install the stops.

I was fortunately about five yards away but the poor guy who was moving the load was almost directly beneath. He escaped by some miracle and stood white and paralysed amid a mess of chain and machinery. Naturally a Board of Enquiry, or something similar, followed.

Shortly afterwards I "remustered" (the service jargon for changing one's trade) to Draughtsman. I had been engaged in similar engineering work before joining the RAF. I thus became a member of the Drawing Office who had their being in the HQ block that I had first visited on my arrival. It comprised a team of about a dozen personnel. We worked under the direction of the Chief Technical Officer, usually staffed by a senior Wing Commander, who was responsible for the technical direction of the unit.

The trade of Draughtsman was a very arcane occupation to the majority of the RAF. No one outside the inner circle quite understood what we did. This was sometimes a great boon and on other occasions a serious handicap. There were comparatively very few service people thus employed, most drawing office staff being usually drawn from a civilian labour pool, the RAF using their own kind to meet their needs on overseas stations. I don't know why this was not the case in 24 MU.

During the period of my stay with the Engineering Squadron we were accommodated in Market Drayton in council houses that were unoccupied and, I think, fairly new. We cycled into work on RAF issue bicycles, all black with the down tube between the saddle and rear wheel painted yellow, no doubt to reduce the chance of theft. It looked like Amsterdam in the rush hour. We dined in a mess on the RAF site. There were no facilities at our quarters in Market Drayton.

The incident of AC Johns (see page 144) occurred during my period in the Drawing Office. We were in the HQ building when the ultra low flight of an aeroplane claimed our immediate attention and we went outside to observe, but it was mostly hidden from our view by the surrounding trees and hangars.

The aircraft, a trainer aeroplane, circled around the airfield, its movements being followed as best as possible by the ambulance and fire tender below. After what seemed an age the machine headed south towards the accommodation sites

Hector Goldsack at work. He was at Tern Hill from 1942 to 1943 when he left to join a mobile drawing office for 151 Forward Repair Unit

where I now slept, and crashed into one of the dormitory hutments where it destroyed itself, the hutment and the hapless pilot.

The story that "went round the bazaars" was that the airman who had carried out this deed had been working in the cookhouse as an Aircraft Hand General Duties. This grade and trade was the most basic of all that existed in the RAF and the only way was up. But it was the position to which a cadet who had failed in his course to be an aircrew member automatically reverted and from which he could subsequently remuster into some other more suitable trade skill.

It was said that this person had indeed been a failed cadet who having been relegated to the menial tasks of the camp kitchen's "tin room" when his whole being cried out to fly, found it more than he could bear. The story continues, that clad in his anonymous, ubiquitous blue overalls worn equally from the aircraft fitters to the "janker wallers" cleaning the ablutions, the airman arrived at the dispersal and climbed into a waiting aircraft. A nearby Flight Sergeant, assuming that here was an aircraft fitter going about his duties, was kind enough to assist the start up of the aero engine. Seeing that all was apparently well he cycled off to the Mess for lunch. Take-off followed and Flying Control was disturbed to see the plane on circuit, but in the wrong direction. At this point the situation hit the fan!

It was said that the pilot threw his forage cap out of the aircraft and this, together with his paybook salvaged from the remains of his burnt corpse, confirmed his identity.

All this is hearsay, but it is contemporary with the incident.

The ownership of a personal cycle by most of the airmen and airwomen was a great boon to all. It gave flexibility, economy, was healthy, gave good opportunities at weekends and for courting (I am told) and was more than half a century ahead of its time in ecological compatibility. But it did require a special section devoted to keeping the show on the road – although it wasn't rocket science. Often a group of us from the D.O. would cycle out in the evening or weekend, sometimes to Hawkstone Park and its Follies, or perhaps to the Bear at Hodnet where the "Mayor of Hodnet" would be elected from among us and wear about his/her neck a pair of WAAF stockings knotted together with a half pint bottle of Worthington in the foot of each, as their "chain of office"

Other sorties took us to Loggerheads to the local village dance with the Land Girls. On really extreme instances we would venture as far as Swinnerton for the exotic "talent"' from the Ordnance Factory. Some lassies had quite pronounced tans when we all looked pale and wan. But we were advised that this was probably the result of associating with some explosive materials. So much for Health and Safety.

On one sally to the south we went down to Wellington and on a glorious day ascended The Wrekin. As we lay on our back gazing at the sky a flight of American Buffalo aircraft homed on our mountain and in formation proceeded to circle round us. We watched in admiration as the dumpy planes banked round, the sun glinting on the pilots in their canopies. Our appreciation turned to horror as one of the planes, for no apparent reason, rolled out of formation, put its nose down and at full throttle went into the field below us, less than quarter of a mile NE. The distance to the ground was only about 1000 feet and it was over in seconds. Just a black hole in a field and a few bits of debris.

This dramatic transition from life to death on a warm summer's afternoon was a jolt back to the reality of war. It happened fairly frequently in those days but it never failed to leave a bookmark in the mind, which still turns the page back after 65 years.

The remaining planes re-formed and headed back to their nearby station. No doubt pondering.

As an aid to our diligence no doubt, it was customary for the draughtsmen who had been responsible for a particular aircraft modification or design to accompany the pilot and crew on the subsequent proving flights if this were practicable. On one occasion it came to pass that I had to join a test flight of a Lancaster that had embodied a modification that had my name on it, so to speak.

Having signed the usual "blood chit" etc. I drew an observer's parachute from the store as required and presented myself on the apron by the "Lanc" whose four engines were ticking over. The Sergeant Air/Gunner in the doorway of the plane looked down at me and shouted above the engine noise 'Chuck your chute up to me lad'. I obliged and as I did so the ripcord hooked into a belt hook on my tunic and the canopy deployed, beautifully wrapping itself around the port tail fin and rudder. It was not something that one could keep to oneself, particularly as I was in clear view of the HQ block. It did not go unremarked.

As you may have gathered, I enjoyed my stay at Tern Hill greatly – in fact I have enjoyed my whole working life greatly.

Below: Two views from around 1918, showing one of the hangars, and a line up of Sopwith trainers. *(RAF Shawbury archives)*

Above: Gloster Gauntlet at Tern Hill in the late 1930s. *(Don Tyrer)*

Were it not for a liberal dose of good luck to balance the bad, Tern Hill airfield could fairly be considered jinxed. Tragedy and narrow escapes have gone hand in hand. Here are some examples of "Tern Hill's luck":

● October 6, 1916, two hangars almost destroyed in a gale. Several injured.

● July 30, 1918, commanding officer, Major C.E. Brisley, killed in unusual circumstances. He fell out of his plane in flight. He was from 13th Training Depot Squadron – a temptation to fate if ever there was one.

● March 9, 1919, aerodrome narrowly escaped total destruction when two hangars burned down.

● October 7, 1936, fire destroyed officers' quarters. October 20, another fire in one of the officers' huts. Arson suspected.

● October 16, 1940, Luftwaffe bombing raid destroyed or damaged over 30 planes. Five hurt.

● July 7, 1941, Wing Commander J.W.C. More DFC, officer commanding fighter sector HQ at Tern Hill, crashed in a Beaufighter near Shrewsbury.

● Around 1944 the Tern Hill soccer team, having beaten most local teams, are reputed to have looked for stronger opposition and, taking to the field, found themselves confronted by the full England team. Tern Hill lost.

● February 20, 1989, IRA terrorists spotted by guards planting bombs at Clive Barracks. Parachute Regiment soldiers were successfully evacuated before the devices went off with devastating effect.

Tern Hill today

Although the main part of the old RAF Tern Hill base is now Clive Barracks, occupied by different Army units at different times, the airfield itself is still in RAF ownership and is in regular use by helicopters from RAF Shawbury.

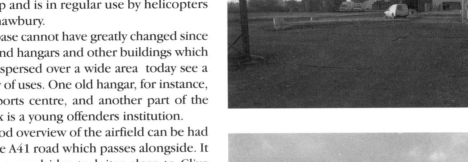

The base cannot have greatly changed since the war and hangars and other buildings which were dispersed over a wide area today see a variety of uses. One old hangar, for instance, is a sports centre, and another part of the complex is a young offenders institution.

A good overview of the airfield can be had from the A41 road which passes alongside. It is not a good idea to loiter close to Clive Barracks, as the guards are armed.

Numerous wartime buildings like these are still in use.

A look down the runway. This view cannot have changed greatly since the war.

Tilstock

RAF Tilstock is probably the wartime air base with which Salopians are most familiar, because two busy main roads pass directly over the site, and the derelict control tower can hardly be missed. But that name of RAF Tilstock is not so familiar, as the modern generation knows it as Prees Heath airfield, which is a parachuting centre just south of Whitchurch.

Yet turn back the clock over 60 years and, instead of the roar of traffic, the roar was from mighty four-engined bombers which were based here.

The huge hangars, which look as good as new, are in use for storage. Hidden away in woods are some of the huts in which the airmen lived.

A section of just one of the three original runways still exists and it is this which is used by light aircraft, keeping alive the flying tradition.

Opened on August 1, 1942, as RAF Whitchurch Heath, it officially became RAF Tilstock the following year, this name being adopted to avoid confusion with an airfield of a similar name.

Its role was training of bomber crews, and later training crews for the towing of gliders. No planes from Tilstock are recorded as having taken part in bombing raids, but some did take part in dropping leaflets over enemy-occupied territory, and some Tilstock-based aircraft took part in the Arnhem operation, although they flew from airfields in the south of England.

Training was in any event dangerous in itself, and as late as March 20, 1945, a Halifax from Tilstock was shot down by an enemy intruder while on a cross country flight near Peterborough, killing three of the crew.

Halifaxes and Stirling bombers were the main "heavies" associated with Tilstock, but there were also Whitleys and Wellingtons, together with the occasional Spitfire or Hurricane for fighter affiliation exercises, and the ubiquitous Ansons.

Fitters and electricians of 1665 Heavy Conversion Unit in front of a Stirling bomber at wartime Tilstock. *(Phil Ede)*

RAF Tilstock was in effect run as a dual airfield with RAF Sleap, and as we have seen in other chapters, there is a myth that Guy Gibson, the famous Dam Busters leader, was once stationed at Tilstock – the confusion has arisen because the one-time station commander was a Wing Commander G.H.N. Gibson.

Flying activity quickly wound down after the war, although the airfield was still occasionally used for Territorial Army manoeuvres in the 1950s, with a Royal Navy Avenger sadly crashing on the edge of the airfield during one such exercise.

Today light aircraft keep the air base alive.

Reg's narrow escape

A change in the weather at RAF Tilstock was to save the life of Reg Hughes. Mr Hughes, who hails from Wellington but now lives in Australia, was a flight engineer who did his initial flying training at Tilstock before joining an operational squadron.

His unit was the 1665 Heavy Conversion Unit. Writing from his home at Thornleigh, Sydney, he recalls that a Halifax on take-off hit the tops of trees and crashed close to two houses on the edge of the airfield, near the Whitchurch to Shrewsbury road. Three crew died, including a good friend, a fellow flight engineer.

"The twist of fate is that I had arranged to fly as passenger with my friend on their 'circuits and bumps' schedule on the day of the crash, but we were put on glider towing on that day. I could have become a casualty of the crash if the weather hadn't have improved."

Mr Hughes says during his time at Tilstock his unit was using Stirling and Halifax planes, and there were also some Horsa gliders on strength. Aircrews were being converted from flying Albemarle twin-engined planes to the four-engined Stirlings and Halifaxes. The conversion course also included training on Horsa glider towing and supply dropping.

The Stirling was good to fly, but difficult to handle on take-off and landing, and take-offs with a glider in tow were always "dicky" and a bit nerve-wracking.

Mr Hughes says he had no undue experiences in the Stirling, but did have a couple of hairy moments when flying as a passenger in a glider.

The first was when the glider was cast off from the tug aircraft and made what seemed to him a near-vertical descent before levelling off at the last second and landing. This, incidentally, was the normal glider approach technique.

"On another occasion, flying as passenger in a Horsa glider somewhere in the vicinity of Whitchurch, the tow rope snapped and the glider pilot was forced to make an emergency landing. I recall that we came down over some trees and over a road and touched down in a beet field, I think it was. We went down a slope and came to rest with the glider very close to the edge of a wood.

"I recall that the glider pilot instructor was not the least bit upset by it – a view that was not shared by his pupil or by his passengers.

"Several local people were quickly on the scene and we left the glider where it came to rest."

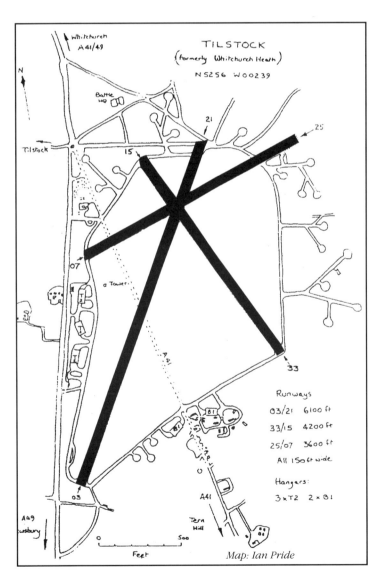

Map: Ian Pride

'I could almost hear voices from the past'

Cyril Wood, of Shoreham, West Sussex was at RAF Tilstock from about October 1945 to February 1946. "I remember that when I went there, there were a lot of Wellington bombers all parked around the perimeter track, just waiting for disposal, I suppose," said Mr Wood, who was at the time a sergeant and during the war had been with a mobile signal unit.

Newly married, he lived out with his wife at Mill House, Tilstock. In the 1990s he returned to relive some memories.

"It was easy to walk into the camp and see all these huts and remember standing there. I could almost hear voices from the past. I can always visualise the place being alive. Everything was there, but was of course overrun with weeds and shrubbery."

Eddie Hall, of West Felton, Oswestry, said: "I was born in 1934 in a cottage down Hollins Lane, and was there until 1944-45. My father worked as a cowman at Fearnall, Alkington Hall. So when the German planes came over in the early 1940s, night after night, they used to fly over our house and frighten the life out of me and help me to grow up tenfold, I can tell you.

"Fearnall had two landmines dropped on their land one night, killing a number of cows. One Saturday lunchtime a German fighter came over our house. We went outside and he was circling around firing bullets at people who were taking food to the school for the children's party.

"The bullets hit the road at the top of Hollins Lane and down by the cemetery gates before the school, and in the pavement. It was said at the time that he got back to Bristol before he was shot down.

"One Saturday afternoon my mother went to town on her bike leaving me alone and an old Avro Anson started going around and around firing flares for about two hours.

Engine fitters at work on a Stirling at Tilstock in 1944. From left, Leading Aircraftsman G.L. Simmons of London, Leading Aircraftsman G. Clyne of Salford, and Corporal Hart of Bolton. *(Picture courtesy of the Imperial War Museum, CH12932)*

Flight Lieutenant Alan Austin DFC leads a Wings For Victory parade down Whitchurch High Street. He was killed on May 8, 1944, when the Horsa glider in which he was a passenger crashed on approach to the main runway. *(Phil Ede)*

Top trio. From left, chief flying instructor Squadron Leader R.R. Glass DFC, commanding officer Wing Commander G.H.N. Gibson DFC, and flying controller Squadron Leader G.T. Yuill. *(Picture courtesy of the Imperial War Museum CH12934)*

I was about eight at the time and it frightened me to death, so I hid in the pig sty, popping my head from under the arch watching him. It seems he had lost the side door and an airman had fallen out. The flares were to indicate where it happened.

"One sunny day my late father and his workmate were cutting beet by hand when suddenly overhead a plane spluttered, cut out, then crashed into the field they were working in. The pilot got out and said: 'I did the same thing with it yesterday.' He wore carpet-type slippers and asked to be taken to a telephone."

Tim Yates was at Tilstock from November 26, 1942, to March 9 the following year when he left for its satellite aerodrome at Sleap. "One thing I remember about Tilstock is that when we got there we hadn't any aircraft. When they built Tilstock they had called it RAF Whitchurch and unfortunately there was an RAF Whitchurch in Hampshire and they had sent our planes there.

"They had Whitleys at Tilstock which was the first time I had been on them. There had been Wellingtons on my operational squadron and at Lichfield. Whitleys were very safe. They were cumbersome and weren't very comfortable inside."

Alan Woolley, of Oakengates, said: "From 1942 until I joined the RAF in 1945 I was a member of Dawley Flight of 1130 Wrekin Squadron of the Air Training Corps and on occasions used to cycle from Horsehay to Cosford,

War diary

1942
September 25: First two Whitley aircraft of 81 Operational Training Unit, based at Ashbourne, arrive.
November 30: Whitley crashed within boundary of the aerodrome. Three dead. Rear gunner severely injured.

1943
January 11: Whitley LA766 crashed into high ground near Wrexham. Five pupils and pilot, navigator, and wireless operator killed.
February 6: Three a/c took part in nickel raid over Paris.
February 10: Pupil pilot killed attempting belly landing when engine caught fire. Six crew of the Whitley bailed out OK.
February 26: Four a/c took part in nickel raid, Rouen, in Whitleys.
March 12: Three Whitleys dropped nickels in Rouen area.
March 23: Nickel raid to Lille. (These leafleting raids continued for several months)
March 24: "The aerodrome was enveloped in dense cloud of vapour of density sufficient to suspend the taking off and landing of aircraft. The vapour persisted for 13 minutes, was slightly irritant to the skin and had a faint unidentified smell."
April 10: Whitley LA771 crashed on aerodrome due to engine failure and burnt out. Two occupants killed, remainder injured.
April 13: Whitley EB346 crashed near Driffield, Yorks, at night. All seven crew killed.
June: Medical summary – "The general state of health of all personnel is very satisfactory. VD is definitely on the decline."
June 1: Name of station officially changed from RAF Whitchurch Heath to RAF Tilstock.

Shawbury, and one time to Prees to see if we could get a flight in one of the training aircraft. In all I flew five times from Shawbury, once in an Airspeed Oxford, and four times in Wellingtons.

"The time I was able to fly from Prees was in a Stirling in 1944 and this aircraft was used to enable experienced pilots of twin-engine planes to convert to four-engine aircraft. My records show we were airborne for 75 minutes doing circuits, bumps and during the flight two or three pilots would sit in turn next to the captain. I was able to stand directly behind the pilots and had a wonderful view of all that was going on.

"When motoring through Prees these days I wonder how I managed to cycle all the way from Horsehay and back, but can only think I was spurred on by the love of flying."

Charles Hindle of Grimsby was at 1665 HCU during February and March 1945 and recalls the night in March 1945 that a Tilstock Halifax was shot down by an intruder.

"I was a wireless operator in another Halifax on that same cross country exercise that night. During the flight I received a radio message from base which, when decoded, read 'Intruders – divert to...' and further instructions which I forget.

"At the time we thought that it was just part of the exercise but the instructions were passed to the navigator and pilot and we obeyed them.

"When we returned to Tilstock we learned that our colleagues in the other aircraft had not returned. I don't think I ever learned the details of what happened or why the

---

1943

July 14: Whitley V dived into ground at high speed near Prees village after completing five hour cross country flight. All six on board killed.

July 27: Whitley V EB366 hit by flak over Cherbourg during nickelling, damaged, but landed safely.

September: Station strength, 1,405 plus 314 WAAFs.

September 28: Whitley struck by an "attacking" Beaufighter of 406 Squadron, RAF Valley, during a night exercise. Five crew members bailed out, but the pupil navigator hit a tree and was killed. A successful single-engined landing was made at RAF High Ercall.

1944

January 1: Tilstock and Sleap transferred from 93 Group Bomber to 38 Group Allied Expeditionary Air Force – a new formation to train crews for towing gliders for airborne troops.

January 5: The first glider - a Horsa - landed at Tilstock.

January 20: Advanced party of 1665 Heavy Conversion Unit (Stirlings) arrived by road convoy from Woolfox Lodge.

January 23: Main party of approx 700 personnel arrive by two special trains.

January 31: Stirling BF444 overshot on landing from night flying and crossed the main Whitchurch to Shrewsbury road. Minor damage to aircraft.

February 15: Whitley V crashed at Snailbeach. All five crew killed. Horsa glider successfully cleared and landed safely.

February 29: Combined strength of Tilstock and its Sleap satellite is 2,818.

May 5: Five die in glider crash. After casting off from tug, went into steep turning dive and crashed into the ground and overhead cables.

May 8: Horsa glider coming in to land on No 1 runway crashed 300 yards short. Two pilots killed plus two RAF pilots who were passengers.

May 16: General Browning (Commander of the Airborne Forces) visited. Gave one and a half hour talk to 300 aircrew of 81 OTU and 1665 HCU.

June 3: Whitley LA770, port engine failed. A/c crashed and caught fire, completely burnt out. Wireless operator died.

July: Four Hurricane aircraft arrived at the beginning of the month (for fighter affiliation).

July 31: Aircraft strength, 31 Stirlings, 28 Whitleys, eight Ansons and seven Oxfords, plus one Spitfire for fighter affiliation

with Stirlings (these figures are likely to include those aircraft at the Sleap satellite).

August 6: USAAF hospital a/c arrive with hospital cases for local American hospitals. Four Hurricanes arrive.

August 12: Stirling EF210 crashes and burns out at Alne, Yorkshire. Five crew die, pilot has multiple injuries.

August 22: Halifax conversion flight within the unit starts about now.

September: Four Stirling IVs normally based at Tilstock used for operational sorties from RAF Fairford and RAF Keevil (for the Arnhem operation). EE889 and LJ828 sustained damage due to enemy action.

September 1: Some air crews attached to RAF Ringway for special parachute jumping course from August 19 to September 1. "Pupils appeared to lack enthusiasm but were glad to have made the descents," says the Operational Records Book.

September 25: Stirling EE972 hits hill in the Cheviots. Two die, other crew are injured.

September 28: Tilstock-based ambulance proceeded to Thunderbolt crash at Blakemere, near Whitchurch. Pilot killed.

October 20: Halifax V LL148 collided with flare tender shed while taxying round perimeter at night. No casualties. Shed badly damaged.

October 23: Halifax V LL501 collided with a crew coach while taxying round perimeter. No casualties.

November 16: Sixty-two Flying Fortresses diverted from Molesworth, Grafton Underwood and Great Ashfield after a daylight raid on France. Aircraft and 560 American aircrew accommodated half-and-half at Tilstock and Sleap.

December summary: "The changeover on 81 OTU from Whitley V to Wellington X a/c has been considerably delayed during the month due to adverse weather preventing delivery. To date, 2 Wellington X a/c have been received."

December 6: Halifax LL281 in fatal accident. During a daylight take-off the port inner engine stopped, but the pilot continued the take-off. The machine failed to become fully airborne and crashed into trees at the edge of the airfield. Pilot, air bomber and engineer died.

December 19: 34 Liberators from Bungay diverted to Tilstock after operational mission to Northern France and Germany. Due to lack of accommodation 200 of the 360 crew members were sent by road to Atcham air base until the aircraft could take off.

December 22: 31 Liberators took off to return to Bungay - three stayed behind unserviceable.

other aircraft had not diverted as we had.

"Looking at my logbook I find that the next day, March 21, 1945, our crew was posted to RAF Earls Colne, 297 Squadron in Essex, because we were needed for the next big airborne attack on Germany, the Rhine crossing which took place on March 24.

"Incidentally my short stay at Tilstock changed the course of my life. At the local dance in the village hall I met my wife and we were married within a year. My wife and her two sisters, Edwina, Eileen and Jacky Green, all married airmen from the camp.

"My rear gunner and close friend Paddy said 'It was a good job for the Green sisters that the RAF came to Tilstock.'"

Don Tyrer, of Arleston, speaking just a week before his death at the age of 87 in May 2006, recalled going to Tilstock in 1943, following operational service with 76 Squadron at Linton-on-Ouse as part of a Halifax crew.

"I was gunnery officer. We had all Whitleys and we used to do such things as leaflet raids down the French coast. I did not go on every one. I had a team of ex operational air crew, pilots, navigators, bomb aimers. We took it in turns.

"We operated with Max Aitken's Beaufighters on Bullseyes (i.e. night exercises under operational conditions with searchlights, interceptions etc). We would make a course out from Whitchurch to Barnaby, on the north east coast. Along the way Max Aitken's Beaufighters would attempt to intercept our Whitleys which worked very well.

"On the particular night I had turned

Gunnery and navigation officers at RAF Whitchurch Heath – as it was then – around April or May 1943. According to Don Tyrer, who loaned this photo, the officer holding his shoulder is indicating where a piece of flak had gone into his jacket.

A Whitley had completed the course but as he came in towards Tilstock he came round by High Ercall and a Beaufighter broke cloud and took his port engine out. The lad was only 18 but had an experienced crew member with him, the wireless operator who had done a tour of operations. Between them the skipper bailed the crew out and they landed the aeroplane.

"The navigator was Canadian, only recently commissioned. After searching half the night we could not find him. We knew he had bailed out because there were only two in the aircraft when it landed.

"We found him about three days later somewhere near Hinstock spreadeagled in an oak tree. The poor chap was dead, impaled on the tree. I have no idea what his name was. (This incident is clearly that recorded as having happened on September 28, 1943).

in around half two in the morning. The duty officer shook me to wake me up. We had trouble.

Coded operational orders sent to 81 OTU for nickelling operations – in this case dropping of propaganda leaflets over Occupied France – in early 1943. (*National Archives*)

"We used to have a Miles Master which was a radial engined job, a two seater, in G flight, as we were a gunnery flight.

"There was one chap named Eagles, who we called Bing Eagles. He had a habit when he started up the Master of revving up until she was warm, and letting her trickle along and start off down the tarmac, and every time on the third bounce he would take his undercarriage up.

"Everybody said don't do it Bing, but he said that on the third bounce she would go up. One day she faltered, and he bent a very nice Miles Master. She went across the Wem road. I think the commanding officer was not very pleased.

"I was there six to seven months. It was a very happy station. I think I finished up there as a Flight Lieutenant – I was a Flying Officer when I went.

"We had a bombing area outside Prestatyn and we also had two Queen Marys. We used these to rig up two Frazer Nash turrets, one at one end, and one in the centre, and made our own hydraulic systems for them.

"We used to take them to a quarry near Hodnet, opposite the Shrewsbury road, and we had mock-up 109s hang on the cliff walls."

1945

March 3: Three Lancasters diverted to Tilstock from their bases at Fulbeck, Leeming, and Binbrook, on returning from operational missions.

March 9: Halifax NA317 collides with Tiger Moth near Abbots Bromley during cross country flying. All die.

March 20: Halifax OG-U shot down near Peterborough by enemy intruder – believed Ju88 – during cross country flight. Pilot, flight engineer and gunner killed.

March 26: 1665 HCU moves to RAF Saltby, Lincolnshire. Whitley training also ends.

April 30: Tilstock station strength, officers 187, other ranks 1,695.

The amazing adventures of Sinbad

One of the more unusual warriors at Tilstock was Sinbad, a battle-scared canine loner who was a bit of a legend on the base. He belonged to a senior officer and would wait at the bus stop on the camp, and then catch the bus into Whitchurch. Later, he would catch the last bus back.

"Sinbad the well-travelled dog was known by many, including myself," said John Willis, of Higher Heath.

"I lived at the time in the house opposite the barrier on the main road through to the headquarters at the base. Sinbad used to come into Whitchurch, get off the bus, walk to the station, get on the train and go to Crewe. That's true. Later he came back. How he knew what train to get on I don't know.

"A Squadron Leader owned him and Sinbad had more battle scars on him than the Squadron Leader.

"I know he got presented with a bill for all Sinbad's travelling. I don't know whether it was from the railways company or from Salopia, the bus company which ran the shuttle service."

Mr Willis' memory is that Sinbad was a white bulldog, although he is in a minority as others describe him as a white bull terrier.

He recalls that Sinbad also travelled by RAF truck to Tilstock's satellite at Sleap.

"He didn't like it and came back."

Mr Willis said of Sinbad's wanderings: "It's one of those things that people don't believe and think you're making up a story. But it's perfectly true."

Mrs N.L. Chambers, of Whitchurch, remembers: "I was stationed at Tilstock from late 1942 to 1944. I was a chef in the officers mess, and Sinbad was a regular visitor.

"He was a white bull terrier and he belonged to Wing Commander Tomkins, who took him everywhere with him.

"He used to come with the Wing Commander at meal times and came to the kitchen to be fed. I used to feed him his meals. Then he'd wander off. It was uncanny how he knew the bus times. He'd go down to the bus stop and sit and wait for the bus and get on.

"Sometimes he would get off in the village of Tilstock, and sometimes go straight into Whitchurch. He'd always manage to get the last bus back. He'd occupy a seat and wouldn't get off for anybody. If the bus was full he wouldn't move – you had to stand.

"Everybody loved Sinbad. He was spoiled. Someone even put Sergeant's stripes on his front legs, so he then became Sergeant Sinbad. When the Wing Commander was posted he left Sinbad at a Mr Wright's, who I think was an auctioneer at the time."

A lady who asked not to be named shed light on what Sinbad used to get up to in Whitchurch.

She said Sinbad used to arrive with a group of airmen off the bus at the YMCA in the old music hall in Watergate Street, Whitchurch, where she worked two nights a week, and they all gave him titbits.

"He had several sausages and chips off us voluntary workers in the kitchen. There was a kitchen, canteen and large recreation room where there was a large fireplace and a good fire burning in the winter. Sinbad would lie full length in front of the fire.

"He was very good tempered usually, but woe betide anyone who tried to remove him from his place. At 10 o'clock when the canteen closed the airmen collected their coats and so on. Sinbad shuffled off with them to catch the last bus back to camp. Regardless of who had to stand, Sinbad assured himself of a seat."

The Driving Force

Memories of the wartime WAAF drivers at Tilstock and Sleap were compiled into a book, called *The Driving Force*, by Peggy Drummond-Hay in 1994. She arrived at Tilstock in January 1944 and quickly discovered the local pubs and cafes near the airfield.

These were the Raven and the Witchbowl Hotel, a cafe called Dirty Lil's, which was the best place to have egg and chips, and another cafe near the camp, called the College, where the girls used to go after night duty.

"Being a wartime camp the main road ran through the airfield but it had been closed for the duration," she writes.

"We were first billeted in the dreaded Nissen huts, which were always damp, but soon moved to some better, and drier, accommodation on the main site, called Laing huts.

"Whitchurch was our nearest town, only three miles away; not very lively but it had a cinema and a decent hairdresser's which I soon visited.

"Gliders arrived in March 1944, which meant we had to keep a special eye out for the towing cable when they were released from the aircraft. Sadly, one glider crew was killed when they hit some wires soon after they became airborne from the airfield.

"Our satellite station was Sleap and to reach it we had to drive through Wem, which was full of black American troops. They used to sit on a wall and make catcalls at us when they were off duty. I can remember one of them had auburn hair.

"One of the more hazardous airfield duties was driving the 'Stop – Follow Me' Standard van which was mainly used for visiting aircraft, to guide them from the runway to their allotted dispersals. There was an illuminated board on the back of the van with the two words written facing rearwards and operated from the cab of the vehicle by the driver.

"On one occasion Pat Kelly put out her Stop light when approaching an intersection to the peritrack but the aeroplane didn't stop and went into the back of her van. She managed to jump out before more damage was done and was unhurt, but very shaken.

"One of the funniest memories I have of Tilstock was of a white bull terrier called Sinbad who, I think, belonged to a Wing Commander. Sinbad used to join the bus queue to Whitchurch in the evenings, unaccompanied, get on the bus and usually onto a seat and woe betide anyone who tried to get him off!

"No-one found out where he went or why. He certainly had many scars to prove his worth. He was always in the bus queue for the return trip to camp.

"It was also rumoured that there was some kind of ghost on the far side of the airfield. The only experience I had of this was when I was driving in the dark around the peritrack on the far side. Suddenly my lights faded and the ignition cut out for a second or so.

"It was an eerie feeling and I drove back to the MT section straight away to have the electrical system checked, but there was nothing wrong with it.

"I heard some time later that some of the other girls had a similar experience, although I never mentioned mine to them, nor had anyone else before."

Drivers of the MT Section 1665 HCU and 81 OTU, 1944-45. *(Phil Ede)*

Why did the bomber cross the road?

Among the most arresting images from Shropshire's wartime airfields are those of a huge Stirling bomber straddling the main A49 road at Tilstock. But there are two versions of how it got to be there.

Mrs Joan Wellings, who was serving on the Shropshire air base at the time, gives the most common version. The pilot, she says, overshot the runway when coming in to land. And so the heavy bomber ended up on the road, pointing in the Shrewsbury direction.

"The crew were all joking that they were just on the way to Shrewsbury," said Mrs Wellings, who was a WAAF driver at RAF Tilstock.

"It was a mid-summer afternoon in 1944. I can remember it quite plainly. It was coming in to land on what they called the short runway. It overshot the runway and landed on the road, and turned to the left and swirled round."

Although she did not see it happen, she saw the bomber on the road afterwards.

"It was left there for a time until the ground crew were all called to it to take it back onto the perimeter track."

Mrs Wellings, nee Price, lives now in Priorslee, Telford, but back then lived at Prees, and she met her husband

Edward, who worked as ground crew, at the airfield while they both worked there.

She recalls another incident at the air base involving an errant bomber which could have had serious consequences.

"I was driving the crew coach and was waiting for a plane to take-off and a Halifax came behind me and chewed up the back of my coach. It did not stop. Luckily I had just dropped the crew off. We had a court case about that on camp."

She said the A49 road skirting the western edge of the base did not close during the war, but the A41 which went across the centre of the airfield was closed.

The photos of the Stirling coming to grief inspired a diorama depicting the incident which is now on display at the museum of the Shropshire Wartime Aircraft Recovery Group at Sleap airfield.

It was created by group member David Amias and the museum guide tells a story which fits in well with Mrs Wellings' account.

According to the guide, the incident was in June 1944 when a solo pupil pilot, flying Stirling Mk III EF210, was engaged in circuits and bumps at Tilstock when he ran into

problems when landing on a short runway with an aircraft that notoriously required a long stopping distance.

At the end he careered through the boundary fence and swung south on to the A49, and the aircraft suffered only a few scratches to its undercarriage and tailplane from the barbed wire fence.

"The pilot was not the only lucky one to survive the experience. A Jeep carrying GIs was travelling along the road at the time the Stirling made its break for freedom through the wire. It finished up in a ditch trying to avoid the breakaway Stirling."

Peggy Drummond-Hay, a driver, recalled: "A Stirling overshot the end of the runway one day and ended up straddled across the main road, but luckily no traffic was moving in the vicinity. And one night another Stirling overshot in the dark and taxied back onto the peritrack of the airfield. The next day we saw the tyre marks to prove it!"

Top, the 1944 drama and above, the same spot today.

John Hughes of Condover has received a different account of the incident from the horse's mouth, Squadron Leader Ray Glass, who was the instructor on board the Stirling and from whose collection the photos originally come.

Mr Hughes has known Mr Glass for years through his involvement with the Stirling Aircraft Association and they have talked about the pictures in the past.

"They were on the perimeter track taxiing along when the wind caught it. I don't know exactly what the pupil was doing but it swung out over the perimeter fence, which was only diamond mesh wire," said Mr Hughes.

Joe Collier of the Wartime Aircraft Recovery Group said as far as he could make out there had been more than one incident in which aircraft finished up on the A49 at RAF Tilstock.

"I have heard of one where the aircraft overshot, broke a fence down, taxied down the A49, turned round and taxied back to the airfield, and nobody owned up to who had done it," he said, adding though that this obviously wasn't the incident depicted in the pictures.

Sergeant R.M. Walton, of Nelson, Lancashire, an airfield controller, dispatching aircraft at Tilstock in 1944. "In civilian life he taught history" said the official caption. *(Picture courtesy the Imperial War Museum CH12933)*

Tilstock today

It's unmissable. Driving along the A41 about three miles south of Whitchurch takes you across the middle of the old airfield.

The old control tower looks out over the site. A surviving remnant of runway, roughly parallel to the main road, is still used by light aircraft. Driving along the A49 also gives a good view of the airfield – it is onto this road that a Stirling bomber once strayed, as seen in preceding pages.

Hangars are now used for storage and in the woods to the south there are the derelict remains of a number of the old accommodation blocks and Nissen huts.

Today Prees Heath is considered a valuable habitat for various species. The common is the home to Shropshire's and West Midlands' only known colony of rare silver studded blue butterflies.

And the control tower still sees flying of sorts. It is in the ownership of Butterfly Conservation, which has turned it into a roost for bats and nesting site for birds.

Thousands of people a day drive past the decaying control tower, which is now a bat roost and nesting site for birds.

The busy A41 cuts across the site.

A derelict Nissen hut.

A fortified headquarters block is hidden in woodland and, left, this sign reveals the new use for the control tower.

Prees Heath Common Reserve

This building is being made available as a roosting site for bats and a nesting site for birds.
Please do not damage the wooden boards, which help to make the building more suitable for these creatures.

Weston Park

For a fleeting period Weston Park, one of Shropshire's smallest and most obscure airfields, was packed with Spitfires.

For the doubters who are getting out their maps, it was indeed in Shropshire, although the bulk of the Weston Park estate is in Staffordshire. Nor is it to be confused with the grass area within the estate grounds which is occasionally used as an airstrip today by microlights and light aircraft during events at Weston Park.

Wartime Weston Park airfield was a satellite landing ground where aircraft would be hidden and stored, often under trees in the grounds of the estate. The landing area was just outside of the estate wall. After landing at the simple grass airstrip, the planes were taken through a gap which had been knocked in the wall. A sliding gate on rollers opened to let them through.

The old satellite landing ground, designated 33 SLG, ran parallel to Offoxey Road. Today it is gently undulating fields, with crops growing, although one or two wartime huts remain to give a clue to the former use.

Weston Park airfield was selected as a SLG in October 1940. Hedges were ripped up, hardcore laid, and a few buildings put up to house the airfield personnel. Initially the planes stored came from RAF Cosford.

It officially opened in April 1942 and records of the parent airfield, RAF Cosford, tell us that by June 1942 the airfield had "settled down to its job, with 13 aircraft being handled in and out in one day. Spitfire aircraft were allocated to the satellite at its opening but in the month under review the first Wellington landed satisfactorily, demonstrating it was satisfactory for all the types held by the parent unit."

On July 31, 1942, 35 Spitfires were on site – it seems possible that at least some of these would be shining new fighters from an assembly plant set up at Cosford.

It closed briefly in October but reopened on December 1, 1942 "for reception of Blenheims for storage."

Later High Ercall air base joined in in storing aircraft at Weston Park and from early 1944 the Royal Navy's blind flying school at RNAS Hinstock took advantage of the airstrip, flying Airspeed Oxfords. RNAS Hinstock was called HMS Godwit, so the navy dubbed Weston Park HMS Godwit II.

Weston Park airfield closed in 1945 and returned to agriculture, its wartime role rapidly becoming a fading memory.

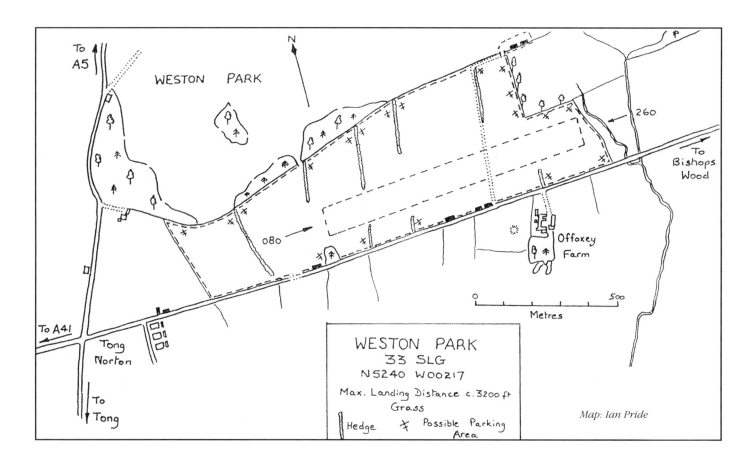

Map: Ian Pride

Sheep on the runway

Sid Lenthall, of Loak Road, Albrighton, was at Weston Park on its official opening day, April 18, 1942, but says the airfield was active before that. "There was no ceremony at all. The landing strip was on the side of Offoxey Road on a slope.

"All that came in on the opening day if I remember rightly was two Spitfires. There was a little office built on the side of Offoxey Road and there was just a Flight Lieutenant who was in charge of Weston and one civvy clerk. The Flight Lieutenant was the commanding officer. I think his name was Staniland. His brother was a test pilot with one of the aircraft manufacturers."

Sid, seen right as a Petty Officer in 1945, said: "It was called 33 Satellite Landing Ground. Brockton was 30 SLG. It stayed open until the summer of 1945 – I can't give you the date as I was in the navy then.

"I worked as an engine fitter. Cosford was still our base and we were still 9 MU employees. Most of the employees travelled by train from Wolverhampton area or Wellington area to Cosford Halt. A wagon would pick them up in the morning and take them to Brockton or Weston.

"I was in digs in Wolverhampton and would catch the 7am bus from Wolverhampton to Bilbrook. I had a friend, Les Butcher, who was also an engine fitter, who lived at Bilbrook. He ran an old Standard Nine and would take me and Jack Smith, an airframe fitter, to Weston."

The aircraft at Weston would take up about half the park, down as far as the lake.

"The way we got into the park was by crossing this field from the office, and quite a wide section of the wall had been dismantled and running gear put down – rollers along the bottom – and we had sliding gates on rollers. It had to be wide enough to take anything as big as a Wellington or Whitley. We rolled the gates along and rolled or pushed the aircraft in. Whether the wall has now

been replaced I don't know. We had a wooden hut, and there was a little brick-built building on the Knoll. Our storeman George Mansfield from Brewood worked in there.

"We started getting Blenheims, Beauforts and Beaufighters and in 1943 the MU at High Ercall dispersed some aircraft to us. And the Royal Navy at Hinstock sent us some Fairey Swordfish to disperse. We serviced them. The navy called Weston HMS Godwit II. And Tern Hill sent us some Harvards. Noisy little things, they were."

Numbers of aircraft kept at Weston varied, sometimes falling as low as a dozen.

"The park still had cattle and deer running around. We had to hide the aircraft under trees. I have flown over there and you couldn't see them. The Ministry of Aircraft Production people built post and barbed wire fences round them to keep the deer and cattle off. Before we could get the aircraft in and out we had to move a section of fence."

Biggest planes kept at Weston were Wellington and Hampden bombers.

"I remember once we had a Blenheim to send to Shawbury and I arranged to go with the pilot and sat in the co-pilot's seat. Then a car pulled up at the little office we had and another RAF chap came out and said can I come with you, so the pilot asked me to lie in the bomb aimer's position.

"Now when you're in the bomb aimer's position you are only about 3ft above the deck on take-off. That was hairy enough. But as we approached Shawbury in a field in line with the direction we were going to land was a damn great muck heap. I thought this is going to be near. I just lay there. The Blenheim didn't have a retractable tailwheel.

"As we flew over I just about skimmed the top of the muck heap but the tail wheel hit it. There was muck flying in all directions. We were taken back to Weston in an Airspeed Oxford and as we approached the landing strip it was covered in sheep, which kept the grass down. They fired a Very pistol on red and we flew around for 20 minutes while the sheep were pushed into the pens.

"For eating arrangements, they built us a hut and we took what sandwiches we had. Another hut was built and a kitchen put in. Cosford employed a cook from Weston village, Miss Beech. She used to cook for us in there. That

War diary

1941

March 7: Flt Lt A. Blomfield and Pilot Officer G.H.A. Freear of Reudell (?), Palmer and Tritton, London, were accompanied to the SLG at Weston Park by the C/O on the matter of camouflage.

June 13: Squadron Leader D.B. McGill from No 51 Wing inspected the SLGs at Weston Park and Brockton.

June 28: Group Captain Shaw and Squadron Leader Gray arrived by air to inspect SLGs at Brockton and Weston Park.

October 22: Pilot Officer G. Staniland reported on posting from HQ 41 Group for duty as Engineer Officer at No 33 SLG.

went on until the place closed.

"There were no toilet facilities. We used to go in the woods.

"I was in the Home Guard based at 9 MU. I was number 2 platoon corporal, F Company, 10th Battalion, King's Shropshire Light Infantry. That was Home Guard. In part of the park was a quarry and we used to go in the quarry for rifle practice. We were equipped with an armoured vehicle, a Standard Ten with armour plating. They called it a Beaverette and it was on a Standard Ten chassis.

"We had a dog unit eventually at Weston with half a dozen airmen with dogs.

"I was a civilian worker and in 1944 I got my call up to the navy."

Weston had two MT drivers, Les Bothwell from Madeley area, and another called Ted from Codsall who used to travel on an old Rudge Whitworth motorbike. ("I can't remember his other name.") There was an electrician, Jack Wooldridge, from Albrighton who kept the newsagents shop in the High Street; an instrument maker; and an engine fitter called Ben Powell, from Manchester. No fire crew were stationed there.

"If there was any flying a fire tender from Cosford would be on duty."

Mr Lenthall also had an adventure when he landed at Brockton SLG in a Wellington X — a particular powerful mark – flown by a Czech sergeant pilot, Charlie Balik.

"When we got over Brockton Charlie said 'It isn't very big'. We went in over this turnip field, landed, and when Charlie pulled up, the nose was over the hedge over the Shifnal road."

Bill Hughston of Blymhill said: "I can remember the airfield being put in. They confiscated the farm land from Offoxey Farm, which was farmed by the Owen family and took a strip straight down the side, between the park wall and Offoxey Road and put in land drainage, levelled it and returfed it and put a tarmac road across it so they had an access to Weston Park.

"They cut a big hole in the sandstone boundary wall around Weston Park and they used to land the aircraft on the airstrip and ferry them into the park with little tractors and put them under the big trees with nets over them for camouflage. Then they created a little camp in Weston Park and the RAF had patrolling alsatian guard dogs all round

---

1942

March 9: Squadron Leader Blomfield of Ministry of Aircraft Production visited and Pilot Officer Johnson attended to discuss with him various features relating to the early completion of this satellite.

April 18: Officially opened at 0900 hours as 33 SLG in accordance with HQ No 41 Group instructions. After two Spitfires, Nos BP881 and BP879 had touched down at 1505 hours, 41 Group and 51 Wing were signalled by 9 MU. Wing Commander A.M. Chalmers and two representatives, i.e. Flt Lt Bunting and Flt Lt Wernher, from 51 Wing, witnessed the arrival of all aircraft, the day's total being four Spitfires.

April 21: Lt Howells, OIC Army detachment KSLI, attended a meeting held, and subsequent defence scheme was formed, and forwarded to 9 MU for approval. This officer expressed every satisfaction with the 3 Beaverettes recently supplied. Three Spitfires touched down and were dispersed in the park.

April 26: Five Blenheim Mark V aircraft landed and were dispersed in site 4.

April 28: Defence conference held, Major the Earl of Bradford and Captain Pearson representing the Home Guard, South Staffordshire Regiment. The chair was taken by Lt Col Lonsdale.

April 29: Mr A.J. Lance of Ministry of Aircraft Production inspected the hides.

April 30: Total aircraft held: 14 Blenheim Mk Vs, four Spitfires.

May 24: Seven aircraft handled on and off the satellite during the day, with only seven employees present.

May 26: Mr Owen, Offoxey Farm, Tong, visited the office to discuss letter received by him from A.M. Lands branch in connection with grazing rights on the landing strip.

May 31: Aircraft holdings: Spitfire I 6, Spitfire Ia 2, Spitfire IIa 2, Spitfire Vb 8, Spitfire Vc 2, Spitfire PRU 4, Bisley 5. Total 29.

June: "The production of operational aircraft during the month was satisfactory, the satellite having contributed its share to the figures achieved by its parent unit. The satellite having settled down to its job – 13 aircraft having been handled in and out in one day – it is anticipated that its production figures will show an early increase. Spitfire aircraft were allocated to the satellite at its opening, but during the month under review, the first Wellington landed satisfactorily, thus demonstrating that the satellite was satisfactory for all the types held by the parent unit. Defence arrangements during the month included an exercise in which the Army detachment and local Home Guard took part."

July 31: Holding of aircraft 35, all Spitfires.

September 30: 33 SLG was practically denuded of aircraft during the month owing to its holding of Spitfires being required for preparation at the parent unit. No further aircraft were sent to this satellite pending the result of certain representations which were being made to HQ 41 Group and HQ 51 Wing concerning the advisability of keeping the satellite open in view of the preoccupation of the main unit with glider production.

September monthly summary: Most of the holding of Spitfire aircraft delivered to the main unit. Firing practice with Thompson sub machine guns by members of unit Home Guard attached to the satellite.

October 4: Authority was received from HQ 41 Group to close No 33 SLG Weston Park until further notice.

October 31: Temporarily closed. The MAP maintenance gang were left in possession and arrangements were made for the site to be visited once weekly by an officer from the parent unit.

November 30: Instructions received to reopen this satellite for the reception of Blenheim aircraft for storage.

December 1: 33 SLG reopened for the storage of Blenheim aircraft.

(From now on many monthly entries in official records simply say: "There is nothing of importance to report.")

the park. At various places they built little brick huts with slate roofs.

"There was only a skeleton staff there with only sleep-

This picture of a hangar disguised as a farmhouse is said to have been taken at RAF Weston Park, in which case it is the only known wartime photo of the base. *(via Alec Brew)*

ing quarters for about two dozen. A civilian in the village used to go and cook up there in the cookhouse, Miss Beech. She lived in the village of Weston-under-Lizard. She used to walk up there every day to do the cooking for these chaps on the airfield.

"I started work at the park in April 1942. There was an Army camp. They (the Army) confiscated part of Weston Hall. The ATS and soldiers were all down the farmyard drive and there was a searchlight battery and all that. I was a bricklayer on the Bradford estate, a maintenance brick-layer. I did 50 years.

"After the aircraft were put in there, they were training the pilots at Cosford to use gliders. They used to drop the rope on Offoxey airstrip and would come out and collect it with a tractor, a great thick rope two to three inches thick. It was attached to the back of the Wellington and to the front of the glider. It would go up at Cosford and go round.

"He would loose the glider when he got over Cosford or thereabouts and then he would come round to Offoxey airstrip and loose the rope so he could land without the rope. They would retrieve it with a little tractor, roll it all up and it was taken by road to Cosford to use again.

"There were all sorts of planes at Weston Park – Mosquitos, fighter aircraft, Spitfires and Hurricanes, and Oxfords. After the war finished I had the job myself of putting the stone wall back with a pair of smaller double doors in where they used to take the aircraft through. The air force

handed it to the farm again for agricultural use.

"The little camp which was made for these fellows was used by the Boys Brigade afterwards as a summer residence. They used to come from Birmingham."

Bryan Brown, of Meashill Farm, Tong, said: "I have lived here all my life and can remember it reasonably well. There was a gun emplacement in Tong, close to the church, and I think there was a searchlight up here, some-where at Offoxey.

"In the fields they ripped out two or three hedges in 1940 and dropped on a lot of con-crete or hardcore and flattened it down to make a grass landing ground there. They knocked large sections out of the park walls – I think they're still knocked out today – and parked these planes under the trees in the park.

"There were some huts in the park and for a few years after the war children used to come out of Birmingham and camp out in these huts.

"Opposite the end of the drive of Offoxey Farm there was a vacant cottage. It think it was a Squadron Leader Chalmers who lived there and was in charge of it. A bit fur-ther along Offoxey Road there's a new house built on the right hand side. That was an officers mess or a sergeants mess at the time. It's been completely demolished and rebuilt as a bungalow."

A surviving hut in 1999.

It looks like a normal rural scene, but over 60 years ago aircraft flew from these fields.

Weston Park today

From junction 3 of the M54 motorway, drive north along the A41 road. After about a mile, turn right opposite the Bell pub, and follow the minor road towards Bishops Wood.

After about another mile, the airfield site is on your left, although there is nothing to see but fields. The runway ran parallel with the road. There is a track which runs across the airfield site into the Weston Park estate. This track has been improved in recent years and has been used as an access for people attending the "V" series of pop concerts held nowadays in the grounds of Weston Park.

A wall painting in a surviving wartime hut. The date it was done is unknown – it may be post-war.